Success with
electronic business

Success with electronic business

Design, architecture and technology of electronic business systems

BERTHOLD DAUM AND MARKUS SCHELLER

An *imprint of* **Pearson Education**

Harlow, England · London · New York · Reading, Massachusetts · San Francisco
Toronto · Don Mills, Ontario · Sydney · Tokyo · Singapore · Hong Kong · Seoul
Taipei · Cape Town · Madrid · Mexico City · Amsterdam · Munich · Paris · Milan

Pearson Education Limited

Head Office:

Edinburgh Gate
Harlow CM20 2JE
Tel: +44 (0)1279 623623
Fax: +44 (0)1279 431059

London Office:

128 Long Acre
London WC2E 9AN
Tel: +44 (0)20 7447 2000
Fax: +44 (0)20 7240 5771
Website: www.awl.com/cseng/

First published in Great Britain in 2000

The rights of Berthold Daum and Markus Scheller to be identified as Authors of this Work have been asserted by them in accordance with the Copyright, Designs and Patents Act 1988.

ISBN 0-201-67482-3

British Library Cataloguing in Publication Data
A CIP catalogue record for this book can be obtained from the British Library.

Library of Congress Cataloging in Publication Data
Applied for.

10 9 8 7 6 5 4 3 2 1

Typeset by Pantek Arts, Maidstone, Kent.
Printed and bound in Great Britain by Biddles Ltd, Guildford.

The Publishers' policy is to use paper manufactured from sustainable forests.

Contents

Foreword

The new structures of electronic business via the Internet have already begun transforming business as we know it at the dawn of the third millennium. And this transformation process will continue at a very fast pace. Business transactions that used to take days and even weeks will be completed in hours. Product design will be increasingly dictated by the customer, not by the manufacturer. Goods will be produced post-sale with fast delivery times, rather than for storage in a warehouse. Goods and services will be aimed at customers' individual needs rather than at general target groups. The point of sale will lose its relevance as a strategic competitive advantage.

In order to support these business models, suppliers, customers, and consumers must be connected to global supply networks. This can only be achieved by integrating IT systems with the World Wide Web to create the infrastructure necessary for these business processes.

The Internet has evolved from a communications medium, and subsequently a forum for advertising (through homepages) and online shopping, to a platform for complete business transactions between organizations. This evolution is irreversible. Only companies that take advantage of the Internet for faster business processes and cost savings will be able to keep their customers.

Many enterprises hope to meet the challenges of this transformation by expanding their ERP (Enterprise Resource Planning) systems. But these back-office systems are geared toward the classical demands of the pre-Internet era. Their monolithic nature is too inflexible for the new global competition. At the same time, online shopping solutions – front-office systems for e-commerce – are not adequate either, unless they can be integrated into the IT structure of an enterprise.

So what is necessary for the enterprises of tomorrow? First and foremost, the future calls for a new technology that supports comprehensive Internet applications. Secondly, a new business process structure that is designed specifically for the Internet is also necessary.

The technology already exists: component-based software with standards like Enterprise JavaBeans (EJB) and the Distributed Component Object Model (DCOM), the Java programming language, and web browsers with HTML (Hypertext Markup Language) for the presentation of information and XML (Extensible Markup Language) for the structuring of information.

The unique focus of this book is on Java technology. Technical, methodological and organizational aspects of this technology are discussed in an easy-to-understand manner and illustrated with examples. These examples represent the wide range of use of Bolero, a development environment for Java applications designed to support high-level electronic business and its applications. Every IT manager will find chapters in this book that represent position: the IT architect, the technology strategist, the project manager, the program designer, the developer.

This book is a comprehensive guide for developing distributed and totally integrated electronic business applications that meet the demands of the new era: web sites that can process transactions; new integrated solutions created from independent applications linked together; use of high-performance integration software, which enables permanent and versatile expansion of existing systems and their connection to the Internet (including existing ERP systems). All of these solutions contribute to safeguarding previous investments in software for the long term.

A few chapters deal with the new Internet standard, XML. It is the foundation for an innovative database architecture that meets the new demands of the Internet and the many types of information that it stores and transports. XML databases will be able to process traditional data just as well as multimedia and other complex types of data.

With this book, Berthold Daum and Markus Scheller have laid the groundwork for the design of IT systems for electronic business. IT experts should consider this book prerequisite reading for bringing their companies up to speed to compete in the business arena of tomorrow. I wish you great success in applying this thought-provoking material to projects in your enterprise.

Dr Erwin Königs
Chairman and CEO, Software AG

Introduction

The press, the machine, the railway, the telegraph are premises whose
thousand-year conclusion no one has yet dared to draw.

Friedrich Wilhelm Nietzsche
The Wanderer and His Shadow, aph. 278
1880

The Internet has been described as the fastest-growing technology in history. This opinion had to be revised after a short time: the growth rate of the Internet was soon outperformed by the growth rate of the World Wide Web, an Internet application, but a technology in its own right.

It seems that this opinion must be revised again. The growth rate of the World Wide Web is now dwarfed by the growth rate of electronic business. Electronic business, as we understand the term and use it in this book, includes not only online shopping, but all human business transactions, whether transactions between supplier and retailer, seller and buyer, citizen and administration, teacher and student, between hospital, practitioner, health insurer and patient, or partners in a virtual enterprise.

Electronic business = business transaction across Internet and web

This is an exciting time, a time where a new continent – the seventh (or virtual) continent – is explored. Stakes are driven into the ground to secure claims, flags are hoisted, kingdoms are gained and lost, and former competitors join in new alliances. It is not a time to sit at home and anxiously watch the borders of one's fiefdom.

This book tries to give the reader an impression of the technological and business revolution that is connected with the Internet, the World Wide Web and electronic business.

About this book

It also implicitly tells the story of a company: Software AG started out 30 years ago as a maker of a database management system (Adabas) and a 4GL programming system (Natural). Until recently not much had happened since then. But now it seems that Software AG has reinvented itself. With Bolero, dubbed The Application Factory for Electronic Business, Tamino, a native XML Information Server, and the middleware product EntireX it has delivered a complete set of cutting-edge products for electronic business and enterprise application integration.

In this book we will explain many concepts with Bolero as our vehicle. This does not mean that these concepts work only with Bolero – but with a programming model that is close to the business model we found that examples were best expressed in Bolero without getting lost in too much technical detail.

Read here what
you get

- In Part 1 of this book we discuss the current trends in the communication and computing infrastructure, we follow the development of electronic business towards a digital economy, and we discuss the implications for information technology in organizations.

- Part 2 is about new thinking. While some of the topics, such as transactions and object orientation, may sound familiar, we reinvestigate them here for their relevance within electronic business. Other topics, such as component-based architectures, aspect-oriented programming, or agents, are fairly new to application programmers but have already found a place in the design of electronic business applications. The concepts are discussed on a philosophical level.

- In Part 3 we discuss concrete technology for electronic business. We give an overview of Java (including Java 2 Enterprise Edition) and XML, and discuss Software AG's Bolero in detail. Bolero integrates the main principles of modern application architecture, such as object orientation, separation of concern, components, and design patterns. We find that the novel concept of long transactions serves as a blueprint for electronic business application design. Finally, we discuss aspects of the integration of electronic business applications with legacy applications. Readers will benefit from a basic knowledge of Java and general object-orientated programming principles.

- In Part 4 we discuss aspects of software reuse and software quality in general. A chapter about Software AG's Software Engineering Lifecycle Model, an object-oriented project development model, concludes this part. Readers will benefit from a basic knowledge of project mangement and object-oriented principles.

- Two case studies are presented in the appendix.

There is one important topic not discussed in this book: the social implications of the digital economy. We know the new technology will have a huge impact on human society, like other revolutionary technologies such as the printing press or the telephone, but we feel that predictions regarding such implications are outside the scope of this book.

At the current speed of developments in electronic business, this book can give nothing more than a snapshot. However, we have tried not to give too much attention to the latest gimmick, but to concentrate on more fundamental developments (at least in our opinion) and on sound engineering practices.

This is obviously necessary. In June 1998 IEEE Software held a roundtable with experts from the software engineering field under the title 'Can Internet-based Applications Be Engineered?'. The very fact that this question was raised suggests that most Internet-based applications are indeed not engineered, but that implementations tend to follow the Q&D (quick and dirty) scheme. This is understandable in a race to be the first. But at a growth rate of 70 per cent per annum electronic business applications will dominate IT in a few years. It is vital to discuss engineering practices for electronic business now if the industry does not want to be faced with problems that will make the Y2K problem appear marginal.

Read it,
and read it quick

This is why we wrote this book. Read it, and read it quick. Please.

Who should read this book

This book is targeted at business managers and professionals involved with online applications, as well as IT decision makers such as IT managers, project managers and also chief information officers (CIOs). We hope that it is equally informative and entertaining for just about anybody involved in computers, software, and electronic business.

It is not a hands-on book. We are talking concepts and architectures in terms of business, not so much nuts-and-bolts. So you won't find advice here on how to code an applet, how to set up a firewall, or how to make RMI work with SSL.

That does not mean that there is no program code in this book. When demonstrating a programming concept, a piece of code is often worth more than a thousand words. We have tried hard not to overdo it.

Acknowledgements

This book was made possible through the help and support of many people, especially from Software AG.

In particular we wish to thank Rainer Glaap, Wolf-Rüdiger Hansen, Peter Mossak and Harald Nehring, for bringing this project 'on the rails'. Their ideas helped to define the final shape of the book.

Valuable feedback was provided by Christof Braun, Christian Gengenbach, Udo Hafermann, Nigel W.O. Hutchinson, Bernd Kiel, Martin Meijsen, Hans-Georg Stork (European Communities), Walter Waterfeld, Christine Zimmermann, and others.

Project management and support was provided by Ellen Engels, Dieter Müller and Thomas Stough. Without their help we would hardly have succeeded in keeping to the tight deadlines. At this point we also wish to thank our publisher Addison-Wesley.

Special thanks go to Annette Abel and Sheila Chatten who had to deal with our slightly teutonic English.

We are grateful to Software AG for supporting this project, and to our family members, partners and friends for their patience.

Berthold Daum   Markus Scheller
bdaum@online.de   mars@softwareag.com
November 1999

Trademark notice

ActiveX, FrontPage, Internet Explorer, J Script, NT Server, Office 2000, VBScript, VisualBasic, Visual InterDev, Windows 95, Windows NT, Windows CE, Windows NT SNA, Windows NT Workstation, Word are trademarks of Microsoft Corporation

Adabas, Bolero, EntireX, Natural, Tamino are trademarks of Software AG

AIX, APL, CICS TS, CICS/390, MQSeries, MVS, OS/2, OS/39, WebSphere are trademarks of International Business Machines Corporation

Alto, Smalltalk, Star are trademarks of Xerox Corporation

Beos is a trademark of Be, Inc.

Boeing 777 is a trademark of Boeing

Delphi is a trademark of Borland International Inc.

Dreamweaver is a trademark of Macromedia

Dynamo is a trademark of ATG

Eiffel is a trademark of Interactive Software Engineering Inc.

Fusion is a trademark of NetObjects

HP-UX is a trademark of Hewlett-Packard Inc.

HyperCard, Macintosh, MacOS, Objective-C are trademarks of Apple Computer Inc.

HotJava, Java, JavaOS, Sun Solaris are trademarks of Sun Microsystems, Inc.

JavaScript, Netscape, Netscape Navigator are trademarks of Netscape Communications Corporation

Jrun is a trademark of Allaire

Jserv is a trademark of Apache

Levi is a trademark of Levi Strauss

Mercedes Benz is a trademark of DaimlerChrysler

Minitel is a trademark of France Telecom

Modula-3 is a trademark of Digital Equipment Corporation

Mosaic is a trademark of National Center for Supercomputing Applications

NetWare is a trademark of Novell Inc.

Opera is a trademark of Opera Software

Orbix is a trademark of Iona Technologies

PalmPilot is a trademark of 3Com Corporation

Portico is a trademark of General Magic

Psion is a trademark of Psion Plc

SAP R/3 is a trademark of SAP

Simula 67 is a trademark of Simula AS

SkyDSL is a trademark of State Medien AG

TRU64 UNIX is a trademark of Compaq

UNIX is a trademark of AT&T

Visa is a trademark of Visa International

VisiBroker is a trademark of Inprise

WebLogic is a trademark of BEA

X-Windows is a trademark of Massachusetts Institutue of Technology

Success with electronic business

Part 1 tries to outline the emerging digital economy, as far as this is poss-ible, and with it the expanding electronic business. We discuss the technical foundations, take a look at interesting web sites, and discuss the need for new software technology.

- Chapter 1 discusses the technical foundations of the digital age, the omnipresence of computers, the ever-increasing and ever-limited bandwidth of communication lines, and standards that shaped electronic business.

- Chapter 2 introduces the exciting and colourful world of electronic business. We discuss new products, manufacturing on demand, supply networks, and safety issues.

- Chapter 3 tries to outline the requirements this new economy imposes on information technology. New software will have to be multi-talented, flexi-ble and responsive.

Information processing at the turn of the millennium

1

This is not the end,
Even not the beginning of the end,
but it may be the end of the beginning.

Winston Churchill

At the turn of the millennium the pace seems to slow down:

According to September, 1999 data from Nielsen//NetRatings, the number of active Web consumers dropped a slight 2.81 percent from 66.8 million to 64.9 million. (Berst 1999)

Between 1996 and 2000 the average yearly growth in the number of Internet users worldwide has been 50 million new users. This has qualified the Internet as the fastest-growing new technology in the history of mankind. The forecast for the period from 2000 to 2005, however, is a mere 20 million per annum, reaching a total of 350 million users in 2005 (Figure 1.1).

Does the Internet get into calmer waters?

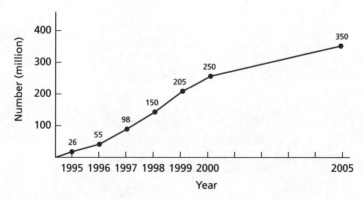

Figure 1.1   Internet users worldwide. (Source: Nua Internet Surveys)

This is still a massive growth rate other industries would kill for. However, it seems that the Internet gets into slightly calmer waters. There are reasons:

- Not until the middle of the first decade in the new millennium will very high bandwidth capacity communication lines be widely available. Until that happens, the online experience remains an experience for the brave and the patient, especially when dealing with rich and therefore bandwidth-intensive content.

- New technologies such as XML, which are necessary to tame the huge amount of information, are still young and large parts are not yet standardized. These technologies will be standardized and find their way onto a dominant percentage of desktops (probably version 6 of Internet Explorer and Netscape) by 2003–2004 (Jacob Nielsen).

User response to the Internet ranges from enthusiasm to nil

On the consumer side the response to the Internet has ranged from enthusiastic to nil, mostly depending on the geographic location (Figure 1.2). While in the US about four in ten households have Internet access (1998), in areas outside the wealthy industrial nations Internet access is more or less restricted to universities, other scientific organizations and government authorities.

But even between industrial countries there are huge differences (Figure 1.3). While in May 1998 about 35 per cent of the population of Finland were connected (Gallup), only 5 per cent of the French were connected to the Internet (Mediangles), mainly because the French already had a popular online device – the Minitel. In February 1998, Iceland scored a per capita Internet access of 45 per cent (Gallup) – which means that nearly every household is connected. In Germany, in contrast, only 10 per cent of the population were connected by March 1999 (GfK).

This means that it is not the complexity of the PC that is the problem, as some media experts claim – or at least that the problem is not that simple. Germany, for example, is an industrialized nation – many people are familiar with PCs and use them in the office. It is unlikely that a German user would have more trouble setting up an Internet connection than a Finnish or Icelandic user.

Africa	1.14 million
Asia/Pacific	26.97 million
Europe	38.55 million
Middle East	0.88 million
Canada & USA	90.63 million
South America	5.26 million
World	163.25 million

Figure 1.2 The phenomenal growth: by May 1999 163.25 million users worldwide were connected to the Internet. (Source: Nua Internet Surveys)

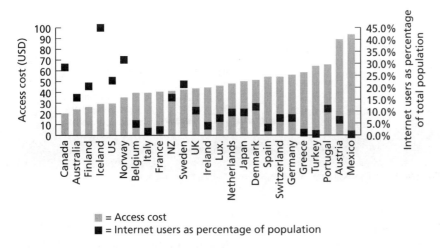

= Access cost
= Internet users as percentage of population

Figure 1.3   Comparison of Internet penetration and access costs, selected OECD nations. (Source: European Commission)

We think that the reason why people connect to the Internet is the value proposition made to them. For people in countries with very big distances, like Australia, the USA and the Scandinavian countries, or in remote countries, like Iceland, the value of the Internet is clear to see: it brings people together, whether in the personal area, in entertainment, science or work.

Value is balanced against cost. For example, people will put up with the pain of installing a browser only if it is worth it, i.e. if the Internet offers so much value that they are not deterred by difficulties. Removing the difficulties will make it easier for the undecided to connect.

Communication costs matter, too. In countries with a flat rate for telephone fees, such as the US or Australia, users tend to connect to the Internet for longer than in countries where call time is metered, such as Germany. Equipment cost is also an issue – in the poorer countries only a few privileged people have access to the Internet or even to a phone or to electric power.

The value proposition of the Internet must balance against user concerns and costs

Security is also a concern. But only to a certain extent: for example, if I have to spend half a day browsing office supply shops and computer shops in search of an ink cartridge for my printer, but can solve the problem from my desktop within five minutes by using the Internet and also get a better price, I am more inclined to take a security risk.

Privacy is another area of concern. Privacy issues matter so much that they have become a topic in high politics. The 'Your privacy' button on US web pages, for example, is a reaction to European complaints about non-existent US privacy laws. On the other hand, current European plans to police web servers could cause users to stop performing financial transactions online.

What we want to make clear is that it is the balance between value and cost that makes people decide to connect to the Internet (Figure 1.4). Both depend on the regional, national, cultural and social context of the prospective user.

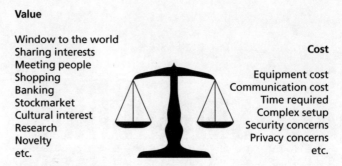

Value

Window to the world
Sharing interests
Meeting people
Shopping
Banking
Stockmarket
Cultural interest
Research
Novelty
etc.

Cost

Equipment cost
Communication cost
Time required
Complex setup
Security concerns
Privacy concerns
etc.

Figure 1.4 The balance between value and cost.

Online shopping growing, but still marginal

So, when the growth of the Internet slows down, how about the development of online commerce?

What about online shopping? While some online retailers such as Dell or Amazon.com have been very successful, the total amount of money spent in online shops is rather marginal. In the US the average person spent about $24 per year on the web in 1997. For 2000, a yearly spend of $99 is forecast (BancAmerica Corp.).

Especially in Europe, only a small fraction of Internet users use the shopping facilities, for example 30 per cent in the UK (Durlacher Research Ltd). The reasons quoted by users are security fears and the lack of online shops. The lack of online shops may be caused by the fact that only 30 per cent of online shops worldwide (ActivMedia, Inc.) are profitable. While it is inexpensive to set up shop on the Internet, the maintenance of a shopping site could cause considerable overhead.

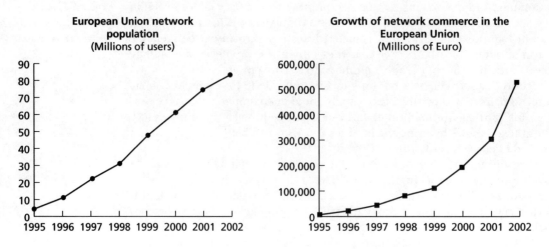

Figure 1.5 The growth in network commerce exceeds the growth in network population: an increasing percentage of Internet users start to shop online. (Source: European Communities)

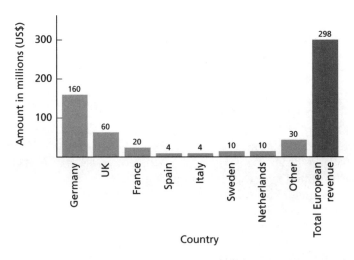

Figure 1.6 Consumer spending in Europe (1998) by country. (Source: Datamonitor)

We expect that the consolidation of Internet technologies and the introduction of security standards will improve this situation. Also, the rising number of users and an increasing percentage of users who use the Internet for shopping will make online shops more profitable, attracting more businesses to the web, which in turn will attract more customers. The 'critical mass' has not yet been reached in most countries.

So, we expect the growth in online shopping to exceed the growth in user numbers (Figures 1.5, 1.6 and 1.7). However, the real business value of the Internet lies elsewhere: in business-to-business transactions.

The Internet's real business value lies in B2B commerce

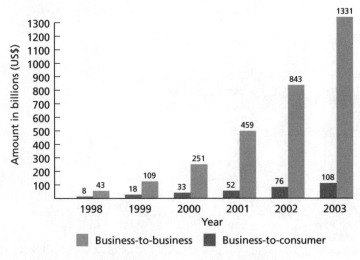

Figure 1.7 US e-commerce 1998–2003. (Source: Forrester Research)

What did we say at the beginning of the chapter?

At the turn of the millennium the pace seems to slow down.

Not quite.

1.1   Computers everywhere

During the age of the steam engine, an industrial plant would have one source of power, a large steam engine. From there the power was transmitted via belts to the machines and tools used for production.

The electric motor has changed this completely. While originally they simply replaced the steam engine, electric motors became smaller, more versatile and an integrated part of machines and tools. Today, we find an electric motor in almost any device – a PC, for instance, employs about 12 motors in hard drives, CD-ROM drives, floppy drives, and fans. Electric motors have become ubiquitous.

Miniaturization and mobility

The analogy with computers is obvious. Whereas 25 years ago a company would have a single computer that filled a large room and could fuel the central heating system, since then computers have crept onto nearly every desktop, then onto laps, and from there into the attaché cases and the pockets of their users (Figures 1.8 and 1.9).

Those are the computers we see. There are also the computers we don't see. They control the output of desktop printers, manage the photocopier, control the motors of our cars; they are found in hi-fi equipment, TVs, VCRs, video and photo cameras, chip cards, automatic teller machines, vending machines, kitchen appliances, washing machines, traffic controllers, telephone switchboards and Internet routers; they control the power supply, water supply, air

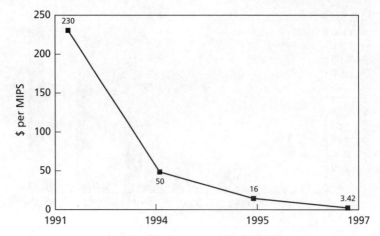

Figure 1.8 Microprocessor prices plummet from \$230 to \$3.42 per MIPS in six years. (Source: Intel)

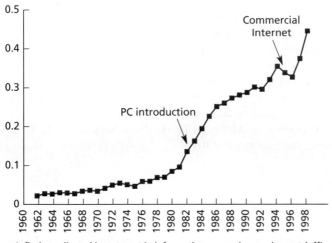

Inflation-adjusted investment in information processing equipment (office,
computing and accounting machinery, communications equipment,
instruments and photocopying equipment) as a share of total private
equipment investment. (0.5 = 50 per cent share)

Figure 1.9   IT's share of business equipment investment. (Source: US Department of
Commerce Bureau of Economic Analysis)

conditioning and central heating. Today, about 15 billion microchips are in use
– 2.5 for every human being.

From the White House

> *The invention of the steam engine two centuries ago and the harnessing of elec-*
> *tricity ushered in an industrial revolution that fundamentally altered the way*
> *we work, brought the world's people closer together in space and time, and*
> *brought us greater prosperity. Today, the invention of the integrated circuit and*
> *computer and the harnessing of light for communications have made possible*
> *the creation of the global Internet and an electronic revolution that will once*
> *again transform our lives.* (White House 1997)

1.2   Wide communication lines?

Patience is the virtue of donkeys.

Honoré Daumier on the invention of photography

'What is more exciting,' was an advertising headline by Intel Corp., 'watching a
web page build up, or watching paint dry?'

The fact is, the Internet is slow. It is also a fact that the Internet is still slow even although we now have fast analog modems and ISDN. The gain in bandwidth was counterbalanced by web pages with graphically rich content, applets, large scripts, animation, etc.

So, we should not expect a much faster Internet even with wider communication bandwidth in the near future. As soon as new capacity is provided, it will be used up by even richer web pages. Wouldn't it be nice to see a video of the new car on the computer screen in HDTV quality before you buy it? But the quality of web video – even over ISDN – is still miserable. So we know what we have to do with the new bandwidth.

The last mile

While high speed networks, like Internet2, are already available to the scientific community, the last mile to the suburbs and family homes is still painstakingly slow (Table 1.1). What we need is a *massive* growth in bandwidth, not just an increase from 33 Kbps to, let's say, 56 Kbps.

The following is an overview of forthcoming communication technologies for public networks.

- **ADSL** (Asymmetric Digital Subscriber Line) was first designed in the US for video on demand, but is now introduced in some countries as a fast Internet access. It delivers up to 8 Mbps transfer rate downstream (from provider to user) and up to 1 Mbps transfer rate upstream (from user to provider). ADSL can use existing telephone wires, so it does not need additional infrastructure. However, the maximal distance between repeater and terminal must not exceed 5.5 to 8 km. This rules out ADSL for country regions – or large investments in amplifiers would be required. At least in the beginning, ADSL will only be made available to metropolitan areas.

- **Wireless** communication like Wiman (Wireless Metropolitan Area Network) is another option. Operating in the radio frequency band between 2.0000 and 2.4835 GHz, this technique delivers up to 128 Kbps transfer rate per user. The maximal distance between provider and terminal is between 5 and 10 km. The advantage of this system is that no rewiring is required. This technology is already an economic alternative to leased line-based services.

- **Satellite**. It is hard to say if direct bi-directional end-user access to satellite-based Internet access will be an economic alternative in the near future. Even for narrow bandwidth satellite phones, connection costs are high.

  Satellites, however, can be used for web casting, combined with digital radio and digital TV. A selected set of content is sent downstream simultaneously to all end users, while the upstream channel is provided by normal phone lines. SkyDSL, for example, uses downstream satellite-based transmission with a maximum baud rate of 4 Mbps. A standard phone line is used for the upstream channel. The system is able to answer individual requests from users but also delivers multicast services to the user base.

- **TV cables**. In some countries TV cables are used for wide bandwidth Internet access. Special cable modems are required, featuring a shared capacity of 1.2 to 27 Mbps. Because this capacity is shared among several end users in a neighbourhood, an estimate for downstream speed is 550 Kbps or more. Newer-generation TV cables can work bi-directionally, while older-generation TV cables can only work downstream. In this case the upstream channel must be provided by a normal phone line in dial-up mode. However, e-mails can be received while the phone line is disconnected. Again, TV cables are usually restricted to metropolitan areas.

  Understandably, using TV cables for Internet access in favoured by media giants such as Bertelsmann or Murdoch.

- **Power line**. Several companies have announced systems to transmit digital information and telephony signals via electric power lines, both from a provider to an end user and as a local area network (LAN) solution. These systems offer access to all electrical devices in an area without rewiring. Power-line systems are not restricted to metropolitan areas but can provide fast Internet access throughout the country. These systems are pushed strongly by power companies, who, of course, want to play a role in the deregulated telecommunications market, but also plan to introduce innovative and value added services along with the electric power supply. Existing services such as power meter reading can be automated. New services and tariffs such as load management, central supervision of appliances, energy management, 'green' power, etc. can also be offered.

  At the time of writing, these systems are in the field test stage. The problem with these systems is that an open standard is required, and standardization usually takes some time. In theory these systems have much appeal: where there is an electric power point there is also Internet access. Suppliers of other communal services, such as water or gas, are probably thinking hard and long about how to use their infrastructure for Internet access.

Table 1.1 Time needed to transfer a 10 MB file.

New technologies for the last mile

Modem speed/type	Transfer time
14.4 Kbps modem	1.5 hours
28.8 Kbps modem	46 minutes
128 Kbps ISDN	10 minutes
512 Kbps Wireless	2.5 minutes
1.54 Mbps T-1 connection	52 seconds
4 Mbps cable modem	20 seconds
8 Mbps ADSL technology	10 seconds
10 Mbps cable modem	8 seconds

However, whatever solution prevails, electronic businesses are well advised to keep their bandwidth usage modest. We have seen that most of the new technologies will only be available in metropolitan areas. Country areas, however, have traditionally been strong in mail order shopping; they will be a strong area for Internet shopping, but also for connecting regional industry within a business-to-business scenario. Not by accident, countries like Australia or the Scandinavian countries, where country people have to travel long distances, have the highest Internet access per capita.

The backbone

The growing number of Internet connections and the requirements for fast delivery of rich content place heavy demands on backbone technology. The Internet is based on telephony networks, and therefore depends on the capacity of these networks. Most telephony networks use a combination of copper cable, fibre optic cable and satellite transmission. Fibre optic offers the most potential: for physical reasons (the atmosphere) satellites cannot broadcast in the short wavelength and high bandwidth spectrum of light. The advantage of satellites is that they can simultaneously broadcast to many receivers (multicast) so they are well suited for the 'last mile'.

Fibre optic bandwidth doubles every year

The capacity of fibre optic cables to carry information is currently doubled every 12 months. New technologies such as wavelength division multiplexing (WDM) allow more information to be squeezed into a single fibre.

- **SONET and SDH**. Telephony lines use multiplexing to squeeze many simultaneous phone calls onto one communication channel. A 1.544 Mbps wide T1 line multiplexes 24 voice channels with a bandwidth of 64 Kbps each. Through the mid-1990s, T1 was the standard access to the Internet for a corporate LAN.

  Telephone carriers in turn multiplex 672 voice-grade channels into a T3 line running at 45 Mbps, or into a T4 line carrying 4,032 voice-grade channels. The bottleneck for faster Internet backbones is the multiplexing/demultiplexing process. This is solved with SONET (Synchronous Optical Network) in North America and SDH (Switched Digital Hierarchy) in Europe. A basic SONET channel carries 51.84 Mbps. The Internet backbone presently uses OC-12 SONET, multiplexing 12 STS-1 channels to achieve 622 Mbps. Specifications exist for OC-48, so eventually the Internet backbone may carry as much as 2.488 Gbps.

- **Internet2**. This project comprises 120 US universities and government and industry partners that have joined to develop advanced Internet technologies and applications (CTR Corp. 1999). As a pilot project for future Internet technologies using fibre optics with wavelength division multiplexing, Internet2 was planned to deliver 1,000 times the bandwidth of the public Internet. Later network implementations such as CA*Net3 in Canada exceed this performance again by orders of magnitude.

● **Project Oxygen**. The Project Oxygen Network is a planned global undersea optical fibre cable network with a first phase comprising approximately 169,000 kilometres of optical fibre cable, 97 landing points in 76 countries and locations, and a capacity of 2,560 Gbps (2.56 Tbps) on trans-oceanic segments (Figure 1.10). This capacity equals the capacity of 5,000 C-band satellites and would be sufficient to transmit 2 million videos in DVD quality simultaneously. Cable installation was scheduled to begin in 1999, with the major trans-Atlantic and trans-Pacific links operational in 2001.

Equally as important as transmission speed are public services that are part of   *Adding value*
the Internet backbone but go beyond pure data transmission. They include computers, storage systems and middleware services, such as security systems, resource management, caching, accounting, monitoring, etc., interconnected by networks. The BetaGrid project led by the NCSA is an example of this technology (Foster and Kesselman 1998). Current grids are used in the scientific and research area. For electronic business future grids could offer commodity IT services and would allow enterprises to outsource certain aspects of their IT business, such as databases, data warehouses, data mining, or deep computing tasks. In addition, they can provide support for collaborative projects between

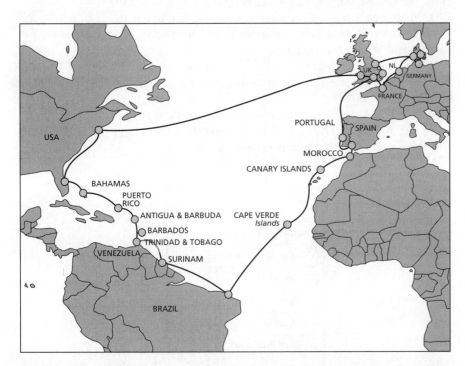

Figure 1.10 Completion of phase 1 of Project Oxygen is scheduled for June 2001. With $10 million per slice, Oxygen is probably the most expensive merchandise offered on the web. But there are some lovely landing points on the way. (NL = The Netherlands)

remote partners (McNealy 1999). These value added services can establish new business models for Internet service providers (ISPs).

1.3 Open standards

The unprecedented growth of the Internet and the World Wide Web was made possible by the existence of open or de-facto standards.

TCP/IP is the Internet's basic communication protocol

TCP/IP (Transmission Control Protocol/Internet Protocol) encompasses both network layer and transport layer protocols of the Open Systems Interconnect (OSI) Reference Model. This seven-layer model was developed by the International Standards Organization (ISO) in 1978 as a framework for international standards in heterogeneous computer network architectures (Figure 1.11).

In TCP/IP the higher TCP layer (transport layer) is responsible for assembling a message into smaller packets and reassembling them at the destination. The lower IP layer (network layer) handles the routing of the packets to the right destination. Packets from the same message may be routed through different paths, but are reassembled in the correct order at the destination.

TCP/IP is a connectionless protocol, meaning that two partners cannot establish a connection that lasts for more than one packet. Each packet sent is independent of previous packets.

TCP/IP forms the basis for higher protocols such as the HyperText Transfer Protocol (HTTP), the File Transfer Protocol (FTP), Telnet, and the Simple Mail Transfer Protocol (SMTP).

HTTP is the WWW's basic communication protocol

HTTP was built on top of TCP/IP mainly for the reason that robust implementations of the TCP/IP protocol were available. The simplicity of HTTP has led to its success: HTTP is powering the World Wide Web.

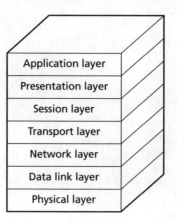

Figure 1.11   The seven layers of the OSI Reference Model

HTTP 1.0 supports three types of requests:

- **GET** returns any information requested.
- **HEAD** returns the server's header information only.
- **POST** is used for posting data, such as electronic mail, news, or forms data.

HTTP 1.0 has no concept of a session, but explicitly opens and closes a connection between client and server for each new request. This causes severe performance penalties, making HTTP about an order of magnitude slower than direct TCP/IP communication (Virginia 1996).

In contrast, HTTP 1.1 establishes permanent connections by default. HTTP 1.1 in addition provides support for

- **access authentication** – the server may request authentication data from the client ('declare yourself');
- **content negotiation** to select the best representation for a given response when there are multiple representations available;
- **caching** to minimize the need to send requests to remote servers. Instead frequently used resources are held locally.

In addition HTTP 1.1 (Fielding et al 1997) provides four more request types:

- GET
- HEAD
- POST
- **OPTIONS** returns information about the communication options available.
- **PUT** stores a web page on the server.
- **DELETE** removes a web page from the server.
- **TRACE** is used for diagnostic purposes and returns to the client what arrived at the final receiver of a request.

The HyperText Markup Language (HTML), the page description language for World Wide Web pages, is an application of SGML (Standard Generalized Markup Language) standardized by the ISO in 1986. SGML is a very powerful construct, suitable for batch processing of documents on mainframes.

HTML is the WWW's basic page description language

HTML pages can refer to each other (and to other resources such as images) by using URLs (Universal Resource Locators). A URL consists of a protocol specification, a domain address for a web server, and a subpath to a document.

HTTP, HTML and URLs are the initial ingredients constituting the World Wide Web. Designed and implemented at CERN (Conseil Européen pour la Recherche Nucléaire) in Geneva by Tim Berners-Lee, the World Wide Web was made available within CERN in December 1990, and on the Internet in the summer of 1991 (Virginia 1996).

NCSA Mosaic, the first web browser, developed by the NCSA (National Center for Supercomputing Applications) at the University of Illinois, was released in 1993, opening a novel and easy way to browse documents stored on the Internet, and fuelling the phenomenal growth of the World Wide Web.

Marc Andreessen, creator of NCSA Mosaic, left NCSA in 1994 to found the Netscape Corporation. This was the beginning of the commercial development of the web, and the major players in the computer industry, such as Microsoft, IBM and Sun Microsystems, would soon discover the web. Microsoft joined in 1996 by releasing Microsoft Internet Explorer.

A browser is the WWW's basic human-computer interface

The last half of the 1990s was characterized by intense competition between players in an effort to set the stakes for the new bonanza. The browser war between Microsoft and Netscape, and the Java war between Microsoft and Sun, were just the public highlights in an intensive struggle for market segments. The competition has certainly accelerated the development of web technology, but on the other hand has also created non-standard HTML dialects which make it difficult to create sophisticated web pages that run on all browsers.

By the end of the decade it had become clear that this situation was counter-productive for the further growth of the web. While complex web pages are not a big problem for desktop PCs, the rising number of low-powered devices accessing the web (web phones, palmtop computers, personal digital assistants (PDAs), etc.) need a simpler technology.

The emphasis in the industry has now turned from adding more 'whiz-bang' features towards consolidation and standardization. The major players like Netscape and Microsoft have promised to compete for the most complete and correct implementation of the standards. We keep our fingers crossed.

WWW technology calls for standardization at all levels

The main standard bodies for the Internet and the World Wide Web are the IETF and the W3C:

- The Internet Engineering Task Force (IETF) is the protocol engineering and development arm of the Internet. The IETF is a large open international community of network designers, operators, vendors and researchers.

- The World Wide Web Consortium (W3C) began operation on 1 October 1994. The W3C is hosted by the Massachusetts Institute of Technology Laboratory for Computer Science (MIT/LCS) in the US, INRIA (Institut National de Recherche en Informatique et en Automatique) in Europe, and Keio University in Japan, with support from DARPA (Defense Advanced Research Projects Agency) in the US and the European Commission. While the IETF is open to any interested individual, membership of the W3C is expensive and only possible for companies and organizations. Members include Netscape, Microsoft, Spyglass, Sun, Apple and many others (Virginia 1996).

After releasing a series of recommendations, as W3C standards are called, the W3C introduced a new document description meta-language in 1998: XML.

Designed as a simple dialect of SGML (the SGML specification covers 500 pages, while the XML specification has only 26), XML had a major impact on standardization efforts in electronic business. XML now forms the basis for nearly every other standardization effort of the W3C.

The new XHTML (eXtensible HyperText Markup Language) specification (W3C 1999-6), for example, is based on XML. XHTML is planned to be the successor of HTML 4.0 and is a major clean-up of non-standard constructs that have crept into the definition and implementations of HTML.

1.4   The omnipresence of the web

At the moment it seems that the 163 million web browsers worldwide far outnumber the web servers. Web browsers have already started to move from desktops into our pockets: hand-held devices, PDAs, palmtop computers, intelligent phones, etc. can all act as web clients.

Mobile computing

Mobile computing adds some challenges to web technology. While the size of screen varies from a few lines in mobile phones and pagers to larger sizes in palmtop computers, the processing and storage capacity and the bandwidth available to such devices is about an order of magnitude lower than in desktop computers. The Wireless Application Protocol (WAP) (WAP Forum 1998) regulates the access of mobile devices to the web and also deals with problems such as intermittent operation: wireless connections tend to be less robust than a stationary connection.

WAP is the basic protocol for mobile devices

Discipline is also required from web authors. The current standard on mobile web browsers is HTML 3.1, while the W3C has published guidelines for using HTML 4.0 with mobile devices. Authors are encouraged to use a particular 'flavour' of HTML 4.0, called HTML 4.0 Strict. This excludes the presentation attributes and elements, and merely marks up the structure of a document. (W3C 1999-2). The XML-based XHTML, successor of HTML 4.0, is an opportunity to extend HTML with specific functionality for domain-specific applications, for example to allow a specific layout for mobile and stationary devices in a single web page.

While *smart proxies* can filter and transform existing web pages for the use of mobile devices, the ideal case is a server that recognizes the client's requirements and sends only specific data to the client. The W3C's Composite Capability/Preference Profiles Proposal (CC/PP) is a mechanism for describing the capabilities and preferences associated with users and the hardware and software they are using to access the World Wide Web (W3C 1998-1).

The web by voice

Eventually, access to the web will not even require a computer. In October 1998 the W3C launched a new activity for a voice browser standard. Based on speech synthesis and recognition, voice browsers will enable anybody with a plain old telephone to access the World Wide Web (W3C 1999-5).

Servers everywhere

Embedded web servers

However, servers are starting a counter-attack. They come in the form of embedded systems. A light switch, for example, is a server. It can be asked for its state and it can be requested to change its state. It may be a server with very limited functionality, but it is a server nevertheless. Connecting it to the Internet would allow us to check from the office if the lights at home are switched off (some may even want to check on the little bulb in the fridge). More complex applications in home control are central heating, security control, web cams, monitoring energy consumption, remote maintenance and so on.

And those are only the applications in the private sector. In an office, for example, we could imagine an intelligent door panel that not only displays which meeting is taking place in the room, but would also reserve the room for scheduled meetings and order lunch for the attendees.

In the health sector, devices such as blood pressure meters, glucose testers or dialysis machines could be connected to the Internet, allowing hospitals and practitioners to monitor patients at home.

In agriculture and ecology we could use the Internet for greenhouse control, pollution control, and: 'I recently read that, in Paris, botanists are putting computer chips in the city's 90,000 trees, so they can continuously monitor their health' (Gerstner 1999-1).

And finally – one cow, one web server?

While this all sounds a bit like science fiction and we feel reminded of Jacques Tati's famous movie *Mon Oncle*, the big players have identified embedded systems as the next big thing in computing.

'Computing will be everywhere' (Gerstner 1999-1). These were not just words. A few months later IBM demonstrated a disk drive with a physical footprint not much larger than a coin.

At the JavaOne conference in 1999, Sun Microsystems launched Java 2 Micro Edition, a dedicated platform for portable devices such as PDAs, mobile phones and pagers, but also for embedded devices. MicroJava includes a new virtual machine (KVM) with a relatively small memory footprint and designed for 16/32-bit processors. Both KVM and standard libraries need only a few hundred kilobytes in size and about 128 KB of RAM or less.

The Java Embedded Server runs on top of this platform and provides web server functionality, such as support for HTTP, servlets, remote administration, logging, etc. Java Embedded Server is targeted at medium-size devices such as set-top boxes or remote-controlled Internet routers.

A different type of server comes from emWare. Backed by Embed, the Internet Consortium (ETI), which includes industry heavyweights such as Analog Devices, Hitachi, Mitsubishi, Motorola, National Semiconductor, Philips, SAP, Siemens and others, emWare has developed the Embedded Micro Internetworking Technology (EMIT), with an embedded, very thin server that can run on 8-, 16- or 32-bit processors and requires less than 1 KB of memory. A group of servers can be connected to the Internet via a gateway, thus sharing one ISP address, and can be controlled via a standard web browser.

Implemented on chips that cost only a few cents, the EMIT servers are targeted at devices such as the light switch mentioned above, but also mobile phones, office equipment, vendor machines, process controllers, etc. With such a small footprint, they might even appear in disposable products.

2 The brave new world of electronic business

In this book, we talk of electronic business instead of electronic commerce. Our understanding of electronic business is wider than that of electronic commerce. Commercial activities such as buying and selling, as the term electronic commerce suggests, are certainly an important part of electronic business but they do not include the full range of electronic business activities (Figure 2.1). The following definition by IBM's CEO, Lou Gerstner, matches closely with our idea of electronic business:

Electronic business defined

> *We coined the term 'e-business' to describe all the ways individuals and institutions derive value from the Net – buying and selling, but also the important transactions between teachers and students, doctors and patients, governments and citizens.* (Gerstner 1999-2)

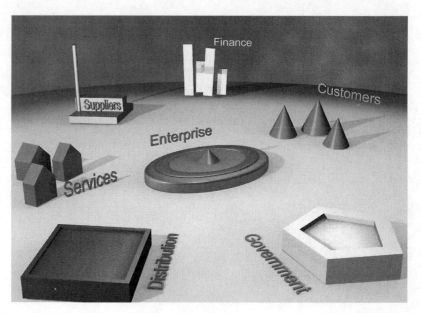

Figure 2.1 Ready for connection – players in electronic business. (Source: Software AG)

Gerstner is absolutely right in emphasizing the 'value' aspect as a key point for electronic business. What remains when the novelty wears off? To be attractive, a web-based service must offer more value than a comparable conventional service. We listed some of the benefits a user can get by conducting business on the web in Chapter 1. But increasingly, as competition gets harder on the web, too, it is not sufficient to rely on the advantages of the Internet alone. Old-fashioned virtues begin to count again, like quality of goods, prompt delivery, after-sales service and customer follow-up.

We can subdivide electronic business activities into the following categories:

Business-to-Business (B2B)

The four categories of electronic business

Traditionally, electronic business networks have been very closed worlds. Using leased lines and value added networks (VANs) to establish an electronic business relation with a partner was a long, complex and expensive process.

The Internet is about to change this:

- Manufacturers are setting up extranets – private networks based on the public Internet infrastructure – especially for supply chains. These are still closed worlds, but within these extranets, the traditional one-to-one approach is increasingly replaced by a networked approach. *Extranets*

- In addition, open markets for buying and selling between businesses are established. These markets may cover the typical small-scale purchases, such as office supplies. But other markets are also created, for example for OEM (original equipment manufacturer) products. These markets attract brokers and intermediaries looking for the best products and the best conditions. It will be a tough, competitive market. Flexibility and service will be instrumental to success. *Open markets*

- Not exactly B2B, but an important market for companies is the market for human resources. Many companies use the Internet to advertise open positions, and many individuals advertise their skills on their homepages. Again, this market attracts middlemen, such as headhunters and human resource specialists. *Human resources*

  The Internet often allows employees to work from home. Using web-based virtual offices, salespeople, for example, need hardly call into the company's office but can do their everyday work from anywhere with web access. *Virtual commuters*

In this new online world, industry associations and guilds play an important role. Involved in the definition of industry standards, and providing online services (knowledge base, consulting, archive, etc.) to their members, they are responsible for the creation of an industry-related online culture. *Associations and guilds*

Business-to-consumer (B2C)

Pioneers

Online shopping had three pioneers. While two of them are well known in this role, the third is popular, too, but for different reasons. We mean Jerry Yang (Yahoo!), Jeffrey Bezos (Amazon.com) and Danni Ashe (Danni's Harddrive). In 1995, at a time when online shopping was still science fiction for many, Ashe went online. The necessary software to exchange adult content against payment was developed in-house. In contrast to Bezos, Ashe made a profit.

However, since then the focus for online shoppers has changed (Figure 2.2). For the Christmas 1997 sale AOL reported a shift in online buying patterns: 'While computer software and hardware were the top sellers a year ago, apparel climbed to No. 1 and books to No. 3 this year. Also popular again this year for AOL shoppers were carryover categories food, flowers, music, and toys' (Clark 1997).

Tangible and non-tangible goods

When selling tangible goods over the Internet, the shipping of the merchandise still poses a problem because of the costs involved. The picture looks brighter for non-tangible goods and services that can be delivered over the Internet. These include travel products, financial services, insurance, software, music, any type of content. We will discuss this in more detail in the next section.

Business-to-administration (B2A)

The business-to-administration category covers all transactions between companies and government organizations. For example, in the USA the details of forthcoming government procurements are publicized over the Internet and companies can respond electronically. In addition to public procurement, administrations may also offer electronic interchange for such transactions as VAT returns and the payment of corporate taxes.

Data collection

In Europe, an estimated €180–230 billion is required every year to collect administration data from 16 million enterprises in the countries of the European Union. In Belgium, for example, 1,500 different questionnaires and data collection forms are in use. A new business has to file about 100 forms during the first year of its existence. The average yearly cost of business-to-administration information interchange is estimated at €2,250 per employee (EcE Conference, Brussels, 1998).

Success in Singapore

Customs is another area where business-to-administration information exchange is a top issue. In Singapore, traders interact with government agencies through TradeNet. Traders have to complete only a single electronic form, which is submitted through the network. TradeNet links all the 18 government agencies involved in issuing trade documents, as well as Port and Civil Aviation authorities. Trade approvals are delivered electronically within 15 minutes. TradeNet saves Singapore traders an estimated $1 billion per year (Howe).

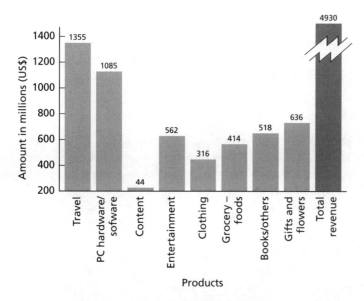

Figure 2.2 Online consumer spending in the US (1998). (Source: Yankee Group)

Consumer-to-administration (C2A)

The consumer-to-administration category is still in its infancy. However, in the wake of the growth of both the business-to-consumer and business-to-administration categories, governments may extend electronic interaction to such areas as welfare payments, self-assessed tax returns, car registration, etc.

Alaska was the first state in the USA to go online with car registrations. Alaska's Department of Motor Vehicles (DMV) has developed a simple and secure way for citizens to renew vehicle registrations, order personalized licence plates and charge these services to a credit card. 'The new system has eliminated thousands of transactions in DMV offices and with it the frustration of applicants who previously waited for hours in line and another six to eight weeks for documents to arrive by mail. The same process now takes an average of less than three minutes without leaving home' (SAGA Software, Inc. 1999).

Car registration in Alaska

This sector also includes consumer relations with large private institutions, such as health insurers or car insurers. Claim processing can be performed across the Internet using digital documents.

The introduction of digital documents may have far-reaching consequences. Once a workflow for document processing is established, it is not even necessary that administration officers involved in the processing of these documents work in the same place – administration can become distributed (Brandsma 1999).

2.1   The products of 2001 – immaterial and transient

The most interesting products for electronic business are products that can be delivered directly over the Internet. These are the non-tangible products and services, including those described below.

Online banking

France processes an estimated 500 million banking transactions per year (1995) over its Minitel network. While Minitels have definitely slowed down the acceptance of the Internet in France, in online banking it has put France years ahead of the rest of the world (Howe).

In the USA roughly 4.5 million households were banking online in 1997. By 2000, as many as 16 million US households are expected to bank online (US Dept of Commerce 1998).

1 cent for one transaction

The advantages for online banking are obvious. For banks, the cost of transactions over the Internet is about three orders of magnitude lower than a counter transaction. In the US, a counter transaction costs $1.07, while an Internet transaction is only $0.01 (Figure 2.3).

For consumers, online banking saves a trip to the bank branch – usually an activity to fill the lunch break. It can also save banking fees, depending on the policies of the bank (Figure 2.4). Some of the early pioneers of 'virtual' banking have failed – mainly because they had to break into an already competitive market, could offer only specialized services, and had big marketing costs. They were absorbed by their 'real' competitors – virtually all of those now offer online banking services, too, or plan to do so.

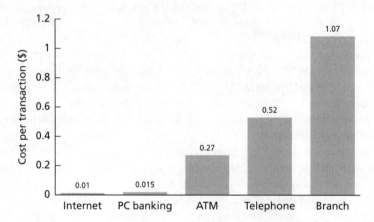

Figure 2.3 Internet banking is cheaper for banks. (Source: Booz-Allen & Hamilton)

Figure 2.4   In the USA, IBM, Visa and 13 major financial institutions have formed the Integrion network allowing financial transactions to be performed over the Internet. The network plans to reach more than 60 million households.

Shares and securities trading

Securities trading occurs over the Internet in large numbers, and analysts have compared the selling of shares over the Internet with an earthquake. In the first quarter of 1999 alone, online brokerage increased by 47 per cent compared to the last quarter of 1998 (Reuters). It is estimated that 16 per cent of all stock trades were transacted online by June 1999. The online trade has opened new possibilities to users: day trading, allowing them to buy and sell shares or options in real time. It is estimated that 10 per cent of German customers that trade online are engaged in day trading (ConSors Discount-Broker).

Insurance

Distribution costs for life, property and casualty policies can be as high as 33 per cent or more of the product's price. The online insurance market is expected to boom in the next few years (Table 2.1). Traditional insurers increasingly meet competition from banks and other financial institutions.

Table 2.1   Expected turnover in the online insurance market.

	1997	2001
Auto	$21 M	$850 M
Term life	$17 M	$108 M
Homeowner	$1.1 M	$152 M
Total	$39.1 M	$1.1 B

(Source: Forrester Research)

Tickets and fares

Airline tickets (and others) lend themselves to being booked over the Internet. In 1996, web users booked $276 million worth of travel. For 1997, online travel sales were estimated to have reached $816 million, and in 2000, online travel sales could reach the $5 billion mark.

Software

Software products should be prime candidates for distribution over the Internet. In fact, shareware authors distribute their programs to a large extent over the Internet. For large products, however, that come in package sizes around 100 MB and above, the low bandwidth of the Internet is still a deterrent – download times are too high. Nevertheless, many companies offer their products (and also try-out versions) on the Internet, often at reduced prices.

Intermediaries

- **Aggregators** help to build seller or buyer communities such as shopping malls or buyer pools.
- **Online auctions** allow sellers and buyers to participate in multiple, real-time auctions simultaneously – without accruing physical-world search and travel costs.
- **Online exchanges** provide sellers and buyers with a trading venue defined by clear rules, industry-wide pricing and open market information. An online industry spot market can operate at a fraction of physical-world cost (Lief 1999).

Education and training

IBM's CEO Lou Gerstner: 'About one-third of all our internal training will be done this year via distributed learning, with savings and productivity gains of $100 million' (Gerstner 1999-2).

Business radio/TV

Used on intranets, business radio or TV broadcasts inform staff about corporate news.

Consulting services

These include web-related consulting services, such as hosting and designing web pages, installing online shops, creating Internet events, etc. Freelance consultants and small consulting firms can also use the Internet to network and form virtual consulting firms.

Healthcare

Networking health institutions, such as hospitals, physicians and health insurers, is paramount to reduce the administration overhead in the health industry.

Compared to other industries, in terms of communication the healthcare industry is antiquated. Only a third of hospitals are electronically linked to other health institutions. It is estimated that one in every four dollars spent on healthcare ($250 billion of $1 trillion) is wasted through the delivery of unnecessary care, performance of redundant tests and procedures, and excessive administrative costs (U.S. Bancorp Piper Jaffray).

The Internet can change this drastically. Not only can healthcare institutions network with each other and share healthcare workflow management such as a treatment plan for a patient, but patients will also have the option to access information online, such as their personal health plan, and to make appointments online, pay bills, lodge claims with insurers and check the status of claims.

Customer service

There are many options for improving customer service over the Internet. Customers can check on the status of an order or a delivery. Troubleshooting, the latest product news, chat rooms, customer help and customer initiatives can be made available online. These features are not only of additional value to the customer, but also mean big savings on call centres for the supplier.

Content

Despite the fact that rich forms of content (music, video) are still hampered by the narrow bandwidth of current Internet technology, newspapers and magazines, radio and TV stations have wholeheartedly embraced the Internet. There are few newspapers that do not offer supporting web pages. Often these pages include archives, allowing users to browse old news, and often additional services such as online classifieds and auctions are provided. This information is often provided free of charge, obviously without negative impact on the print run of the paper-based original, while TV stations experienced a slight drop in rates. Nearly 90 per cent of web users go online to get news and information.

Advertising

Internet advertising in the USA surpassed outdoor advertising in 1998 with $1.92 billion in revenues compared to $1.58 billion. From 1997 to 1998, online advertising revenue grew by 112 per cent (Internet Advertising Bureau).

2.2   Towards a digital economy

Digital content management is crucial for successful electronic business

At present, about 4 million employees in Europe work in the content-related industry, an industry with a yearly turnover of €376 billion. This industry will be transformed under the impact of the new technologies. Springer Berlin Heidelberg, for example, a publisher of scientific books and journals, has been a pioneer in digital publishing, largely because the scientific clientele were online long before everybody else. Springer publishes abstracts of scientific articles on the web for free. Only subscribers have access to the full version. Because the electronic version offers richer forms of presentation such as animation, 3D or virtual reality, paper-based versions of such publications have become second choice. The publisher has now announced an 'online-first' policy for several journals: articles are published on the Internet months before they appear in print. A new system allowing authors and editors to edit articles online is in development and should further decrease the time to publication.

Digital content production, however, will not only augment or replace traditional content. In fact, content production will be the business of any business that moves to the web. It is not possible to sell goods and services online without producing content for web pages.

Web content publishing requires a much lower capital investment than the traditional paper-based counterpart (Figure 2.5). The content of a newspaper or magazine does not have to be printed and delivered to newsstands or doorsteps across the country – steps that add 30 to 40 per cent to the cost of the product. Once the content has been created and stored, there is little or no extra cost to send it to one reader or 1,000 readers (US Dept of Commerce 1998).

Knowledge and information are the assets of a digital world

In fact, in the digital world physical assets become less important, and are replaced or complemented by virtual assets, mainly knowledge. While the introduction of colour photos on the cover of the *New York Times* required an investment of $350 million in a new printing press, the investments to make articles available on the web have been negligible in comparison and readers got more value: not only are the pictures in colour, but articles can contain radio or video clips, are updated every 10 minutes, and can provide links to in-depth information.

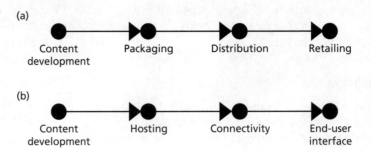

(a)

Content development   Packaging   Distribution   Retailing

(b)

Content development   Hosting   Connectivity   End-user interface

Figure 2.5   (a) Traditional publishing value chain; (b) interactive content value chain.

Digital forms of music and video production allow film and music makers to replace expensive studio equipment by software running on computer workstations, or even Macs and PCs. The Internet allows the output to be distributed, almost without cost, to the whole world. Music groups can now easily self-publish their titles over the web using technologies such as MP3.

Similar developments are currently happening in the video sector. Digital video technology and the ever-increasing processing power of computers allow individuals to create videos of professional quality, edit them on a notebook computer, and submit them to the Internet – a new form of journalism. In an Australian TV experiment, ABC television sent eight young amateur journalists, equipped with small digital video cameras, on a *Race around the World*. Each week their reports were broadcast over TV and discussed; a web site was established for fan support. The series was a huge success.

Future wide bandwidth communication lines will allow a direct connection from content producer to content consumer. While technology will allow producers to reach large audiences with very little investment, and will result in a plethora of small web-based video stations, that does not mean that everybody is able to produce quality content. Experiences with community television, for example, show that it is not easy to produce quality TV. In the future digital economy, what will count are not physical assets, but the combination of individual knowledge, the ability to organize the cooperation of people effectively, and the ability to market a product successfully (Figure 2.6).

An example is the software industry. While nearly everybody in the industrial countries is able to buy a PC and start software development, the fact is that software products have become extremely complex and the development costs for a new product are measured in millions of dollars. Microsoft's success, for example, relies on the ability to react quickly and massively to new developments in the market. 'Time-to-market' is essential in the software industry.

Time-to-market is the key to electronic business

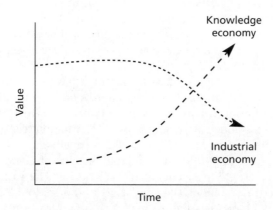

Figure 2.6 The knowledge economy vs. the industrial economy.

In the Internet-based digital economy, these trends will be even more dominant. In a market where it is possible to launch a new product to hundreds of millions of potential consumers almost instantaneously, companies have to respond to new developments fast.

A major industry   A European study (Frost & Sullivan) predicts that by 2004 over 40 per cent of revenue in electronic commerce will be generated by what the report terms 'intangible' consumer goods, namely online services and information. Business products will generate 20 per cent of revenue, followed by 'tangible' consumer products. By 2002, about 5 per cent of the GDP of the European Union will be either directly or indirectly related to the use of digital networks.

In the USA, by 2006, almost half the workforce will be employed by industries that are either major producers or intensive users of information technology products and services (US Dept of Commerce 1999).

2.3   From store front to production line

Just-in-time delivery was a concept developed by the retail sector to keep inventories low. Lower inventories mean less storage cost and less capital cost. They also mean less outdated stock when a new product version arrives. Just-in-time delivery was enabled by the installation of electronic point-of-sales (EPoS) systems – in a supermarket usually equipped with a scanner. When the customer checks out, the barcodes of the merchandise are scanned in. The computer can therefore maintain a close image of the actual inventory (if we ignore shoplifting). Orders are sent to suppliers when the inventory goes below a certain level, and suppliers guarantee that new stock is delivered within a specified time frame. The system also has some drawbacks – suppliers now have more work. They must keep to schedules and probably make more and smaller deliveries. Because not much stock is held locally, safety margins are thin.

Similar techniques are used today in business-to-business transactions in the supply chain. Large companies, such as General Motors, for example, rely on thousands of smaller suppliers. Just-in-time delivery from these suppliers has a substantial cost-saving effect for the buyer. Just-in-time delivery was certainly one of the driving forces when General Motors introduced electronic data interchange (EDI) to its suppliers.

While one aspect of supply chain management (SCM) – also known as supplier–retailer collaboration (SRC) – is the improvement of the flow of physical goods, another important aspect is to enhance the flow of information. Reducing non value-added activities by using information technology results in cost reduction, improved data accuracy and less paperwork.

A European study identified the potential benefits of computer-based SCM to be approximately 2.5 per cent of the retail price. The total logistics costs would be reduced from about 10 per cent of retail price to 7.5 per cent. In the US, the potential benefits were estimated to be a maximum of 10 per cent (Simon 1998).

Successful SCM requires that the partners share knowledge and information effectively. Restrictive information policies towards partners are counterproductive in an SCM scenario. Instead, companies have to learn to trust their partners. Supply chains that implement strategies of shared knowledge management and knowledge transfer can better respond to the needs of the customer and to changes in the market. Knowledge shared with partners may include information such as analytical sales data, sales forecasts and internal logistics figures, even more qualitative information regarding purchasing behaviour, consumer requirements and changing demands.

Now, with more and more consumers ordering online through the Internet, there will be a paradigm shift. In fact, our heading should rather read 'From browser to production line'. Just-in-time delivery will remain for traditional trade, but online trade works differently: on-demand-delivery and on-demand manufacturing are the concepts that work. One example is Dell: customers not only select a PC from an online catalogue, but can also configure the PC according to their specific requirements. After the customer has submitted the order, the data is sent to Dell's suppliers who then start assembly. Three days after the order was submitted, the PC is delivered to the customer's doorstep. There is no need for an inventory of finished products.

On-demand delivery and manufacturing

Many manufacturers today are able to build an end product in a very short time. Production processes are highly flexible and highly integrated, allowing highly customized products. Delays in delivery are caused more by the fact that administration is not quite as well automated and organized as production. For example, we hear from DaimlerChrysler that, in terms of manufacturing, 24 hours would be enough to build a customer-specified Mercedes Benz. This contrasts to the administrative process which takes about three weeks. But what are three weeks when the queue for your dream car is 18 months long?

2.4   From supply chain to supply network

Contrary to their name, VANs (value added networks) did not initially support the concept of business networks. Instead, electronic business relations were almost always one-to-one relations. Examples are the traditional EDI (electronic data interchange) solutions. Many small and medium-sized suppliers are connected to a large manufacturer on a one-to-one basis. Even when sub-suppliers are connected to a supplier, we still have a hierarchical situation – a supply chain (Figure 2.7).

The closed world of supply chains will continue to exist, but Internet-based technology – extranets – will change it to a world of supply networks.

- The ANX network initiated by General Motors is such a network. It addresses the concerns of enterprises about Internet technology (security, reliability, responsibility, etc.) by setting up a VPN (virtual private network) relying only

GM's Virtual Private Network

on certified and trusted providers, and by using a company that acts as an overseer and is responsible for the stability and security of the network. ANX went into production in 1998, connecting the automotive industry with 15,000 trading partners in the USA and 50,000 worldwide.

Spare parts

● In November 1996, Boeing's spare parts business 'went web', allowing Boeing's airline customers around the world to check the availability and pricing of spare parts, to order parts, and to track the status of orders. Less than a year later, about 50 per cent of Boeing's customers used the Internet for 9 per cent of all parts orders and for a much larger percentage of customer service inquiries. Boeing could handle 20 per cent more shipments per month with the same staff numbers, and as many as 600 phone calls to customer service representatives are avoided each day (US Dept of Commerce 1998).

Procurement

● In 1996, General Electric Lighting piloted the company's first online procurement system. Before, the company's corporate sourcing department received hundreds of requisitions for quotes each day from GE factories. The requisition process needed about seven days and was so complex that the sourcing department sent out bid packages to only two or three suppliers at a time. With the new extranet-based system the bid can be evaluated and awarded the same day. The labour costs for procurement have dropped by 30 per cent, while the material costs have declined by up to 20 per cent because a wider base of suppliers is reached (US Dept of Commerce 1998).

● And IBM: 'We'll procure $12 billion in goods and services over the Web this year, saving $240 million in the process' (Gerstner 1999-2).

The ANX network is a good example of the driving forces behind these developments. The automotive industry is already operating in a global environment and is highly networked. Competitors are more often than not collaborators, working with each other in a mutual client–supplier relationship. The new connectivity was introduced because the economics in this industry community required it.

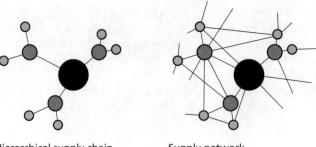

Hierarchical supply chain   Supply network

Figure 2.7 From a hierarchical supply chain to a supply network.

Over the next few years, we will see other industries establishing similar communities. Closed trading networks, such as ANX, that use a shared set of rules and a shared vocabulary, are necessary to establish a working relationship between partners.

2.5   The virtual enterprise

Adidas and Nike don't manufacture shoes; PCs with the Dell label to the value of approximately $50 million a day are sold, but Dell does not produce PCs. The German electronics company Dual is run by only four people, but can look at a palette of 60 innovative products and a turnover of DM 70 million.

What these companies have in common is that they follow the concept of a virtual enterprise (Figure 2.8). Such an enterprise does not need to own factories, distribution chains, or outlets. What is required is a relatively small group of dedicated people with mobile phones and laptops, and the ability to build networks of suppliers, distributors, franchisers, etc. *Virtual enterprise defined*

What virtual enterprises are about is the branding of supply networks, marketing and quality control. Virtual enterprises don't outsource. Instead, they tap into the expertise and the resources of external partners. In the virtual model, a lead organization creates alliances with other groups, both internal and external, that possess the best competencies to build a specific product or service.

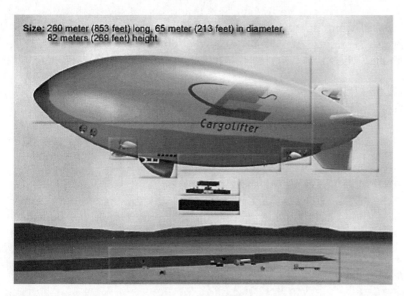

Figure 2.8   Virtual reality: the German company, CargoLifter, was founded in 1996 with a starting capital of DM 50,000, but plans to have a worldwide fleet of 260m long airships up and running by the first decade of the new century.

Virtual enterprises may prefer to work in narrow market segments, like the Boston Beer Company. Their label, Samuel Adams, is brewed regionally all over the USA by external breweries. 'We want to produce better beer, if we own the breweries or not doesn't matter', says Boston Beer's owner James Koch.

Others diversify: Virgin, for example, started as a record company, but now runs under its label the Virgin airline, Virgin balloons ('At Virgin we know hot air balloons work'), Virgin travel, Virgin hotels, Virgin cola, etc. By 'componentizing' the value chain and networking the components, the company is able to exploit synergy, at the same time multiplying the mind-share of the Virgin label.

Virtual enterprise in operation

Traditional and well-established companies are detecting the operative power of virtual enterprises, too. Boeing, for example, 'virtually' designed and manu-factured the new Boeing 777. Boeing teamed up with engine, airframe and electronics makers and suppliers, customers and even competitors spread around the world. They used digital technology to share design and manage-ment information and to develop and sustain parallel engineering efforts across distances and between the different organizations (Brandsma 1999).

For some of the virtual enterprises, the Internet with its ability to reach hundreds of millions of potential customers almost instantaneously has been an instrumental part of their success. In January 1997, Dell Computers was selling less than $1 million of computers per day on the Internet. During the December 1997 holiday period daily sales reached $6 million several times, and continued to climb to $18 million by April 1999 (US Dept of Commerce 1999). Eighty per cent of the consumers and half of the small businesses who purchased from Dell's web site had never purchased from Dell before. Dell expects to conduct half its total business online shortly after 2000 (US Dept of Commerce 1998).

2.6   A buyer's paradise

So, where is the value for the customer?

Customer's benefits

- *Convenience.* Online shops are open 24 hours a day, seven days a week, and the shop is only a few mouse clicks away.

- *Price.* Online shops can offer a lower price because of reduced overhead, or by cutting out the middleman (Figure 2.9). For example, consumers buying and selling stocks through the Internet commonly pay $8–30 per trade, while traditional brokerages charge approximately $80 per trade on average.

- *No sales pressure.* There are no pushy shop assistants (well, almost, if we ignore the occasional pop-up window).

Figure 2.9   With 4.7 million titles (1999), Amazon.com is the largest bookstore on earth. Amazon sells exclusively online – as a virtual retailer, Amazon has no physical store infrastructure. Rent and depreciation represent less than 4 per cent of Amazon's sales compared to 13 per cent for the traditional retailer. Books turn over 20–40 times per year versus two to two-and-a-half times per year for the traditional retailer, allowing Amazon to offer substantial discount to shoppers.

- *More and better information*. Online shops can provide better, more complete, and more up-to-date product information than their traditional counterparts. While individual advice to customers is a strong point in favour of traditional shops, in many cases the information provided online far exceeds the scope of the average shop assistant.

- *Greater choice*. Consumers can choose from a wide variety of shops. Customers are not restricted to walking or driving distance but can shop nationally and internationally (Figure 2.10).

Figure 2.10   Electronic business from Cuba – this site specializes in Cuban rhythms. And yes, you can pay in dollars.

- *Larger selection*. Online shops can offer a wider variety of goods (Figure 2.11).

- *Mass customization*. In many cases, consumers are able to specify their wishes on the web browser in a far more detailed way than a shop or a printed catalogue could allow. A carpet that is woven to the customer's design, a computer that is exactly configured to the requirements of the prospective user, a travel package that is custom tailored, and online magazines that present on the front page the articles that are most important to the reader, are all examples of a unprecedented customization level.

- *Better customer support and service*. Companies can provide better product information via the Internet. Ordering and distribution of spare parts is streamlined. Registered customers can be informed about product upgrades. Customers can get up-to-date information about the status of their order.

  Federal Express is an often quoted example of a company that has improved customer support by using the Internet. By quoting a tracking number, customers are able to access the FedEx web site and query the status of a delivery. While this provides transparency to the customer, it has also saved FedEx (and clients) many calls to call centres. Other courier and mail services, such as DHL and UPS, have followed. UPS has launched a new system, using wireless terminals. As soon as an item is accepted for shipment, the tracking number is entered into the system and can be queried even before the pick-up truck leaves the scene. UPS' web site receives 800,000 tracking requests a day.

- *New products and services*. New products, especially in connection with the telecommunications sector, become available. Listening to e-mail messages on the phone, sending written messages to pagers and making international phone calls across the Internet are just a few.

Figure 2.11 Selling furniture: the customer has the choice between 72 different versions of one single chair at Herman Miller's web store.

One example is General Magic's Portico, a virtual personal assistant. The system can be used via a web browser but also controlled by voice over the phone. It can work as a message bank, screen incoming calls, juggle appointments, keep track of contacts, and access stock quotes and news and read them to the user.

There are, of course, benefits for the trader, too: *Trader's benefits*

- *Novel business opportunities*. The main problem of the Internet is the vast amount of unstructured information. When the whole world is at your fingertips, it is not easy to decide which offer will suit your needs best. A digital globalized economy will bring opportunities for intermediate services: directories, agents, brokers, contact services, advisers.

- *Attracting new customers*. That is the usual reason why any trader would open a new outlet. The Internet is no different in this respect.

- *Lower sales and marketing costs*. While web presence certainly does not come for free, as costs for IT and content creation are involved, sales costs may be lower than with traditional outlets, because there is no rent to pay for real estate, and staff and inventory costs are significantly lower.

    Marketing costs can vary widely. When supporting a new market or a niche market, marketing costs can be very low. However, when well-established traditional markets are targeted, marketing costs can be very high. This is one reason why Amazon.com still has problems with its bottom line (first quarter, 1999).

- *More efficient and effective customer service* (Figure 2.12). 'For instance, Cisco reports that its customer service productivity has increased by 200 to 300 percent, resulting in savings of $125 million in customer service costs. Dell estimates that it saves several million dollars a year by having

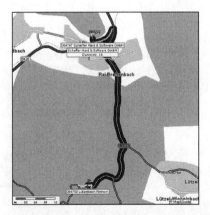

Figure 2.12   Customer friendly: EPSON Germany's web site not only informs customers which distributors exist close to them but also tells them how to get there.

basic customer service and technical support functions available on the Internet' (US Dept of Commerce 1998).

● *Better inventory management.* By integrating the ordering system with the supply chain, stock can be greatly reduced. In particular, it is not necessary to keep shelves of stock to allow customers to select from product samples – instead the customer selects from a digital catalogue. In many cases it will be possible to manufacture to order – selection and configuration data is directly fed into the production system.

● *Cutting out the middleman.* By bypassing distributors, wholesalers and retailers, a manufacturer that sells directly to the public can substantially improve its margins. However, tangible products require door-to-door delivery, so the traditional distribution channels are replaced with mail and courier services.

   For non-tangible products like film, video, music, magazines, newspapers and software, the implications are even more dramatic because they can be delivered at virtually no cost over the net.

● *No shoplifting.* While in some cases the number of disputes over payment has increased, online shops are safe from shoplifting. For example, in the traditional book publishing industry the typical value chain for books looks almost like this: printer 20 per cent, publisher and authors 20 per cent, distributor 20 per cent, bookstore 20 per cent, shoplifters 20 per cent.

2.7   How safe is the web?

That depends mainly on how enterprises treat their employees!

External vs. internal security breaches

According to a 1999 IDC study, about 90 per cent of IT security breaches are internal and more than 45 per cent are carried out by disgruntled employees. These findings are opposed to the popular belief that hacker attack or eavesdropping by criminals is the main security risk. In fact, server security is the crucial issue.

Opportunities for security breaches grow with the size and complexity of sites. Security management can tie up a considerable amount of human resources, especially in heterogeneous environments with different security systems in place. 'One-stop' multi-platform security systems can improve this situation.

The credit card

Consumer fears

The fears of many users regarding sending credit card numbers over the Internet are understandable. But they are not justified – not because the web is so secure, but because the whole credit card business is insecure. Transmitting a credit card number over the phone, for example, is a fairly insecure operation.

So is transmission between a point-of-sales terminal and the server. When the shop assistant swipes a card through the magnetic card reader, the credit card data (including credit card number and expiry date) is transmitted in plain ASCII to the server, making eavesdropping easy.

Compared to cheque fraud Internet-related credit card fraud seems to be rather marginal: the American Bankers Association estimated that cheque fraud costs banks $10 billion a year, while online fraud is running at only about 0.05 per cent of that ($5 million a year). Visa USA's experience with electronic commerce is that the level of fraud involving credit card transactions over the Internet is comparable to that of other 'card-not-present' situations, such as mail order or catalogue orders.

Visa's experience in Asia, however, was different. Although only 2 per cent of Visa Asia-Pacific's credit card business related to Internet transactions, 50 per cent of its disputes and discovered frauds were in that area. Most of these transactions are cross-border transactions – between 70 and 85 per cent of overseas e-commerce sales flow into US-based digital merchants. Disputes over transactions were more common than outright fraud, a common case being consumers denying they had ordered goods or services from sites, that they were charged too much, that they did not get what they ordered, or that delivery was too late (IDG News Service).

The decision whether or not to make a transaction over the Internet does not really rely on hard facts, but on the perception of the public. It is therefore necessary to take measures to improve this perception, a task that will take time.

Public perception dominates over reality

Another fear of consumers is the fear of building up a data shadow. Because every purchase with a credit card is documented, the buying behaviour of individuals – even their current location – can be monitored.

The data shadow

The cash card

Another technology could change this picture. Cash cards have the potential to replace the credit card in 'card-not-present' and in point-of-sale situations. Cash cards are based on chip cards. Loading a cash card at a bank branch or an ATM is equivalent to withdrawing cash from an account. The cash card can then be used to pay for goods and services in the same way cash is used. The payment is totally anonymous, as it is with cash. This also means that when the card is lost or stolen, the money is gone.

The cash card has a few implications, though. Tax departments won't like it because transactions are anonymous. Governments would lose control of another part of the monetary system. The amount of circulating cash is determined by the banks, who decide how much they allow for downloading to the customer's card. Also, the security problem could appear in the new form of counterfeit cash cards (or unauthorized charging of cards), keeping the counterfeiters busy.

Security technologies for the Internet

In any event, security for Internet transactions is a major concern. Usually, secure Internet connections encrypt the messages sent over the net. Because encryption needs computing power, secure systems do not scale well. Two general approaches dominate this area:

- *Virtual private networks*. VPNs simulate a private network by running a TCP/IP stack (private) on top of another TCP/IP stack (public). This allows the VPN to encode/decode data at the physical level and provides application-independent security. The advantage of a VPN is that it provides virtual ISP addresses without limitations on the number of domains. Encoding/decoding can be run on dedicated machines, removing the additional load from the server.

- *Packet-level encryption*. This method applies encoding and decoding at higher levels of the TCP/IP stack. It has the advantage that the relatively complex setup of a VPN is not required (Bolding 1995). The most widely used security protocol on the Internet is SSL (Secure Sockets Layer), introduced by Netscape Communications Corp. but also supported by Microsoft's Internet Explorer. SSL fits in between TCP and the application (Treese and Stewart 1998).

The most common form of network security on the Internet today is the regulation of which packet types can move between networks. Techniques used are:

- router traffic regulation (on the way through the net);
- firewall traffic regulation (for example, when entering an intranet);
- and to a lesser extent host traffic regulation (at the destination) (Bolding 1995).

For a further discussion of security concepts, please see (Kosiur 1997) and (Treese and Stewart 1998).

3 Getting ready for RITI[1]

On Saturdays around noon, Melbourne's Victoria market meat hall is probably the noisiest place in town. About two dozen butchers are advertising their products, and they do it at the top of their voices. Tactics and policies are changed by the minute, and rumpsteaks or schnitzels are sold by the kilo, by the tray, or by the tried-and-trusted buy-two-get-one-free strategy.

Similar noise can presently be heard from the telecommunications industry. In a deregulated market, policies are changed almost from day to day, advertising battles rage, but the merchandise is very similar. Failure to answer a competitor's move promptly can cost a company dearly, as it did AT&T, for example.

The electricity power market will show similar symptoms when this market is deregulated. Pricing and tariffs will be subject to fierce competition. Electricity companies are already honing their skills by joining the telecommunications battle.

The US Manufacturing Futures Survey from 1992 revealed the following outlook on managers' expectations for their companies' business environment (Rolstadås et al 1995):

- increasingly globalized markets, resulting in greater competition, but also cooperation;
- stronger focus on customer expectations with regard to quality and time;
- changes in the workforce with respect to attitude, competencies and capabilities, task structures and compensation mechanisms;
- increasing concerns for environmental issues, followed by national and transnational regulations;
- declining or stagnating domestic markets;
- increasing speed in technology development and shorter product life cycles.

This was before the World Wide Web and electronic commerce became an issue!

The challenge for corporate IT departments today is not to follow changes, but to lead the way. While a decade ago IT was mainly regarded as a tool for supporting the daily operational work of a company, today it is considered as a major enabler for organizational redesign.

A responsive information technology infrastructure (RITI) (Killen 1998) will be instrumental for the revolutionary changes that have already started.

---

[1]. Responsive Information Technology Infrastructure

3.1   The amalgamation of web and corporate world

The emergence of the Internet and the World Wide Web clearly had a disruptive effect on traditional information technology (IT). Not long ago, IT managers would look suspiciously at Internet technology. 'Sure we will support it, we have supported BTX and Videotex, so why not' was an often heard statement. Even Microsoft, usually very fast when picking up on trends, at first underrated the importance of the Internet.

Culture clash

Today things look different. Traditional IT managers now have to deal with things like web servers which don't even need air conditioning, and are confronted with design issues: not application design, but graphical design! The information technology infrastructure they set up (and did overtime in order to achieve it) is all of a sudden now called 'legacy'. IBM now sells more mainframe computers (S/390 servers) than ever before, but most of these machines are now used as web servers and the benchmarks are now measured in hits (to web pages) per second. CICS is sold as 'IBM's enterprise e-business server'.

Manufacturers of database management systems (DBMSs) have turned to web technology, integrating DBMSs with web servers, or supporting web-related data formats such as HTML and XML directly. Software AG, for example, a maker of enterprise DBMS, has launched the Tamino Information Server, a high performance XML database that integrates with web servers.

From the opposite direction come the web page designers, the 'pony tails'. These people, many of them with a background in graphical design, used HTML and JavaScript to make a page 'real cool'. They moved on to Java applets, and are now confronted with XML, servlets, Enterprise JavaBeans, database transactions and big iron (Phipps 1999).

3.2   Re-engineering for responsiveness

In 1989, Michael Hammer, a former professor of computer science at the Massachusetts Institute of Technology (MIT), published an article in the *Harvard Business Review*. He claimed that the major challenge for managers is to obliterate non-value-adding work, rather than automating it. Companies should reconsider their business processes in order to maximize customer value, while minimizing the consumption of resources (Hammer 1995).

BPR helps managers to obliterate non-value-adding work, not automate it

This article started the Business Process Re-engineering (BPR) movement. BPR was quickly adopted by the corporate world and widely exercised. BPR focuses on the business process, which may span several business functions (Figure 3.1). BPR is 'the fundamental rethinking and radical redesign of business processes to achieve dramatic improvements in critical contemporary measures of performance, such as cost, quality, service, and speed' (Hammer and Champy 1993).

BPR is customer centric: each step in a business process must improve the outcome (add value) for the customer – it must respond to the requirements of the customer.

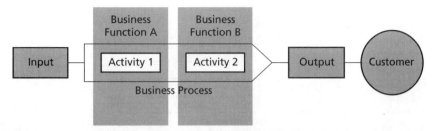

Figure 3.1 A business process usually contains several activities that can relate to different functional sectors of an enterprise. Adding value for the customer must be the purpose of each activity.

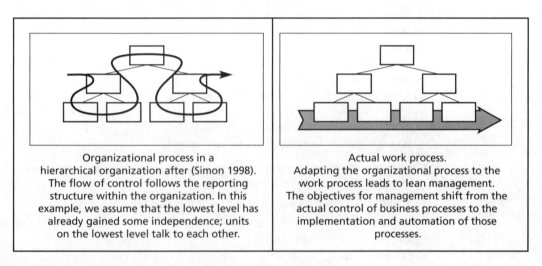

| Organizational process in a hierarchical organization after (Simon 1998). The flow of control follows the reporting structure within the organization. In this example, we assume that the lowest level has already gained some independence; units on the lowest level talk to each other. | Actual work process. Adapting the organizational process to the work process leads to lean management. The objectives for management shift from the actual control of business processes to the implementation and automation of those processes. |

Figure 3.2 Organizational and actual work processes.

The consequence for information processing is obvious. As business processes can cut across the functional sectors of an enterprise, and information processing is organized along these functional sectors (Figure 3.2), supporting and automating business processes requires the integration of independent enterprise applications (Figure 3.3).

The growth of electronic business will have dramatic effects on the work organization and information infrastructure of enterprises. Nearly two decades ago the printing industry experienced a major transformation: the introduction of computer-based typesetting almost abolished the profession of typesetter, and thoroughly changed the work profiles of journalists, editors, authors and many others.

For electronic commerce the consequences are not yet felt: in 1999 less than 1 per cent of the US retail volume went through electronic commerce. At the present growth rate a share of 20 per cent might be reached by 2006. Some

Electronic business requires flexible organizations in both process and technology scalability

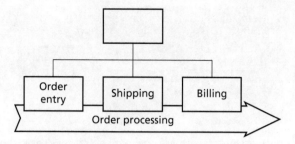

Figure 3.3 A business process spanning several business functions needs to integrate separate IT applications into one automated process.

industries, such as the stock trade, already feel the pitch and speak of an earthquake. It seems the shake-up in the printing industry in the late 1970s was a sandbox quake when compared with what is to come.

In such a time of rapid change, an extremely flexible IT organization is paramount. It is necessary not only to streamline processes and to integrate separate business functions into seamless processes (and of course connect them to the Internet), but to keep these processes so flexible that they can be swiftly adapted to changing situations.

Technologies instrumental in this task include:

- An ever-increasing amount of computing power – computational power doubles every 18 months (Moore's law).
- Systems that support a programming model close to the business model.
- Systems that allow planners and developers to define, verify, test and monitor business processes visually.
- Repository-based application warehouses that store components relevant for the development of electronic business applications.
- Repository-based 'soft coded' business rules.
- Systems that integrate existing applications – including Enterprise Resource Planning (ERP) applications – by embedding them into a rule-based business process. This includes protocol conversion for proprietary applications.
- Component studios that allow developers to regroup and replace components quickly, possibly guided by artificial intelligence-based wizards.
- Component brokers that support the distributed execution of components, automate deployment and version control and allow the hot-swapping of components.
- Simulation software that allows planners to predict the effect of new business processes and business rules by testing them in artificial worlds populated by intelligent agents. While this sounds a bit like SIMULACRON-3 (Galouye 1964), the first models of artificial worlds have been tried out for the insurance industry (Casti 1997) and for supermarket supply chains (Venables and Bilge 1998).

3.3 Multi-client, multi-tier, multi-platform, multi-threaded, multi-component, multi-cultural, multi-everything: the new IT environment

The Internet is a global phenomenon, despite the fact that it originated in the USA. Figure 3.4 shows how usage is split between the different regions in the world.

The industrialized nations clearly dominate the Internet world. In the poorer countries of the world Internet access is simply not affordable to ordinary people of average income. In Mexico, a nation of close to 100 million, for example, only about 1 million people have access to computers and only 10 per cent of those presently access the Internet. Even in a country such as South Africa, which has made great strides in recent years, the problems are formidable. In 1994, less than 25 per cent of South African households had telephones; now 35 per cent are linked to the telephone system (US Dept of Commerce 1999).

Nevertheless, the Internet is shifting to more and more cultural diversity. The non-US market is growing faster than the US market, mostly because the US market is close to saturation. But even within the industrial countries there are large language groups that make the picture even more fragmented: in the USA there is the Spanish-speaking group and in Canada the French language community. In Germany, about 3 million people speak Turkish, while countries such as Switzerland or Belgium are multilingual by design. As most industrial countries can maintain their population level only by immigration (because of low birth rates), this trend will continue and societies will become even more diverse.

Successful Internet-based business must scale to cultural diversity

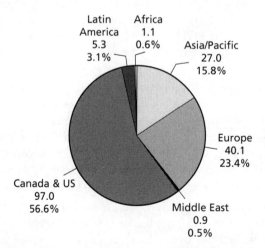

Figure 3.4 Distribution of global Internet users by language, OECD Nations, May 1999. Figures show the number of Internet users in millions followed by the percentage of PC users who are also Internet users. (Source: Nua Internet Surveys)

It is clear that software production cannot ignore these facts. The internationalization (see Section 15.2) of applications is an important topic, not only in globalized applications but also in national applications that must address different ethnic groups in their native languages (such as consumer-to-administration applications).

Most modern software products recognize these requirements. For example, newer web browsers such as Microsoft's Internet Explorer 5 come with optional modules to support alphabets such as Cyrillic, Chinese, Korean, Arabic, Hebrew, etc. Newer programming languages such as Java and Software AG's Bolero support Unicode, different calendar systems and resource bundles allowing multilingual texts in labels and messages.

But multicultural features are only one area in which modern software systems must provide flexibility:

The multi-everything paradigm of the electronic business society

- *Multi-client*. Because web applications run in an open network, they can encounter any type of client that can connect to the web: PCs can run under a variety of operating systems, such as Windows 9x, Windows NT, Linux and Beos. Then there are other hardware architectures, such as Macintosh or UNIX workstations. Increasingly, mobile devices such as hand-held computers (Windows CE machines, PSION), or PDAs (PalmPilot) are connected to the net. Web browsers are integrated into telephones (both stationary and mobile) and TV sets.

  Clients can use web browsers of different origin, such as Microsoft Internet Explorer, Netscape, HotJava or Opera with varying version numbers, or can connect to the net via Internet-enabled applications, such as Windows or Java-based applications.

  When operating in such a diverse environment, electronic business applications should restrict the client features used to the lowest common denominator, such as HTML 3.1. This *thin client* concept, together with server-based business logic in the form of servlets, is easier to create and to maintain.

- *Multi-platform*. What applies to clients also applies to servers. Web servers may run on different hardware and operating system platforms, such as PCs under Windows NT or Linux, UNIX servers, or mainframes. While the environment is more controlled (a web application usually runs on a known server), issues such as scalability may require applications to be portable to other platforms – when business flourishes it might be necessary to upgrade from a PC to a UNIX server or even to a S/390 mainframe.

- *Multi-tier*. A multi-tier architecture identifies separate layers of components, where each layer can be upgraded or modified independently from each other. A popular architecture is the three-tier architecture, consisting of the presentation tier (probably running on a desktop computer), a middle tier containing the application logic, and a database tier. Figure 3.5 shows a four-tier architecture.

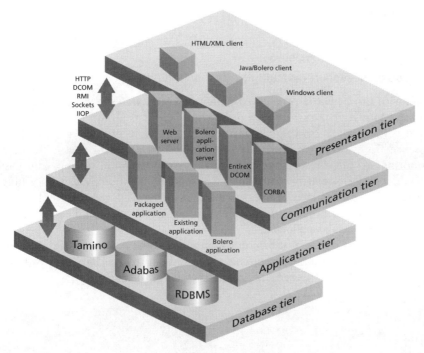

HTML/XML client

Java/Bolero client

Windows client

HTTP
DCOM
RMI
Sockets
IIOP

Web
server

Bolero
appli-
cation
server

EntireX
DCOM

CORBA

Packaged
application

Existing
application

Bolero
application

Tamino

Adabas

RDBMS

Presentation tier

Communication tier

Application tier

Database tier

Figure 3.5 A four-tier architecture. The middle tier is split into an application tier and a communication tier. (Source: Software AG)

- *Multi-threaded*. Multi-threading and other concurrent architectures are required in distributed environments to hide latency times caused by communication, download times, computation, database accesses, etc. Usually, user interfaces employ multi-threading techniques to avoid keyboard and mouse lock while the CPU is busy with computational tasks or waiting on a response from the server. In distributed environments multi-threading and asynchronous execution become an issue, too, for business processes. Notoriously difficult to test and to debug, the use of multi-threading requires sound engineering methods.

- *Multi-component*. Actually, we mean multi-component model. Three major enterprise component models have evolved: Enterprise JavaBeans, COM/DCOM and CORBA. Because any of the three has advantages and disadvantages it is likely that a large application has to deal with components implemented in two or more component models. While Enterprise JavaBeans and CORBA are growing together, bridge technology between DCOM and CORBA exists, too.

It is clear that all this variability comes at a price. For example, supporting six end-user languages, eight different client platforms and three different server platforms would theoretically require us to build and test 144 different versions of the same application.

It is therefore important to select development tools that support concepts for

- internationalization;
- client and server portability;
- transparent support for multiple component models.

Even with those features, the development of a large web site is a complex task, and its maintenance can be even more complex. As is always the case in software development, testing can confirm the presence of bugs, but not their absence. To avoid later surprises and downtime in production, it is therefore important to provide mechanisms for the early detection of bugs and easy exchange of erroneous components. Component technology can help here, because only the affected component need be exchanged, not the whole application. Deployment of new component versions to clients should be automatic, as is the case with Java applets.

It has been said that programming computers is the most complex engineering task that mankind has faced. This seems to be true, especially for web-based applications. Also in this sense we reach 'the end of the beginning'.

New thinking for new challenges

Part 2 gives an overview of concepts in software technology that have shaped the industry or will do so. Readers will not require knowledge of a particular technology. The concepts here are discussed on a philosophical level with little or no reference to existing technology, but are referred to when technical questions are raised in Part 3.

- Chapter 4 discusses the concept of, alas, transactions, a fundamental concept in commercial programming.
- Chapter 5 and Chapter 6 present the history of object-oriented programming, starting as early as 1967.
- Transactions are processes, and processes create problems in the context of object-oriented programming. Chapter 7 analyzes these problems and shows how to solve them.
- In Chapter 8 we discuss the principles on which these solutions are obtained, such as separation of concerns. There is a world after OO.
- Components certainly belong in this world, and they are discussed in Chapter 9.
- Chapter 10 finally discusses new developments in user interfaces, including systematic user interface design methods that can be utilized for electronic business applications.
- Chapter 11 discusses application concepts that allow multiple users to collaborate in a task or process.

Transactions 4

A t the heart of commercial programming is the concept of the transaction. The concept became an issue when terminals were connected to central computers and business transactions were performed on these terminals. Core technologies of that time were database management systems (DBMSs) and transaction monitors.

Before, business data was processed in batch jobs. Batch jobs that run as the one and only process on a computer do not require a transaction concept. When a batch job fails, you simply restore the backup.

Database transactions are at the heart of enterprise computing

Not so in a timesharing system, where multiple users initiate tasks against the same set of data. The data set is changed continuously, so it is not possible simply to return to a backup copy of the data set when an exception occurs.

Let us consider a flight booking system as an example of a transactional database system. During the course of a booking several transactions are made for a passenger:

- Flight reservation
- Payment and confirmation
- Cancellation
- Check-in
- Check-out.

Several operators are connected to the system: travel agents, airline personnel at airport counters, etc.

The requirements for a database transaction are indicated with the term ACID (atomic, consistent, isolated, durable):

Database transactions are ACID in their sense

- **Atomic.** A transaction is an indivisible unit. It cannot be divided into several transactions and cannot contain other transactions. In the flight booking system, all the transactions are atomic, but the whole process from reservation to check-in cannot be seen as one atomic transaction – the customer could decide not to confirm the flight, the flight could be cancelled, etc.

- **Consistent**. A transaction must guarantee to transform the data from one valid state into another valid state. This requires that each transaction has a clearly marked begin and end. If a transaction fails or is interrupted because of a hardware or system error, the data must still be in a consistent state, i.e. the state before the transaction was started must be recovered (rollback).

For example, if a customer reserves a flight, it is necessary not only to reserve a seat, but also to store the customer's address. In a flat file system this would require updating two files. A system crash could lead to the situation where one file was updated but the other was not. A database system can guarantee consistency of data across multiple tables.

- **Isolated**. A transaction must not be influenced by other concurrent transactions. In our flight booking system, concurrent transactions must not be allowed to access the plane's seat allocation at the same time, otherwise a seat could be allocated twice. This isolation is achieved by locking the data elements (e.g. table rows) that take part in a transaction so that no other transaction can access them. This is of course a performance issue – other transactions have to wait until the locks are removed. In cases of bad application or database design, deadlocks can occur when two transactions mutually lock each other's access paths. Several strategies (optimistic locking, pessimistic locking, timed locks) exist to improve performance and to avoid deadlocks.

- **Durable**. The effects of a transaction must persist as soon as the transaction is completed. The state of the data at transaction end must even survive a system crash. In the case of the flight booking system, confirmation made by paying for the flight must persist as soon as the transaction is acknowledged by the system. For applications that require high reliability, DBMSs replicate databases on different disk drives, so that data survives even a head crash. Log files allow the most recent and consistent database state to be recovered from the last backup.

The ACID transaction model has served enterprise computing well in both hierarchical database systems (CODASYL) and relational databases (RDBMSs). Usually each business task (such as reservation or confirmation) is mapped onto one ACID transaction.

Relation to business task and business process

The containing business process (from reservation to check-in) does not have an equivalent in software technology, but is represented by state information in data elements and by organizational structures. Human operators initiate the individual business tasks. When something goes wrong in between, they can start a compensating task, such as a cancellation (which of course must be implemented in the system). The whole area of orchestrating individual business tasks is left to the operator.

This is going to change. As we discussed in the previous chapter, enterprise application integration is about integrating individual business tasks into one seamless process – an automated process, that is.

Relation to electronic business requirements

Similar requirements come from electronic business. The business processes running in an electronic business scenario usually should not require the intervention of a human operator (apart from the client). The system must therefore guide the client through the business process. Each process can include many tasks and many ACID transactions. In the case of our flight booking system the customer would reserve his flight through the Internet. He would specify his preferences for seating, meals, etc. At a later time, in another session, he would confirm his flight and pay with a credit card. The final check-in is at the airport in the traditional form. Until check-in the customer may ask for cancellation (also through the Internet) and depending on the type of ticket he may get a refund. The system must make sure that only valid tasks are offered to the customer or are accepted from the customer. Cancellation before reservation is nonsense and cancellation after check-in is possibly fraud.

Business processes can last a very long time. In the example above, the process could last several months. In other cases, such as an insurance policy or church membership, they could last a lifetime.

ACID transactions vs. business transactions

Usually a business process is identified by one business object. This identifying object usually starts its existence with the start of the business process and ceases to exist when the process ends. It does not always represent a real-world object but may be purely virtual. In the example above, the identifying object would be not the customer, nor the plane, but the booking of customer A to flight B. In an online shopping process the virtual shopping cart might act as the identifying object. In other cases we can identify a group of objects as the identifying object. If, for example, we regard a marriage as a business process, the married couple would be the identifying object.

Similar long-running processes are found in many areas. Early experiences with such processes were made in design-oriented computer applications, such as CAD or CASE. Design processes usually take a very long time, from days to months or even years. But for each single step within the design process the principles of ACID transactions apply.

Several techniques have been developed to implement long-running processes that allow a varying degree of transaction granularity.

Implementation of business transactions

Nested transactions

This technique is used with some CAD systems and relies on specialized database systems that support nested transactions. Here also, a locking concept is required that supports a varying degree of granularity. When, for example, during the construction of an airplane the outer shape of the airplane is modified, the whole airplane design must be locked. When only a wheel is modified, it is not necessary to lock the whole airplane design, but only the wheel elements.

For enterprise applications, however, nested transactions are not suitable. Most existing commercial DBMSs do not support nested transactions and business processes can span multiple, heterogeneous and distributed databases. There is currently no technology in sight that can manage nested transactions across such a diverse environment.

State transition diagrams

Within a business process we can identify several states. In our flight booking system, for example, the following states can be identified: START, RESERVED, CONFIRMED, BOARDED, STOP. A state transition diagram describes which business events (reservation, confirmation, cancellation, check-in) lead from one state to another (Figure 4.1).

State \ Event	Reservation	Confirmation	Check-in	Check-out	Cancel
START	RESERVED (*Reserve seat*)				
RESERVED		CONFIRMED (*Process payment*)			STOP (*Free seat*)
CONFIRMED			BOARDED		STOP (*Free seat and refund*)
BOARDED				STOP	

Figure 4.1 State transition table for the flight booking example. Valid combinations of state and event result in a new state. A business task (in parentheses) is in most cases executed during such a transition.

State transition diagrams are a well-used technique in the design of electronic circuits that have to monitor processes. The process control of appliances like dishwashers, washing machines or answer machines can all be described using state transition diagrams.

State transition diagrams are at the heart of the long transaction concept defined in Software AG's Bolero, so we will discuss them in more detail in Chapter 15 (Sections 15.9 and 15.10).

Petri nets

A Petri net describes processes in terms of *places* and *transitions* (between places) which are organized as a directed graph. Places can contain *tokens*. When all places pointing to a transition have a token, the transition 'fires', removes all tokens from the input places and sets tokens to the places it points to (the output places).

Petri nets are fun to exercise on paper (draw circles for places, rectangles for transitions, and use beans or similar for tokens); they are a powerful instrument for modelling concurrent processes, for example a workflow, where a process can split into subprocesses which join again at a later stage (Figure 4.2).

Petri nets are a well-researched topic in computing science, and computer-based simulators and verifiers exist to check whether a given design will run or not.

However, the abstract character of Petri nets has not advocated their use in the commercial world but has limited their use more to scientific and technical applications.

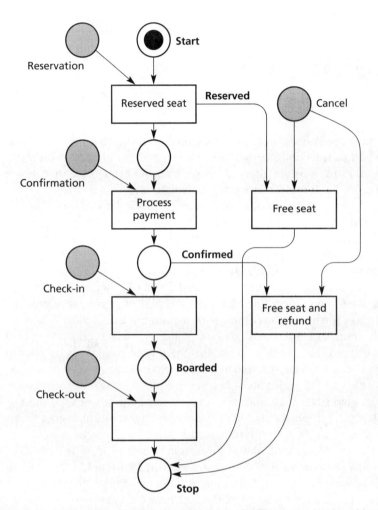

Figure 4.2   Petri net for the flight booking example. The game is played by placing tokens on the grey circles to simulate business events, then following the rules. Note that there is already a token (black dot) on the START.

5 Simulating objects

OO-thinking is new thinking for enterprise computing

Talking about object-oriented (OO) programming seems to be a bit odd in a part of the book entitled 'New thinking'. After all, object-oriented programming is more than 30 years old. But it is true: in commercial programming OO is still a relatively young discipline.

Object-oriented programming was invented in the far north of Europe. Two computer scientists at the Norwegian Computing Institute, O.J. Dahl and Kristen Nygaard, developed a computer language that would be useful for simulating large industrial processes such as steel mills, warehouses, etc. The language was called Simula, it was based on the Pascal ancestor Algol, and because it was released in 1967 it was called Simula 67. Remember that this was the time when computers filled factory halls and programs were punched on cards to enter them into the computer (Dahl and Nygaard 1966).

Objects model real-world business processes

When simulating real-world processes it makes sense to built a model of the real world that is as realistic as possible. One way of doing so is to describe the world as a set of objects that relate to each other. Each object has an internal state which it has to maintain, it can receive messages from other objects and modify its own state as a reaction to the message, and it can send messages to other objects. Each object also has a life cycle: after creation it goes through a series of state changes until it is discarded.

Let us take a closer look at the simulation of a steel mill (Hills 1973). Steel ingots are created when liquid steel is poured into a mould. The steel in the mould is allowed to set, then the mould is broken open. The ingots are removed and loaded into soaking pits. There they are held for a period of time until they are ready for rolling. Rolling turns the ingots into slabs, the end product.

During their time in the soaking pits the ingots cool down. In a non-object-oriented simulation a monitoring routine would update the ingot data periodically to model this process realistically. In object-oriented simulation, in contrast, external instances are not allowed to modify the state of an object directly. The temperature-over-time function is purely the business of the ingot object itself. Finding out about the temperature of an ingot requires sending a query message to the ingot object, which answers with the value of its current temperature.

A steel mill produces many individual ingots which all have an individual state (like temperature) but in terms of data structure (not data content) and program logic they are all identical. So it makes sense to describe the data structure and message processing methods in one *class* definition that is valid for each ingot object.

So, a class definition contains the definition of the internal data structures of an object, and the definitions of the methods (functions) for message processing. A client that wants to use an object must first create it. This is done by sending a New message to the class, which in turn sends the handle of a new object instance to the client. Clients can then send messages to this object instance by calling a method and specifying the object handle. *Classes define an object's internals*

We see that class definitions can contain methods that are not applied to an object instance but to the class itself. The New method is such a method – it is interpreted by the class.

Today, we understand three features as being characteristic of object-oriented languages:

- **Data encapsulation**. This means that the internal data of an object cannot be accessed directly from the outside. It is only possible to send a message to the object that subsequently leads to the modification of the object's internal data and state. This restriction has been softened in modern languages by allowing objects to publish some of their internal fields, thus allowing direct access and modification from the outside. This is equivalent to the definition of specific get and set methods for each of these fields, so it is not a violation of data encapsulation. *OO language characteristics*

- **Polymorphism**. This means that clients can call methods without caring about the class membership of an object. If, for example, both ingot class and mould class define a method get_temperature, a client can call this method without caring if the correspondence object is an ingot or a mould.

- **Inheritance**. Inheritance allows a class to be implemented by referring to the definition of a similar class. Features that are different are overridden. By applying inheritance repeatedly a hierarchic tree-like structure of inheritance relationships is created. It is often the case that class definitions in the tree-top are not used to create objects – they simply serve as prototypes for other class definitions which are derived from them. We call such class definitions *abstract*.

Simula had all that: encapsulation, polymorphism and inheritance were already defined there. Simula even had a garbage collector. In Chapter 12, when we discuss the merits of Java, we will also explain why an object-oriented language needs a garbage collector.

It was soon discovered that Simula could do more than just simulations. Simula became a general-purpose object-oriented language which also has good simulation facilities. The language is still in use today.

Simulations for steel mills, warehouses and similar processes are today best performed by using a ready-made simulation package. The focus of object-oriented languages has shifted in the meantime to general-purpose programming tasks. Contemporary object-oriented programs are often populated with objects that have nothing to do with real-world items, but represent traditional,

OO has paved its way to general-purpose programming

often functional constructs in object-oriented clothes. What, for example, is the real-world counterpart of an `Iterator` object?

The object-oriented paradigm, however, is deeply rooted in simulation. Whether we are modelling a real-world scenario like an order entry system, designing a graphical interface consisting of windows, buttons, menus, scroll bars, selection lists, etc. (all objects), or using the Document Object Model (DOM) API to navigate in an XML document, in all cases it helps to think in terms of virtual worlds and simulation (Kay 1977). When using object-oriented methods for analysis, design or implementation, instead of asking 'What can I do with this object?', one should ask 'What can this object do for me?' (Budd 1997).

Back to the future: a Star is born

6

From the early 1970s to the mid-1980s the Xerox PARC laboratory was the source of an astonishing amount of groundbreaking ideas. The inventions made were combined in the Alto computer and later the Star office system which anticipated modern networked office computer landscapes by more than a decade.

The inventions made included:

- Desktop computer
- Graphical user interface
- Mouse
- Ethernet
- Smalltalk.

It seemed that PARC had set out to invent the paperless office. It would not come to this – at the same time the laser printer was invented, too, at PARC.

The influence of the Alto and the Star on the computing community was immense. When Steve Jobs was given a demonstration of the Alto he knew what to do: build the Apple Macintosh.

The same principles applied in the Star system are found today in the Windows operating system, and in presentation managers such as X-Windows.

The researchers at PARC had the goal of putting a computer on every office desk. The design of the system was clearly motivated by user acceptance studies: the invention of the mouse was motivated by applied psychology. To get a computer on a manager's desk, it was necessary to find a way to operate the computer without using the keyboard too much. Managers usually cannot type as fast as their secretaries, so operating the computer via a keyboard would make them look silly. A mouse, in contrast, allows them to operate the computer in a slightly reclined and relaxed position, communicating an air of authority and superiority.

Mission: to put a PC on every office desk

The mouse (invented by Douglas Engelbart) has an important function in the overall concept of the system. The graphical user interface of the Star system represented a virtual reality scenario consisting of real-world replicas, such as folders, waste-baskets, desktop, in-tray, out-tray, which were represented as small images – icons. The mouse acts as the extension of the hand. With the mouse I can move things around, open a folder or a document, drop it into the waste-basket, etc. The icons resembling the familiar office environment and the mouse were what made this user interface so intuitive.

Virtual worlds are basically simulations, except that they do not simulate an existing real world but a world that could exist. It comes as no surprise that the language created to develop the software of the Star system had to be object-oriented again – Smalltalk.

Programming in objects also went well with a distributed system. Objects that communicate with each other define a natural way to decompose a complex system into a distributed application. Each network node hosts a set of objects which talk to each other, either locally or across the wire. One object cannot be distributed over several nodes.

Smalltalk was invented by Alan Kay (Kay 1993). Kay knew Simula and realized that the object-oriented paradigm was what was needed. While Simula still carried some legacy baggage from Algol (Simula could aptly be named Algol++), Kay went for a radical solution. Smalltalk was designed as an object-oriented language from scratch. In Smalltalk, everything is an object and everything is expressed as a communication between objects. In Smalltalk, computing the expression 3+4 means sending the message '+4' to an integer object with the value 3 (the result of 7 was first computed in 1972).

The first Smalltalk interpreter was written in BASIC and was very, very slow. Smalltalk was initially designed as an interpreted language (and therefore not fast). Because there was no compiler, the language design did not have to provide syntactical means for compile-time checks. So Smalltalk is dynamically typed – data type incompatibilities are detected at runtime and not at compile time (there is no compile time). Today, several implementations provide compilers which deliver efficient executables. However, because the language does not support it, compile-time checks are not possible to the same degree as in languages designed with compilation in mind. This disadvantage, in our opinion, makes Smalltalk problematic for the implementation of large enterprise applications.

Mission accomplished, let's move on!

The merits of Smalltalk lie in making the object-oriented approach popular. Simula had been a niche language, but Smalltalk made the US (and the rest of the world) aware of object-oriented methodology. A number of implementations exist today, one of the most prominent being IBM's Visual Age for Smalltalk.

Processes and objects

7

lready defined in Simula 67 was the concept of a process. During a process the state of one or several objects is changed. Each process is defined by a thread of execution.

In today's electronic business systems, we have to deal with multiple processes that compete with each other for resources, but also communicate. In a graphical user interface alone, several processes are at work: for example, one is rendering the screen, while another reacts to mouse movements. Using only a single process for everything would, for example, prevent the mouse and keyboard reacting while the system renders the screen or waits for the completion of a distributed transaction.

Relation to electronic business applications

In Chapter 4 we discussed ACID database transactions, which are a good example of processes. When a database transaction is started it forms a new process (in the DBMS), which runs concurrently with the (main) process that started it. During the lifetime of the transaction both processes communicate with each other: usually several objects are updated during the course of a transaction. The transaction process finishes when the main process commits or aborts the transaction.

We also mentioned that DBMSs set locks to objects accessed by a transaction in order to stop other concurrent transactions accessing the same objects at the same time (Figure 7.1).

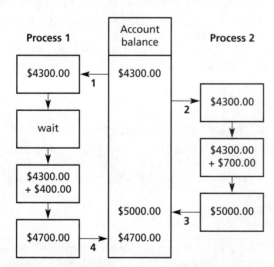

Figure 7.1   The classical problem: two processes are updating the same object. The effect of the second process is lost, because the result is overwritten by the first process. We have lost a deposit of $700 and have one angry customer.

Objects and database transactions

Objects in database transactions have the same requirements as objects in general processes (Holmes et al 1997):

- **State constraints** define the conditions under which certain methods can be applied to an object.

    For example, removing order lines from an order object is only possible if there are order lines left.

- **Exclusion constraints** define which methods of an object are allowed to be executed concurrently.

    For example, two processes must not be allowed to modify a customer address concurrently, but one process modifying the address and another concurrent process retrieving the customer's account data would not cause a problem.

- **Transaction constraints** deal with the need to perform operations involving several independent objects atomically.

    For example, transferring an amount from one account to another is a transaction that involves two objects. It is necessary, in this case, to exclude concurrent access to the account objects during the whole transaction.

While state constraints and exclusion constraints can be handled individually by each object, this is not advisable for transaction constraints. Transaction demarcation is not a concern of business objects: the reusability of these objects would suffer if their methods contained implicit transaction control.

But even the inclusion of exclusion constraints in business objects is problematic. When the object class is extended and a method that has exclusion constraints is overridden, there is no guarantee that the overriding method contains appropriate exclusion constraints. The developer extending the class may not even know of the existence of exclusion constraints in the original method.

For state constraints no such problem exists – they are part of an object's business logic. In addition they can be secured by contracts, as discussed in Section 15.2.

7.1   Controlling processes by using monitors

Monitors explained

The concept of monitors goes back to C.A.R. Hoare (Hoare 1974). Monitors are used to protect critical sections of code that must be accessed by concurrent processes. Each monitor protects a single section of code and can be owned by only one process at a time.

A monitor consists of:

- An *entry set*. This is a queue where one or more processes can wait before one of them is chosen to enter the monitor.

- A *critical section*. This is a portion of the program in which at most one process can be active at any time.

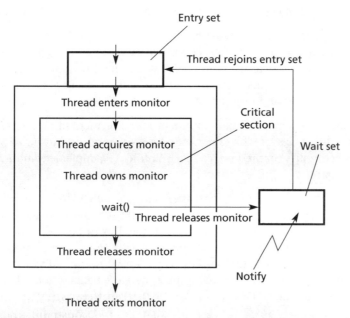

Figure 7.2 Monitors.

- A *wait set*. This is a queue in which one or more processes can wait for a 'notify' signal from another thread (or until a specified period of time elapses).

When a process enters a program section that is protected by a monitor, it enters the monitor after it has passed through (and, if necessary, waited in) the entry set (Figure 7.2). The process can then proceed to acquire the monitor. The process is now said to own the monitor, and it can proceed to process a critical section of code. After processing the critical section of code the process releases and exits the monitor.

In addition, monitors can facilitate communication between processes:

- A process, which must be the owner of the monitor, can wait until a 'notify' signal is sent to the monitor by another process, or until a time-out occurs. During that waiting period the process joins the wait set and releases the monitor. After notification the process reacquires the monitor: it must pass again through the entry set.
- A process, which must be the owner of the monitor, can send a 'notify' signal to the monitor. This 'notify' signal can wake up either one or all processes waiting in the monitor's wait set.

Monitors can be introduced into object-oriented programming without too much conceptual difficulty. Each object can own a monitor, and the object's program code (the methods), or parts thereof, can be protected. A thread entering a protected section of program code also has to enter the object's monitor. This ensures that only one thread can execute protected code at a time.

Monitors in OO programming

In the context of object-oriented programming, monitors have drawbacks:

- Sometimes the 'all-or-nothing' exclusion policy introduced by monitors is too coarse. For example, an object has two methods A and B: two concurrent processes must not execute method A at the same time, nor method B at the same time, but they may execute A concurrently with B. This policy cannot be expressed with an object-based monitor.

Because the monitor logic is part of a method's implementation, problems arise with the reuse of classes. This is not only true for monitors, but for all synchronization techniques that require code within method implementations, such as locks or semaphors.

- When a class is extended via inheritance, a newly-added method may require changes in synchronization logic that require most methods to be rewritten. For example: the new method requires to be executed only after method A, but not after any other method. This requires the introduction of a Boolean variable which is set TRUE by method A and FALSE by any other method – each method in the class must therefore be rewritten. This is called 'inheritance anomaly' (Matsuoka et al 1990), (Papathomas 1995).

- Synchronization policies are part of a method's implementation, but do not show up in the interface specification of a class. Remember that it is a declared goal of encapsulation techniques (and OO is one) that the implementation of a module is hidden from its user.

  A developer that extends a class and in this process overrides a method may remove necessary synchronization logic or add logic that is not compatible with the synchronization logic in the other methods.

The last two problems can be eased by separating the synchronization logic from the business logic (Figure 7.3).

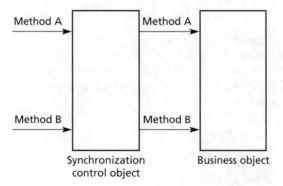

Figure 7.3 Separating synchronization logic and business logic.

Now, all synchronization logic is contained in the synchronization control object, while the logic in the business object is freed from synchronization issues. The business object can now be extended easily, and the synchronization control object can be extended without the need to rewrite all the business logic. There is one disadvantage, however: it is now not possible to protect only part of a method with a monitor.

7.2   Communicating sequential processes (CSP)

CSP was a later development by C.A.R. Hoare (Hoare 1985). CSP was a building block in the definition of the Occam programming language, a language designed to program arrays of parallel processors (Inmos Transputer).

The advantage of CSP is its simplicity: CSP knows only processes and chan- *CSP defined*
nels. There are no processes that compete for shared resources: each resource that would be accessed by concurrent processes is encapsulated into its own server process. The client processes can access the resource by communicating with the server process.

Processes communicate via channels. In the simplest case, a channel synchronizes two processes so that they can exchange messages (Figure 7.4). The sender process dispatches a message to the channel and waits until the reader process has read the message. Vice versa, the reader process waits at the channel until a sender writes a message.

Channels are unidirectional. If two-way communication is required, two channels must be used. Other channel types include buffered channels, which allow messages to be dispatched asynchronously, and one-to-many channels to dispatch messages to many receivers.

CSP fits well into object-oriented architecture. Channels are first-class objects   *CSP in OO*
themselves and contain all synchronization logic. Objects participating in con- *programming*
current processes must not call each other's methods but communicate by

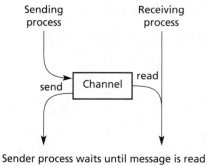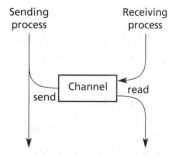

Sender process waits until message is read   Receiver process waits for message

Figure 7.4

sending messages to each other. This requires the receiver to interpret the message and dispatch it to the addressed method. Therefore, using CSP requires developers to design applications in terms of processes and channels.

The advantage of CSP is that it is based on a sound mathematical theory which allows the correctness of designs based on CSP to be proved. Especially in component-based systems and in connection with Message-oriented Middleware (MoM), CSP is a valuable theoretical tool.

Beyond OO   8

malltalk had started the OO train. In the following years, dozens of object-oriented languages were designed and implemented. Some were based on new concepts, while others tried to add object-oriented extensions to existing non-OO programming languages.

The race was finally won by C++ which became the de-facto standard in object-oriented programming (Stroustrup 1994). The strength of C++ (interoperability with C) is also its weakness: the inclusion of non-object-oriented constructs such as explicit pointers, and the lack of garbage collection, led to a complicated and sometimes dangerous to use language. However, C++ was the breakthrough for object-oriented programming. It brought OO to the masses of C programmers.

Developed at the same time as C++ (1988), Eiffel is another notable member of the OO family. Designed by Bertrand Meyer (Meyer 1997) and named after Gustave Eiffel, constructor of the famous tower, Eiffel is a pure object-oriented language, with an easy to read syntax and many innovative concepts. The two top change requests for the Java programming language are features known from Eiffel: parameterized types and contracts (Sun 1999). We will explain these features in more detail in the chapters about Java and Bolero.

The tables were turned with the advent of Java (Gosling 1996). The success of Java lies in the fact that some newer developments in software technology were directly integrated into the language: support for Internet technology, component technology and platform independence. In addition, while keeping the C-like syntax, Java did away with some of the not so nice features of C++: there are no pointers, and Java does have a garbage collector.

With object-oriented technology now maturing, and object-oriented languages now used to implement large and mission-critical applications, the deficiencies of object-oriented technology are becoming more visible. Researchers have now turned to topics beyond OO. New programming paradigms pop up like mushrooms after warm rain – and each research lab has its own. At Xerox PARC it is open implementations and aspect-oriented programming, at IBM's Watson Research Center it is subject-oriented programming and hyperspaces. Don't get us wrong: none of these researches would consider dropping object-oriented technology; all of these new concepts are based on OO or include it.

Meta-programming concepts beyond OO

These new concepts have one thing in common: they do not define new programming languages. Instead, they are concepts of meta-programming, meaning that a programmer describes how to transform existing program code to meet a certain goal.

Also, all of these new concepts follow Dijkstra's principle 'separation of concerns'. (Edsger Dijkstra was one of the fathers of ALGOL '60 and inventor of structured programming (Dijkstra 1968)). In fact, object-oriented programming itself follows this principle in parts.

Main concepts explained

In the following we briefly discuss the main new developments.

8.1   Open implementation

Open implementation (Kiczales 1996) is a reaction to the fact that one of the main principles of object-oriented programming, data encapsulation, is sometimes counterproductive. Data encapsulation hides the implementation from the client. The user of a software module knows only the interface specification of the module; how methods and data structures are implemented is not the user's concern, but the concern of the author (or owner) of the module. In some cases, however, the client knows best which implementation works best. For example, in the case of a sorted list object, the best sort algorithm depends on the application: if we are dealing with very small lists, the bubble sort may be appropriate, for large lists the Quicksort algorithm may be appropriate, and in the case of short sort keys a binary sort could work best. Open implementation postulates that the user of an object should have an influence on the algorithms used. It suggests providing a second interface through which the object user can specify the implementation to be used. The disadvantage is that the object owner must provide all selectable implementations.

8.2   Aspect-oriented programming

Aspect-oriented programming (Kiczales et al 1997-1) evolved from open implementation. It recognizes that very often the implementation of an object contains many aspects that have nothing to do with the business logic, such as persistence, transaction control, thread synchronization, exception handling, contracts, etc. This leads to the situation that the code implementing business logic is intertwined and tangled with code that has nothing to do with business logic but organizes the more technical and auxiliary aspects mentioned above.

Aspect-oriented programming removes this code from the object and separates it into extra code units. Before an object is compiled, the code in the object unit and the separate aspect units are merged by an 'aspect weaver'. A meta-language is used to describe the relationship between object code and aspect code.

8.3   Subject-oriented programming

Subject-oriented programming (Harrison and Ossher 1993) addresses a problem that exists when using object-oriented programming techniques for large software systems and in large development groups. Let us consider an example: the real-world object *Customer* is implemented as a reusable business object. This software module is to be used by several applications, or sub-applications. Each of these applications has a specific view of this object. The sales department, for example, is most interested in the sales history of a customer. The shipping department is most interested in shipping data, such as the mailing address, etc. The accounting department is most interested in the customer's accounts. The question now is: who owns the software object *Customer*? Somebody has to be responsible, and it will probably be a programmer in the Core Business Objects group.

If any of the above departments want to change their part of the *Customer* object, they have to talk to the object owner. This causes bureaucracy and delays.

To solve this problem, subject-oriented programming transfers responsibilities for an object partly to the users (subjects) of an object. Each application using the object (or each department) is responsible for its part – for its view – of the object and is allowed to make changes to this part only. The development system is responsible for merging the different object views into one consistent object definition.

8.4   Hyperspace

Hyperspace (Ossher and Tarr 1999) is a recent (1999) development. The hyperspace programming model recognizes that subject-oriented programming and aspect-oriented programming are very similar, indeed that both models are about separation of concerns. The hyperspace model integrates these concepts into one consistent model.

Hyperspace identifies the individual concerns and organizes them into separate dimensions. Because dimensions can be added freely, hyperspace can cover not just the programming phase, but the whole software development life cycle. Here is a typical example of the concern dimensions we can identify in a simple order entry application:

- Object-related dimension: Customer, Product, Order, Invoice.
- Subject-related dimension: Sales, Shipping, Accounting.
- Aspect-related dimension: Persistence, Transaction control, Contracts, Exception handling.
- Artefact-related dimension: Requirements, Design, Code, Tests.

In addition, each dimension also contains a non-concern element. Concerns that overlap must be placed in separate dimensions.

These dimensions define an n-dimensional matrix. Each element in the matrix corresponds to a separate software unit (or is empty). The final program is composed by the hyperspace development system.

The concept of hyperspace is the most systematic approach to separation of concerns we have seen so far. If there is a critique, it is this: in large development systems the number of units (matrix elements) explodes and could become almost unmanageable. Matrices could easily reach millions of elements (i.e. software units).

Components 9

In the following we give a short description of common principles of component-based systems. However, we do not go into the details of concrete component models such as CORBA, DCOM or Enterprise JavaBeans. These systems are covered in more technical detail in Sections 12.7 and 15.4.

9.1 Components are objects, or?

In the most common sense, yes. Components are objects in the same sense as flowerpots, tables, computers or programs.

Yes, but...

Similar to objects in object-oriented programming, components maintain a state (information kept in the component) and exhibit properties and behaviour (request/response) through one or several interfaces.

But components do not necessarily belong in an OO context. Components can be created with traditional non-object-oriented languages – most component models are in fact language neutral and support bindings into several programming languages. In object-oriented programming, objects are first and foremost entities on a source code level. The primary purpose of object-oriented programming is to provide a way to organize source code in an intuitive and logical way, not to produce plug and play software modules that can be deployed independently.

Components are language neutral

Components, in contrast, do not add value to the code-writing process (in fact they make this process more demanding), but they facilitate the construction of software applications from pre-built ready-made modules, thus enabling software reuse on a higher level and on a larger scale. The decision to build an application in a componentized way makes sense when there is already a large pool of components that can be reused, or if the reuse of new components is likely. Thinking in components also means thinking in application *families*.

Components facilitate software reuse

There are some common features that distinguish components from normal software modules:

- *Publishing of features.* Components can inform (other components, applications or builder tools) about their features (what requests are accepted by the component and which properties are public).

Components are proactive

  Builder tools can be used to construct larger pieces of software from components. With builder tools it is possible to 'wire' components together, so that they can interact. A popular example of component-based builder tools is GUI-builders, where buttons, widgets and text field components are combined to form a larger component of a graphical user interface.

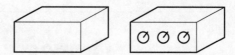

Figure 9.1 Components without customization are just dumb bricks – like a hi-fi amplifier without controls. Components with customization are smart bricks.

Components are flexible

- *Customization.* Components that cannot be customized are of limited use (Figure 9.1). While in object-oriented programming customization is achieved through inheritance (requiring recompilation), components contain special logic for dynamic customization.

  Customization is usually performed at 'plug'-time, when the component is embedded into a larger context by a builder tool. For example, in a GUI-builder a button component is customized by changing the caption text in the button's property sheet. For complex customization components may offer a special property editor. In extreme cases the code required for customization exceeds the code required for the component's functionality.

Components have interfaces

Most component models combine semantically related methods and properties in interfaces. Instead of publishing single methods and properties to clients, the interfaces are published. A component may implement and publish several interfaces, allowing different clients a different view of the component. For example, a database component may offer an interface for the retrieval and update of data, but may also offer an interface for administration. An accounting component may offer an interface for account maintenance and another interface for risk assessment, etc.

Components and polymorphism

Just as one component may implement several interfaces, a given interface may be implemented differently by different components. For instance, components that represent printable documents such as text, images, spreadsheets, etc. could all implement a `Printable` interface containing methods to print, for printer setup, etc. A client that wants to print out documents can use this interface without caring about the type of document. Through this interface all components look equal and can be treated in the same way.

9.2   Design issues

Decomposition

Components as building blocks for electronic business applications

The first step in the design of a component-based application is to identify a proper segmentation of the application into individual components. While software libraries order classes by categories (for example, all classes that deal with file I/O, or all classes that deal with SQL), an application is segmented into components by coherence – meaning that classes that interact strongly should be located in the same component. In contrast, the interaction between different components should be rather loose. This is especially important for distributed components – where the interaction between components means line traffic and latency.

An application can be organized into an *n*-tier architecture:

> *A computing architecture in which software systems are structured into three networked tiers or layers: the client or presentation layer, the business logic layer, and the data layer. PCs usually provide the presentation layer, PC servers the middle tier, or business-logic layer, coordinate relations between the user (client) and the back-end tier. The data tier often includes a variety of PC and non-PC systems.*
> (Gates 1999)

From the horse's mouth

While Gates postulates here *n*=3, we are able to identify additional tiers in an electronic business scenario:

Multi-tier architecture

- The **database tier** consists of enterprise databases and other data sources, such as messaging systems. Each of these enterprise resources can be seen as a component.

- The **application tier** contains the business logic. The business model defines the way to componentize this tier: we can identify business processes, business tasks and business objects.

- A **navigational tier** supports the user in navigation between information nodes. A user's view of a site may be vastly different from the internal structure of a site (see also Sections 10.1 and 10.4). A navigational layer is required to map the user's navigational model to the actual business model.

- The **presentation tier** handles the presentation of information items and interaction with the user. This tier can be subdivided into a server-side presentation tier (such as dynamically generated HTML pages) and a client-side presentation tier (such as HTML pages, JavaScript and applets).

Persistence

Components can be either transient or persistent:

- A **transient component** only exists within a defined scope, for example within a session: when the session ends, the component's life cycle ends, too.

- In contrast, a **persistent component** is not scoped; its life cycle ends only when the component is explicitly destroyed. For example, a persistent component can maintain its state across several sessions. This is achieved by storing the component's state on some non-volatile medium, for example a database.

For persistent components, and especially aggregation of components (see below), the question of transactional behaviour becomes important. We discussed transactions in Chapter 4 and the relation between transactions and objects in Chapter 7. The statements made there also hold for components.

```
Order.Header.setDate(d)
```

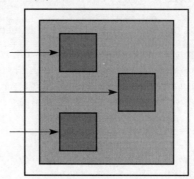

Figure 9.2   Aggregated objects within a component are accessed directly by reference (dot-notation).

Composition

The following techniques are used to combine several objects or components. The same techniques are used in object-oriented programming.

- **Aggregation**. Components contain other components (*aggregates*); for example, the component `Customer` could contain several `Order` components. Methods of the aggregates can be called by referencing the aggregate directly (Figure 9.2). This requires that the main component makes the aggregates public.

  In a scenario of business tasks and business objects, aggregation is suitable for business objects. An `Order` component, for example, could be modelled as an aggregated component. The main object `Order` could contain aggregates like `Header`, `Body`, and `Trailer` and publish these components to the client.

- **Delegation**. Here, components do not include each other but exist on a peer-to-peer basis within a package. However, there is a hierarchy in method execution. A client only calls methods of the main component, which in turn calls methods of subaltern components.

  In a transactional scenario of business tasks and business objects, for example, the delegation model is the preferred method: the business task accepts all requests because only the methods of the business task can start and end transactions (see Section 15.7), but delegates business logic functions to the business objects.

  In the `Order` example, the `maintainOrder` business task would accept all requests for the `Order` object and forward requests to it or its sub-objects (Figure 9.3).

- **Internal delegation** is a mix between aggregation and delegation. A component contains other components (aggregates) but does not allow the

```
maintainOrder.setDate(d)
```

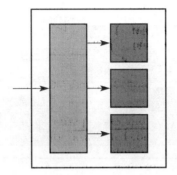

Figure 9.3   A dispatcher component delegates incoming requests to cooperating components.

```
maintainOrder.setDate(d)
```

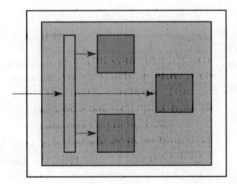

Figure 9.4   Dispatcher and cooperating objects are contained in a main object in the internal delegation model.

sub-objects to be accessed by reference (it does not publish the fields referencing the aggregates) (Figure 9.4). Instead it accepts all requests itself and dispatches them to the aggregates. Internal delegation is the delegation model in DCOM.

In a scenario of business tasks and business objects, internal delegation combines the advantages of aggregation and delegation and can be used to model both business objects and business tasks.

Component systems

By 'component system' we understand an application sub-system consisting of many components. These systems do not exist as a single physical entity and

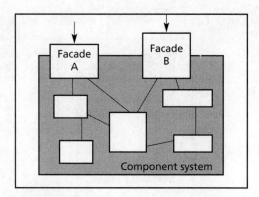

Figure 9.5 A component system.

their parts may be deployed and exchanged individually. But the design of such a component system follows the basic design principles observed for components (Figure 9.5):

Facade components are entry points to component systems

- Access to such a system is restricted to clearly defined *facade* components, which play the same role as the interface does for a single component (Jacobson et al 1997).

- A component system may have one or several facade elements.

- Components other than the facade components are private to the component system, and may not be accessed from outside the component system.

Variation

Reusability gains with variability

Reusability requires a certain amount of variability in a component. A component that is too specialized is hardly reusable. For example, a component `Order` that allows only one possible syntax for product numbers is hardly reusable in other contexts. Components must therefore provide mechanisms to customize some of their features. Jacobson (Jacobson et al 1997) introduces the term *variation point*. A variation point defines the location (or locations) within a component at which the variation occurs.

Some of the techniques for the variation of components are similar to those found in object-oriented scenarios:

- **Inheritance**. Inheritance can be used to extend or specialize a given component by overriding its features or introducing new features.

  This includes inheritance from an abstract component but also from a concrete component. Overriding or addition of features includes the introduction of new sub-objects into an aggregated component.

- **Parameterization**. Parameters contained in the source code are replaced with supplied values by a preprocessor when a component is compiled. By supplying different parameter sets developers can create components with different behaviour.

- **Customization**. Customization is similar to parameterization. However, the parameters are not supplied when the component is compiled but at plug-time, when a component is embedded into a larger application context. Customization, therefore, requires that a component can make the customization parameters permanent. It also requires that the component implements and publishes a customization interface. A typical example is visual components that are plugged into a graphical user interface with a GUI builder tool. The GUI-builder presents the customizable features in a property sheet to the GUI designer. In more complex cases a component may implement its own property editor.

- **Configuration**. A component may implement an interface which allows clients to modify the configuration of a component instance after creation of the instance.

Finally, we wish to stress that too much variability is no good, either. Too many degrees of freedom make a component difficult to build, to debug and to maintain. The art of component architecture lies in finding the right balance between adaptability and specialization.

How much variation is good for you?

9.3   Communication

Remote procedure call

The remote procedure call (RPC) is the basis for all communication between distributed components. While the concept of RPC is simple – send a function identification and parameters to a remote module and receive the result – the practical implementation requires a lot of attention to detail:

RPC is the backbone to component communication

- The procedure called may rely on global variables. This requires synchronizing global variables on client and server.

- The procedure may rely on environmental variables. For example, the collation sequence could be different on the server platform, resulting in a wrong sort sequence for the client. A policy must be devised to deal with environmental differences between client and server.

- The procedure could access peripheral devices. For example, it could require input from an operator, but the server machine runs unattended. Again, a policy must be devised to deal with this situation.

- The procedure could raise an exception. This event must be transmitted to the client and an exception raised in the client's environment.

- The remote platform may represent data differently. For example, UNIX (and Macintosh) platforms represent integer numbers differently from how they are represented on a PC. Character code tables on mainframes (EBCDIC) are different from those on UNIX and PCs (ASCII). Parameter values must therefore be converted before and/or after a transmission.

- Parameter and return values can contain complex data structures. To transmit this data across a wire, data structures must be 'flattened': nested data structures are *marshalled* or *serialized* into a sequential stream of data.

Marshalling and serialization

In component-based systems components can be implemented in different languages. These languages may implement data types and structures in a different internal format. For example, one language may store a string by prefixing it with a length byte, the other may store a string by suffixing it with a null byte. One language may store an array in one contiguous memory block, while the other implements arrays by using pointers and small memory fragments. And so on.

The marshalling process must therefore translate data structures on the sender's side into a language neutral format. *Unmarshalling* on the receiver's side translates this data stream into the internal representation of the receiver. Marshalling and unmarshalling require considerable computational overhead.

Remote method invocation

RMI extends RPC to component-based architectures

In object-oriented or component-based architectures the notion of the procedure has been replaced by that of the *method*. For the remote invocation of methods we use the term *remote method invocation* (RMI) which relies on RPC but introduces additional features:

Supports complex call parameters

- In object-oriented systems a method parameter or a result can be another object. This requires transmitting not only the data structures (the state) of the object or component: objects are active entities. The receiver may invoke a method of the object that has been transmitted from a remote location. This requires that the program code of that method is made available to the server: if the class definition of the object resides only on the client side it must be transmitted, too.

Supports distributed garbage collection

- Objects and components can now refer to each other over distributed locations, a situation that cannot be properly handled with local garbage collection algorithms. RMI implementations must therefore support distributed garbage collection.

Ping

- The death of a server could leave the client in limbo (or vice versa). Resources that had been allocated by the partner would remain allocated. This is solved in most implementations by 'pinging' the partner (periodically sending a signal). If the signal stops, the partner can run the necessary clean-up operations.

Interface definition languages

IDL describes a component's interface to the world

Most component models use an interface definition language (IDL) to describe the features (methods and properties) of an interface. An IDL is typically independent of and neutral to the implementation language of the component. Language bindings define how the definitions made using the IDL are mapped onto the implementation language. IDL compilers translate IDL definitions into the implementation language.

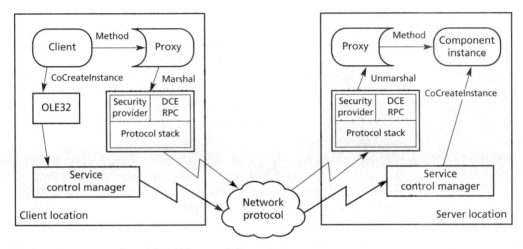

Figure 9.6 Proxy and stub in DCOM (Source: Software AG).

Most component technologies use proxies and stubs (or skeletons) to implement the runtime environment for distributed components (Figure 9.6).

The *proxy* acts at the client side as a substitute for the remote component and accepts all method calls from the client. It marshals the method data structure (parameters) and sends the resulting data stream through the transport layer to the server. There, the data is passed to the *stub*, which acts as a substitute for the client. The stub unmarshals the data stream (reconstructs the parameters in the format of the server platform) and then calls the appropriate method of the server-side component. The result is passed back likewise.

Proxies and stubs are key to distributed component architectures

Event-based architectures

While RPC and RMI are a powerful concept for distributed processing, they have one disadvantage: they work synchronously. A client that calls a remote method must wait until the method returns. This can lead to unacceptable response times and is also not what we expect from distributed processing: it should be possible to execute tasks asynchronously.

This requires the ability to handle asynchronous events (see also Chapter 7). Most component models support – on top of RMI or RPC – an event- or message-based architecture. Most component architectures predefine several event-related interfaces. The methods of these interfaces can be implemented by components that wish to take part in event-driven processing.

Several mechanisms for the exchange of asynchronous messages exist:

- *Point-to-point.* The connection between sender and receiver is 'hard-wired' – sender and receiver are connected by a channel. The channel may act synchronously (wait until a message is delivered before it accepts a new one), or it can queue messages.

Techniques for asynchronous event processing

Receivers can act

- synchronously: the receiver requests a message and waits until the message arrives;

- asynchronously: the receiver registers with the provider. When a message arrives the provider notifies the receiver by calling the receiver's notification method. The receiver can then read the message.

Point-to-point connections are also possible between multiple senders and receivers (multicast).

A message from the publisher

- *Publish-and-subscribe*. The publish-and-subscribe concept works on a content-related basis. Receiving components can subscribe to a data item (which could be a component, too). When a sending component (publisher) modifies the data item, all subscribers are notified.

Observers want to be notified

- *Observer-observable pattern*. This pattern relies on the publish-and-subscribe mechanism. Observer components (for example, a representation unit) register with an observable (for example, a business object). When the observable changes its state, it notifies all registered observers.

Managers facilitate communication

- *Dependency manager*. These are used to separate event notification logic from the business logic. Both observers and observable register with a dependency manager. When the state of an observable changes it notifies the dependency manager, which takes further action to notify the observers.

Software bus

- *Bus*. Bus systems allow several components to join the bus. Components can place a message on the bus which forwards the message to all participating components. The receivers look at the content (or only the header) of the message and decide whether they want to process the message or ignore it.

Tuple space

- *Tuple spaces*. Tuple spaces work like a whiteboard. Components can place messages into the tuple space. Each message consists of an *n*-tuple of label/value pairs. Components that want to receive messages issue a query to the tuple space. Queries consist of tuples of label/value pairs, too, but the value part of a tuple element may contain a variable or placeholder. The tuple space returns the messages that match the query to the receiving component.

Example:

Sender places	`(Make=Porsche, Model=911, Year=1990)`
Receiver requests	`(Make=Porsche, Model=?)`
and gets	`(Make=Porsche, Model=911)`

Receiving components can either read the matching tuple and leave it in the tuple space, or remove the tuple from the tuple space.

Some implementations allow queries to be posted asynchronously. The receiver registers a query with the tuple space. When a matching tuple is stored in the tuple space, the receiver is notified.

Asynchronous event-driven processing requires middleware infrastructure

All of these concepts require some infrastructure to facilitate the exchange of messages, such as a channel, a bus or a tuple space. This infrastructure is usually implemented as a component, too. In the simplest case it can be contained in the sending or receiving component, but in an enterprise situation these services are often provided by Message-oriented Middleware (MoM). Examples are IBM's MQSeries or Software AG's EntireX.

9.4   Names and directories

In traditional monolithic applications the modules of a system are linked together after compilation. The problem of locating a component thus does not arise.

In component-based systems, components are deployed independently of each other. Before using the services of a component it is first necessary to locate the component within the distributed environment.

How to find a component?

Several mechanisms have been developed to provide a component with an address:

- *Global unique identifiers* (*GUIDs*). A global identifier is a string which is unique worldwide. GUIDs provide a component (or an interface) with a unique identification, but do not specify where the component is found. They rely on registries that map GUIDs to a location. This allows an application to be reconfigured (for example, a component to be moved to another machine) by changing only the registry entries.

GUID

- *Name spaces*. Here, the address of a component is defined by a composite name, consisting of a domain name and a subpath. The names can be easily made unique by using World Wide Web domain names. The names used for components do not usually specify a physical location but specify a location in a virtual name space. The mapping to physical locations is facilitated by directory services which allow virtual names to be mapped to physical locations.

- *Directory services* allow resources to be addressed by name (white pages) or by features (yellow pages). Because features (interface definitions) do not usually qualify a service sufficiently, additional attributes can be used to describe the functionality of an interface. The X.500 standard defines common attributes for resources.

White and yellow pages

- More sophisticated services for feature and attribute-related addressing are provided by *traders* (ISO/IEC 1995). In a component scenario a trader acts as a matchmaker. Components register their attributed interfaces with a trader. Other components that require a service ask the trader for components that could fulfil the service. If a suitable component has been found the trader passes the address of this component to the querying component.

Traders

Within a component studio, traders can also support developers during the construction of a component-based application in finding the right component for the right purpose.

10 User interfaces for the masses

10.1 A new metaphor

The computing industry of the 1990s fully adopted the graphical user interface metaphor pioneered by Xerox PARC in the 1970s. This metaphor, first explored by the Smalltalk system on the Alto, was already defined in most aspects when the Xerox Star was introduced in 1980. The concepts of WYSIWYG editing, overlapping screen windows, and the direct manipulation of system objects as icons had all been thoroughly demonstrated.

Emancipation of the GUI

The following decades saw considerable refinement of the original ideas, first in the Apple Macintosh, later in OS/2 and Windows '95. By providing human interface guidelines and an API (application programming interface) to the GUI, Apple and Microsoft ensured that applications written for these platforms have a user interface that is consistent with those of the operating system itself and all other applications.

The intuitive graphical user interface has made the PC popular. What had started as a research project in Palo Alto has become an everyday item on the desktops of millions.

Writing software that is intuitive to use is easier today than it was in the days of the Xerox Star. We do not really have to simulate an office environment. Today's office workers do know how computer applications work and they have certain expectations regarding how an application is to be used. They expect a menu bar under the title line. Also, the sequence of menu items does not leave much choice:

```
File Edit View ... Window ?
```

Point and click as user interface

The web browser has introduced a new metaphor for how to use a computer. The point and click interface of a web page is superior to a menu-based interface which requires considerable manipulation to call a function. Recently we have seen more and more web pages equipped with a menu bar – old habits die hard.

The discipline of web page design is still quite young, so there is still a lot of room for experimentation.

Usability issues

One problem is that web pages are designed by graphic designers (if a designer is used at all). Graphic designers know how to make a page look 'real cool', but they are not experts in usability and ergonomics. Graphical user interfaces (including web pages) for heavy-duty applications should be designed by industrial designers who have specialized in software ergonomics.

Things are different when web pages are designed not for in-house use but for a public web site. The web site will probably be used by computer novices, or by people new to the web. Here we are in a similar situation as Xerox was with the Star system back in 1980. And we resort to the same means: we use metaphors that people know from everyday life, like the shopping cart. We can also use metaphors that are part of the majority of other sites, because they are well known to web users. Jakob Nielsen reports an experiment where an online shop for winter sports products used a 'shopping sled' instead of a shopping cart. The result was that 50 per cent of users did not understand this concept (Nielsen 1999-2).

Beware of eclecticism

Creating a large successful web site, however, needs more than just good intentions. It requires field studies, experimentation and measurement. It also requires implementing different navigation models for different groups of users. A customer probably has a different view of a company from a staff member. A supplier again may have his or her own mental model of this company. When the structure of the web site matches only the view of the staff, customers and suppliers will get lost. This does not matter so much with suppliers (they are not so easily turned away), but a customer may give up quickly in frustration and switch to the competition.

Adhere to mental models of target groups

10.2   Reducing the strain

The mental hazards are accompanied by physical dangers – a topic that should not be taken lightly. The mass introduction of desktop systems did not go without victims: before the age of the PC, RSI (repetitive strain injury) was a phenomenon that was common among data typists and secretaries. The omnipresence of the PC and the mouse have now spread this problem over the whole community of office workers, including developers and managers. Severe cases of RSI can even lead to permanent disability.

This is not just a case of selecting the right mouse, keyboard, desk and chair. It is also a concern of good software design. Software that requires many mouse movements and mouse clicks certainly adds to the strain caused by the hardware. Manufacturers such as Microsoft have recognized the problem: newer versions of the Windows operating system and Internet Explorer have reduced the number of mouse clicks significantly by replacing the double-click with a single click. The former single-click action is now achieved just by hovering over an item.

Ergonomic software

Other ways of human–computer interface (HCI) representation should be considered as well. Speech technology is becoming more and more mature, but it is not applicable in all environments. One problem is that existing applications are not yet built around speech technology.

Speech technology

The same problem applies to web pages: graphically rich web pages do not really scale well to speech synthesis. But speech access to web pages may become an important topic in the near future. In October 1998 the World Wide Web Consortium (W3C) started a new activity for a voice browser standard. The aim is to open the web to a vast number of people by providing access through the plain old telephone service (POTS). Immediate applications are seen for accessing e-mail, voice mail, diaries and information services, for travel, resource tracking, financial news, weather and traffic updates, directories, etc. (W3C 1999-5).

10.3   Adapting to the user

To guide users through the vast amount of information, services increasingly use techniques to gather information about users. They use this information to make educated suggestions to the user. Because it is practically impossible to implement such recommendations 'hard wired', adaptive techniques are used, such as neural networks, genetic algorithms or statistical methods.

Collaborative filtering

Collaborative filtering (Breese and Kadie 1998) (*Recommender systems* (Resnick and Vaian 1997)) is one such adaptive technique to assist users in information retrieval. Based on previous choices made by the user, the system makes suggestions that will match the user's preferences with high probability. In an online shopping system such virtual recommenders replace the real shop assistant. At Levi Strauss's web site, for example, customers are asked about gender, and preferences for music, look and fun. Based on these choices, the system recommends shirts and trousers to the customer. There is still room for improvement: the system does not ask for hair and eye colour, complexion or age.

A serious research site for collaborative filtering is found at `http://shadow.ieor.berkeley.edu/humor`. After registering with the system the user is asked to rate 15 jokes. Thereafter the system continues to tell jokes but tries to avoid the bad ones. Because rating continues, the system can improve its selection strategy during operation. The only problem that remains: when no more bad jokes are told, the good ones seem less funny.

User clustering

Collaborative filtering systems need a certain startup period, until enough statistical data is gathered to make a recommendation, and until the preferences of an individual user are determined. In many cases user clustering can help to shorten the startup phase: as soon as a user is identified as belonging to a certain user group, the group preferences can be used as the initial preferences for the individual user.

Privacy

Privacy is a concern. User preferences are personal data. The exchange of user preferences between different sites can certainly be useful because the recommendation process does not have to start repeatedly from scratch with the construction of user profiles. The exchange of user preferences, however, is a breach of privacy which the user must authorize. The W3C has addressed this problem with P3P (Platform for Privacy Preferences) (W3C 1999-4). P3P allows users to specify what kind of personal information they are willing to disclose to web-based systems. Users can delegate decisions to their software agent. P3P-compliant systems inform the user if the user's privacy preferences are not consistent with the privacy practices of the site accessed. While P3P is a standard for the implementation of privacy-aware systems, privacy laws – especially in European countries – must be considered in addition when privacy-related information is stored or exchanged.

10.4   Systematic design of user interfaces

The design of user interfaces for electronic business is still a young discipline. The liberal use of JavaScript in particular has allowed web designers to invent all kinds of non-standard surfing experiences. This has reduced the usability of the web considerably. Jakob Nielsen has published a whole list of dos and don'ts for web design (Nielsen 1999-1).

But while guidelines like 'The back button should always lead to the previously opened pages' are certainly useful and much needed, what is required is a systematic approach to the design of web-based user interfaces.

Fortunately, there is some help. Several research groups have developed *Hypertext* design methods and tools for multimedia applications, such as multimedia encyclopedias or virtual museums and galleries, usually for the CD-ROM market. What these applications and web-based applications have in common is that they are both based on hypertext. Users can follow links to other information nodes (web pages). In both application domains content is organized in a non-linear fashion, and both domains' information nodes can contain rich multimedia items. Hypertext systems are much older than the web.

> *The history of hypertext goes back to 1945, when Vannevar Bush published the* *History of hypermedia* *idea of associative indexing in an article 'As We May Think' (Bush 1945): 'It affords an immediate step, however, to associative indexing, the basic idea of which is a provision whereby any item may be caused at will to select immediately and automatically another.'*
>
> *The terms 'hypertext' and 'hypermedia' were coined in 1965 by Ted Nelson. In an article published by Literary Machines, Nelson explained: 'By "hypertext" (we) mean nonsequential writing – text that branches and allows choice to the reader, best read at an interactive screen.'*
>
> *The first Hypertext system was developed by van Dam for IBM in 1967 and was later used for project documentation in the Apollo space program. Other landmarks include: NLS by Doug Engelbart (who also invented the mouse) at Stanford Research Institute in 1968; the Aspen Movie Map by Andrew Lippman of MIT Architecture Machine Group in 1978; the never implemented Xanadu by Ted Nelson in 1981; Xerox' NoteCards in 1985; HyperCard by Bill Atkinson of Apple Computer in 1987. (Nielsen 1997)*

In the meantime commercial multimedia titles have reached a high degree of sophistication. So it is certainly worth taking a look over the fence to see what concepts from the hypermedia area can be used for electronic business.

If we consider that the conceptual design of the business model is done, then *Storyboard* the design of an electronic business user interface starts – no, not with a user manual – with a *storyboard*. An electronic business application should be intuitive and self-explaining. It is not possible to ship the traditional user manual to millions of prospective users.

Storyboarding is a pencil and paper technique for designing and testing user interfaces. Although it is not as immediate as a prototype it has the advantage that it can be done without a computer, allowing designers to follow their personal preferences.

Navigation structure

A storyboard shows the sequence of events and specifies the user actions that cause them. The result is a scenario of information nodes that the user can navigate.

Different user groups

It may be necessary to design several such storyboards, one for each user group. Staff from a trading partner will certainly have different access rights from an enterprise's own employees, thus the navigation structure of the web site will be different for both groups. Experienced users may have different requirements from novices, and so on.

In the following we give a short overview of OOHDM (Object-Oriented Hypermedia Design Method), a design method that was developed for the systematic design of hypermedia applications (Schwabe et al 1996; Schwabe and Rossi 1998).

Systematic HCI design with OOHDM

OOHDM knows four design activities which are applied in an iterative and incremental way:

- **Conceptual design**. This is where the business model of the application is designed. Here the conceptual objects and the relationships between them are defined. In our terminology conceptual objects comprise business processes, business tasks and business objects. The business objects form the basis for what the user will eventually see.

  We can use traditional methods such as UML (Unified Modelling Language) for conceptual design.

- **Navigation design**. Here we define navigation objects, which are views of the conceptual objects. We separate interface issues from navigation issues. For example, not every mouse click leads to a new information node. Some mouse clicks may just change the state of an element (such as a radio button) in the current information node. This is not considered as navigation.

  We also have to define how navigation objects relate to business objects. This is not necessarily a 1:1 relationship. On the one hand, a complex business object could split into several web pages. On the other hand, several business objects could be displayed on the same web page, for instance in a list, a table or a synopsis. Because business objects can change in the course of a session, navigation objects and business objects must implement the observer/observable pattern, so that navigation objects are updated when a business object changes.

  The transitions (links) between navigation objects must be defined. These transitions define the possible paths of users from navigation object to navigation object. As the user moves through the navigation space, the set of transitions may be transformed: links can be enabled or disabled depending on the position (and history) of the user.

The possible path of a user through the navigation objects depends on the *navigation context*. Different user groups may have different access rights or information requirements. The navigation context also depends on the access structures (links, paths, indices, guided tours, etc.) a user has chosen. In OOHDM a navigation context is a set of active navigation objects, links and other (nested) navigation contexts.

- **Abstract interface design**. Navigation objects are not directly perceived by the user; rather, they are accessed through *interface objects*. Interface objects are responsible for mediating user interaction with navigation objects. The interface model specifies which interface objects the user perceives; which user events cause state changes in the interface objects; and which user events or state changes cause navigation events. OOHDM uses *abstract data views* (ADV) (Cowan and Lucena 1995) to model the abstract interface.

- **Implementation**. During implementation the conceptual objects, navigation objects and interface objects are mapped onto technologies, such as server components, servlets, server pages, HTML pages, scripts, applets, etc.

By clearly separating conceptual design, navigation design and abstract interface design, OOHDM allows the later modification of each single layer without impact on the other layers. For example, it is possible to change the look and feel of a site without touching business logic and navigation logic. Or, the navigation structure may be changed due to observation of user behaviour, without touching the business logic and the GUI.

11 Collaboration

I n a digital economy, collaborative applications become more and more important, applications that allow multiple users to cooperate in different roles to achieve a common goal.

Collaborative computing spans a wide range of applications and implementation strategies. The range reaches from simultaneous or sequential collaboration between end users in a single business transaction over workflow systems to the collaboration of independent electronic business applications across company boundaries.

Collaborative systems are traditionally found in the large engineering and construction projects. The car and aviation industries, for example, use globally distributed construction processes to shorten development cycles: development takes place in the US, Europe and Australia, and while everybody is working from nine to five, the project is worked on continuously, 24 hours a day.

Many electronic business scenarios have collaborative aspects. For example, processing a health claim at a health insurer may involve three persons in different roles: the patient, the responsible officer and a medical expert. Instead of trusting that all participants will eventually e-mail each other, the system manages the flow of information and control between them.

From the perspective of an end user, collaboration happens in multi-party sessions simultaneously (like online auctions) or in sequential non-overlapping sessions (workflow):

- Compared to single user sessions, multi-party sessions require additional session control methods. Users can not only start and finish a session, but may also join and leave existing sessions that were started by other users.

- Workflow systems are characterized by multiple users performing a sequence of tasks to achieve a common goal. Each task is performed by a single distributed workflow component (worker), i.e. there is no collaboration of multiple workers within one task. Each participant has a special role. The task sequence may split into several concurrent sequences, and concurrent sequences can join to form a single sequence. The dynamic behaviour of workflow systems is usually modelled using Petri nets (see Chapter 4).

The following strategies have been developed for collaborative systems:

- Collaboration can happen **synchronously** (user actions are immediately broadcast to the other users of the same session), or **asynchronously** (recording of events and data streams and later replay).

- Users can collaborate in editing the same information item, or they may specialize in editing different partitions within a larger context. It is often necessary to **partition** information objects into objects of finer granularity, to allow collaborative processing of a large information object.

- The application may enforce full information **consistency** over all user views, or it may allow less strict consistency policies.

- Information can be stored:

  - **Centralized**. Centralized storage can use simpler concepts of event serialization and locking. Frequent update of all user views, however, may require transmitting high data volumes.

  - **Replicated**. Replicated storage allows more responsive applications because updating user views can be handled locally. However, events must be replicated and sent to all users. Object locking must be controlled by a central lock manager, requiring additional messages.

  - **Mobile**. Moving the whole application information state to another user can be appropriate for workflow systems, where tasks are executed sequentially rather than simultaneously.

- Synchronization in multi-party collaborative systems is achieved by:

  - **Floor control**. Before a user modifies the information state, the session is locked to other users: *Everybody is quiet when I speak*.

  - **Event sharing**. When a client changes the state of a local application a message is sent to all other clients. Event sharing can be applied on different layers of an application:

    - Sharing of GUI events. This technique provides 'collaboration transparency', allowing a conventional single-user application to be used in a multi-user environment. For Java-based applications this can be achieved by modifying the Java AWT. However, waiting on mouse movements transmitted through the Internet requires a lot of patience.

    - Sharing of navigation events. The three-layered architecture as described in the discussion of OOHDM in Chapter 10 allows navigation events to be shared with other users. This technique synchronizes navigation between navigation nodes, provided that all users share the same or compatible navigation contexts.

    - Sharing of business events. This type of event sharing only ensures that the state of the business process is the same for all users. This technique should not be used in an architecture comprising a separate navigational layer: business processes and navigation processes could go out of sync, leading to disorientation of the user.

    Event sharing can lead to event queues – events may be already out of date when they are served. Thus semantic consistency checks are required.

- **Object locking**. When a user starts a transaction, all objects that are involved in the transaction are locked, and unlocked after the transaction is committed (check-in-check-out). Granularity is an important issue. Fine-grained object locks allow users to work simultaneously on different object regions. A problem is the handling of relationships between objects. For example, a user may delete an object that is referenced in other non-locked objects.

There are several locking strategies, ranging from individual locks (one per information object) to centralized locking managers.

One example of a system based on object locking is Software AG's Bolero Component Studio. Its *team repository* allows multiple users to work simultaneously on the same repository. Users that plan to modify a development object can lock this object to other users. After the required modifications have been made the lock is released and the development object becomes available again to other team members.

- **Promises and guarantees.** A flexible approach to collaboration is taken in (Dourish 1996). Operations on an information object requested by a user promise certain properties, but also ask for guarantees. Access to the object is only granted when there is no conflict in guarantees. For example, an operation used to attach an additional information item to an existing object can promise that it will not change or remove existing information, but will ask for a guarantee that the target object exists.

- **Divergence.** In case of a locking or guarantee conflict, the system can allow the existence of diverging versions of an information object (Dourish 1996), (Haake and Haake 1993). At some point inconsistencies between the diverging versions must be reconciled by the users. The advantage is that many users can work simultaneously on the same object. For example, after the draft version of this book was created, it was sent to several reviewers. The reviewers' comments and the author's improvements were reconciled to create the final version. Using a locking technique (allowing only one reviewer at a time to review the book) would have delayed the review process by months.

Collaborative computing is the subject of many ongoing research activities. A number of pilot systems have been developed. We will briefly discuss two of them as examples:

- *Habanero* (Chabert et al 1996). Developed at the National Center for Supercomputing Applications (NCSA), the Habanero framework provides state and event synchronization for multiple copies of Java-based software tools. Habanero is client based and works by replicating applications across clients and sharing all local state changes between the application clones. In addition, Habanero provides a general floor control object, an arbitrator, that controls the events that can be performed at a given time. It can also lock application resources. Habanero supports multiple concurrent sessions per client and provides extensive session management facilities (session information, invitation service, participation list).

- *Tango Interactive* (Beca et al). Developed at the Northeast Parallel Architectures Center (NPAC), Tango exists as a plug-in for Netscape browsers and as an ActiveX control for Microsoft Internet Explorer. It provides APIs for several languages, including Java and JavaScript, and supports collaborative applets as well as collaborative stand-alone applications. Similar to

Habanero, the architecture of Tango is based on event sharing. Applications are replicated for each client. When an application changes its state it sends a message to the other applications in the same session. Which state changes cause messages can be defined by the application programmer. It is therefore possible to implement fine-grained or coarse-grained coupling between applications. Tango provides means for session control (user authentication, starting and ending sessions, tracing participants' activities, changing user privileges), and support for multimedia streams (sound, video). It provides a logging mechanism, so all user activities may be stored and retraced if necessary. Tango is a client-based solution. The data is always obtained from the Internet server infrastructure, such as HTTP servers, audio/video servers, or JDBC-connected databases.

Enabling technology

In Part 3 we discuss technology, mostly Java and XML-related technology, for electronic business. Readers will benefit from a basic knowledge of Java and general object-oriented programming principles.

- Chapter 12 presents Java and its main architectural principles. This includes a discussion of the Java 2 Enterprise Edition architecture.

- Chapter 13 follows Java's path from the applet to the server. The Java Enterprise Application Model and new developments like application servers are discussed.

- Chapter 14 discusses the importance of XML for electronic business applications.

- In Chapter 15 we introduce Bolero, Software AG's commercial Java-based programming language and development system. We highlight the differences from Java. Bolero's concepts are discussed in detail in areas important to commercial programming, such as the Internet, component models, databases, XML, and the relationship between business model and programming model.

About Java 12

12.1 A new computing platform

The genesis of Java started in mid-1991, long before the web was an issue. But then, Java wasn't even called Java. The name was Oak, named after an oak tree standing outside James Gosling's office. The name did not survive a brand name search, so the language was later renamed Java. The name change was a lucky one: Java is the kind of name that puts a grin on every programmer's face, at least in the coffee-drinking nations – some programmers measure productivity in lc^3 (lines of code per cup of coffee). The connotations would have not been so obvious with Oak – the practice of using roasted acorns as a coffee substitute has ceased considerably since World War II.

Java (as we call Oak from now on) was developed to sell modern software technology to consumer electronics, computer chips built into TV sets, VCRs, household appliances, toys, etc. Programs suitable for such devices must be:

Java started as a workhorse for industrial programming...

- small – in devices that are far less expensive than a PC, computer memory even today *is* a cost factor;

- portable – devices use chips from different manufacturers, and applications should run on different platforms without recompilation;

- robust – applications must run without any maintenance and without the reset/reboot cycles known from PC usage.

The strategy in the design of Java was to concentrate on tried-and-trusted techniques in object-oriented programming, not so much on the implementation of the latest cutting-edge concepts. Java was to become a workhorse for industrial programming.

By mid-1994 the web was the dominant force in Internet computing. It turned out that the virtues of Java (small footprint, portability, robustness) were also the virtues that could make a great language to implement distributed applets for the web:

- A small application footprint is required to deploy software components across today's narrow bandwidth connections.

... and became the preferred web application language

- Portability is necessary because clients are machines from different manufacturers (PCs, Macs, UNIX workstations, etc.). Distribution of software in source form and recompilation on the target platform – as required with the C or C++ programming language – is not feasible.

● Robustness. A web-based application should be able to run without any intervention and should be isolated from the features of other components.

12.2   The Java architecture

The concepts used in Java to achieve these goals are indeed among the tried and trusted. It was more the blend of technologies and the timing that made Java a success.

Java Virtual Machine (JVM)

JVM

Java source code is compiled into platform-independent and compact *byte code*. This byte code is interpreted and then executed by a platform-specific interpreter, the Java Virtual Machine. This technique was pioneered by UCSD Pascal. Fourth-generation language systems, such as Software AG's Natural, use similar techniques to achieve both platform independence and small modules.

Java Application Programming Interface (API)

Java API

While the JVM abstracts from the hardware and the operating system, Java Class Libraries abstract from operating system services. The `java.awt`, for example, abstracts from a concrete windowing system. A Java program can execute identically without change under Windows, MacOS or UNIX (Figure 12.1). Because Java Class Libraries are deployed with the JVM to form a client-based Java runtime environment, applications can use these library functions without having to include library modules into the application module, resulting in a small application footprint.

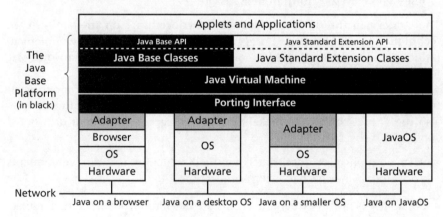

Figure 12.1   The Java Base Platform is uniform across all operating systems. (Source: JavaSoft)

Late binding

Late binding is a technique used by most 4GL languages. After compilation, *Late binding* modules are not linked together to form one big executable, but can be deployed (and exchanged) on a module-by-module basis. The actual linking process (binding of entry points and variables) is performed just before execution. Java uses this technique on a class-by-class basis. This makes it possible to deploy only the class that contains the `main` or `run` method; all other classes can be loaded and bound when needed – the Java class loader is also able to load classes from remote locations.

Garbage collection

In the context of object-oriented programming languages garbage collection is *Garbage collection* old hat. From the early days of object-oriented programming with Simula 67, all genuine object-oriented languages, such as Smalltalk or Eiffel, were equipped with garbage collectors.

Most non-object-oriented languages, however, like Fortran, Cobol, Pascal, C or PL/I, don't need garbage collectors. All memory usage is *scoped* – memory areas are only used within the scope of a procedure call or a program block, and can be released immediately afterwards. This can be implemented efficiently by using a stack that grows and shrinks as required (Figure 12.2).

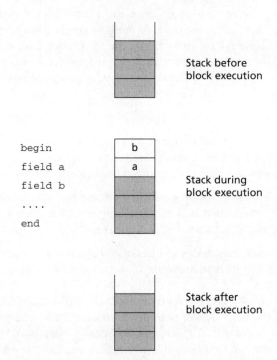

Figure 12.2 Stack allocation and de-allocation in a block frame.

Object-oriented languages, on the other hand, create object instances that live beyond the scope of the block where the object instance was created. For that reason objects cannot be stored in the stack. They are instead stored in a second memory area, the *heap*. Object instances, as a matter of fact, can become obsolete. For example, an event object is no longer needed after the event has been processed. Such objects must be detected so that their memory can be reclaimed. There are several techniques to detect obsolete objects:

- Counting the references to an object (use count). When the use count is zero the object is obsolete. (This method fails if cyclic object structures are involved.)
- Mark and sweep. Starting from active references (e.g. references contained in the stack) directly and indirectly referenced objects are marked. Unmarked objects are regarded as obsolete.

The process to detect obsolete objects and to reclaim the occupied memory is called *garbage collection* (Figure 12.3).

Typically, languages that implement object-oriented features on top of an existing non-OO language, such as C++ or Delphi (based on Pascal), do not offer automatic garbage collection. This leaves the task of detecting obsolete objects and reclaiming memory to the programmer. Humans make mistakes, and sometimes they forget to reclaim the memory of obsolete objects. This is called a *memory leak* (it is unclear if this term relates to the memory of the computer or to that of the programmer). Unfortunately most of these errors do not show up during the testing phase, and even during production they may become apparent after days or weeks of faultless continuous operation – when all memory leaks have added up such that the application runs out of memory.

The fact that Java is equipped with a garbage collector and features a C++-like syntax must appear as a godsend to many C++ programmers.

No pointers

Pointers

The pointer problem is the other side of the coin. In C++ or Delphi, objects are referenced via explicit pointers. Pointers are physical references (addresses) to data structures, and languages such as C even allow arithmetic operations on pointers.

> *Pointers are like jumps, leading wildly from one part of the data structure to another. Their introduction into high-level languages has been a step backwards from which we may never recover.* (C.A.R. Hoare)

When the programmer makes a mistake and releases an object that is still in use, the result is an open (dangling) pointer. A routine that uses this pointer will usually crash.

Again, in genuine object-oriented languages this situation cannot arise, because the programmer leaves memory management to the system. Explicit pointers are not necessary, and not wanted because they make garbage collection extremely difficult or impossible to implement. Objects are addressed via references, and as long as there are active references to an object, the object continues to exist.

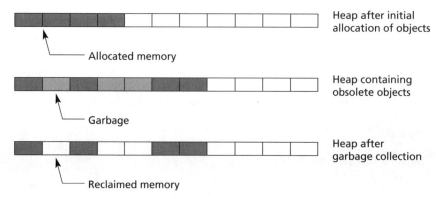

Figure 12.3 Heap allocation and garbage collection.

Strong typing

A language is called strongly or statically typed if the type of an expression can be determined at compile time, which contributes to robust applications. In the object-oriented family, with the exception of Smalltalk and Objective-C, all languages implement strong typing to a varying degree. Java implements strong typing, but also allows the programmer to use *type casts* to evade strong typing. Type casts can cause type errors at runtime, but are necessary in Java, because there is no concept of *generic* (parameterized) types, as in Eiffel, Bolero or the Standard Template Library (STL) in C++.

Typing

Serialization

Originally known as 'pickling' from Modula-3, serialization is a technique to represent the state of an object (possibly including a whole tree of aggregated sub-objects) as a single data stream that can be stored on persistent media – or can be sent to a remote destination using RMI. Deserialization reconstructs the object from the serialized data stream. We explain serialization in detail in Section 12.8.

Serialization

Reflection and introspection

Known from C++ and Smalltalk, *reflection* provides methods to dynamically access the definitions of classes, fields, arrays, methods and constructors, allowing applications to find out about the features of a class. So it is possible to interrogate a compiled Java class about the methods, fields and parameters contained in the module.

Reflection and introspection

Based on reflection is Java's *introspection* which allows builder tools, such as a component studio, to find out how a component (JavaBean) works. The same introspection can be used by applications to inspect the features of pre-manufactured components to adapt their behaviour accordingly.

It would be unfair to say that Java did not break new ground in object-oriented programming. Some features in Java are quite unique:

Separate concepts for class (behaviour) and type

Well, almost. While a subclass is also a subtype, Java in addition allows the concept of types to be applied independently of classes (Budd 1997). The construct for subtypes is the `interface`. An `interface` is a type specification but does not specify an implementation. A class definition that implements an `interface` must provide an implementation for each method specified in the interface (unless the class is defined as *abstract*).

Example:

```
public interface Printable {
  void print();
}

public class Document implements Printable {
  void print() {
  ....
  }
}

public class Image implements Printable {
  void print() {
  ....
  }
}

public class Spooler {
  void addElement(Printable) {
  ....
  }
}
```

Polymorphism

The interface `Printable` defines that each class implementing `Printable` must have a method `print()`. The classes `Document` and `Image` implement this interface and both implement a method `print()`. Instances of both classes can then be used as a parameter of the `addElement` method of class `Spooler`. The parameter of this method was defined as of type `Printable` – the type of the common interface of both `Document` and `Image`.

```
Spooler s = new Spooler();
s.addElement(new Document());
s.addElement(new Image());
```

Java allows a class to implement multiple interfaces, but to extend only one class. So, multiple inheritance is restricted to data types – a compromise between the inflexibility of single inheritance and the minefield of multiple inheritance.

Multi-threading

Java is one of the first commercially available object-oriented languages (besides Perl) to implement multi-threading. Concurrent execution of applications in multiple threads and processes is a cornerstone for smoothly operating user interfaces and efficient distributed processing. We will discuss multi-threading in detail in Section 12.5.

Multi-threading

Network support and distributed objects

The Java Class Libraries include an extensive set of routines that support TCP/IP protocols like HTTP and FTP. This allows programmers to access objects across the net via URLs with the same application programming interface (API) as if accessing the object from a local file system.

Remote class loader

Network support is also built into the JVM class loader, allowing program modules to be loaded across the net via URL.

Remote method invocation (RMI) supports method calls of remote objects across the network transparently. We will discuss this in more detail in Section 12.4.

These features support the implementation of distributed (multi-tier) applications. Objects running on a client can interact with objects running in a different JVM, possibly on multiple remote servers.

Built-in security

Security features are built into the Java Class Libraries and into the Java run-time environment:

Java security

- If the class code is not local, the Java Byte Code Verifier is called by the class loader before a class is passed to the JVM for execution, ensuring that the file contains valid Java byte code.

- The Java Security API allows programmers to include security features in their applets and applications. These features include cryptography, encryption and authentication.

- Until Java 1.1 untrusted applets did not have access to system resources (sandbox model), while local application and trusted applets did have unrestricted access to system resources.

  Java 2 adds Security Policy Files that allow fine-grained access control for both applets and applications. So it is possible to restrict access rights to certain files, or to allow only read access but not write access. Policy files can be defined by users, programmers or administrators.

  These security policies are controlled by the Security Manager. The functions of the Security Manager are called by the JVM and by various methods throughout the Java libraries before those methods perform sensitive operations.

On-demand compilation

Compilation

The byte code layer that makes Java independent from hardware platforms needs interpretation by the Java Virtual Machine. This interpretation causes overhead. Several techniques have been developed to boost the performance of Java:

- *Just-in-time (JIT) compilers.* A JIT compiler translates Java byte code into machine code, just before execution. Because the compilation happens on the target machine, programs remain portable.

- *HotSpot compiler.* Introduced with Java 2, the Java HotSpot Virtual Machine promises superior performance levels relative to Java 1. Among other performance improvements like faster thread switching, method inlining and faster garbage collection, this virtual machine includes the adaptive HotSpot compiler. The most frequently used code parts are compiled into optimized native code based on statistical information gathered from runtime usage. The HotSpot technology is able to adapt the optimization dynamically to client behaviour – to change optimization when client behaviour changes. Sun claims performance levels equal to or better than C++ (Griswold 1998); however, soon afterwards Symantec claimed that JIT 4.0 beats HotSpot. The race is still on.

- *High performance compilers* (IBM) exist for many platforms. High performance compilers compile Java byte code into native machine code. Elaborate optimizations are applied. The resulting code is not portable, and the compiled modules are usually much bigger than Java byte code modules (`.class` files). There are also limitations regarding dynamic code derived from reflection.

  However, for server-side applications these compilers are useful instruments for performance optimization.

12.3   From chip card to mainframe: J2ME to J2EE

The Java Virtual Machine and Java Standard Libraries are available on almost any platform. JVM and libraries are integrated into popular browsers such as Netscape Navigator or Microsoft Internet Explorer, or are deployed as part of the operating system. A Java plug-in is also available for most browsers.

The Java Base API (or Java Applet API) is the minimum functionality that developers can safely assume for deploying Java applets and applications. This platform applies for network computers, desktop computers, workstations, enterprise servers, and mainframes, running under operating systems such as Windows 9x/NT, MacOs, UNIX, NetWare, JavaOS, MVS, etc.

Beginning with Java 2, Java has been reorganized into three specialized editions. These editions provide the support for a homogeneous and consistent computing environment from the smallest device to the most powerful mainframes.

J2ME

Java 2 Micro Edition (J2ME) is intentionally small, designed to fit reduced memory devices. The range of devices spans across top-level consumer devices like personal digital assistants (PDA) or hand-held computers, over embedded systems such as industrial controllers, automotive devices, or printers, down to chip cards (SmartCards). This edition features a specialized virtual machine, the KVM (K Virtual Machine), which has been optimized for a small footprint. J2ME includes the following APIs:

Micro Edition

- The Personal Java API is intended for top-level devices which require graphical user interfaces or communication features. The Personal Java API offers only a limited functionality but needs fewer resources than the standard Base API.

- The Embedded Java API is targeted for embedded devices. The functionality of the Embedded Java API is even more limited. Support for a GUI, for example, is not required.

- The Java Card API consists of a minimal API. It is targeted for SmartCards.

J2SE

Java 2 Standard Edition (J2SE) provides appropriate functionality for desktop/workstation devices.

Standard Edition

- *Java Foundation Classes*. This library includes Swing, Drag and Drop, and Java2D classes. **Swing 1.0** includes GUI Components and Services, Pluggable Look and Feel, and Accessibility class libraries. **Drag and Drop** classes allow Java and non-Java applications to share data using an extensible data-type system based on the Multipurpose Internet Mail Extension (MIME) standard. **Java2D** provides support for windowing, colour, fonts, vector-based and pixel-based graphics, and printing.

- *JDBC*. Provides a uniform interface to a wide range of relational databases. JDBC allows the user to connect to a database, send SQL statements to it and process the results. (See Section 12.9.)

- *Java Interface Definition Language* (*IDL*). Provides interoperability with CORBA (Common Object Request Broker Architecture). Java IDL supplies the mapping of the OMG CORBA 1.0 APIs to the Java programming language. It includes an IDL-to-Java compiler and a lightweight object request broker (ORB) that supports IIOP. (See Section 12.7.)

- *Remote method invocation* (*RMI*). Allows remote class methods to be called in the same way as local class methods. The actual communication process via sockets and streams is hidden from the programmer. (See Section 12.4.)

- *Collection classes*. These classes implement collections that can host groups of objects. Typical examples are sets, bags or lists.

- *Java extensions support*. Allows new packages to be added easily to the Java platform.

J2EE

Java 2 Enterprise Edition specifies all the functionality required for heavy-duty enterprise systems. Most of this functionality is not provided by J2EE itself. J2EE instead specifies the application programming interfaces (APIs) for enterprise services, such as message systems, transaction managers, directory services, etc. Makers of those systems can equip their systems with such an API, thus providing a standard interface to their product.

J2EE includes the following APIs:

- *Enterprise JavaBeans Specification*. The specification defines an API that allows developers to create, deploy and manage EJBs (Enterprise JavaBeans). See Section 12.7.)

- *JavaServer Pages*. The JSP technology provides a platform-independent way to create dynamic web pages. (See Section 13.5.)

- *Java Servlet*. The Java Servlet API provides web application developers with a consistent mechanism for extending the functionality of a web server, similar to the way an applet extends the functionality of a web browser. (See Section 13.5.)

- *Java Naming and Directory Interface*. JNDI provides developers with unified access to multiple heterogeneous naming and directory services across the enterprise, allowing objects and services to be referenced via a name. Among the supported naming services are the RMI registry, the CORBA Naming Service, LDAP and NDS. JNDI is extensible for other naming services.

- *Java Message Service*. The JMS specification provides developers with a common API for multiple vendor enterprise MoM (Message-oriented Middleware) services. These services support the asynchronous exchange of data and events through queuing, publish-and-subscribe communication and various aspects of push/pull technologies. (See Section 12.6.)

- *Java Transaction Service*. The JTS specification provides system developers with a common low-level API for multiple vendor transaction services, such as resource managers, transaction processing monitors and transaction managers. Most JTS interfaces are Java mappings to the CORBA Object Transaction Service (OTS). JTS is not usually required at the application programming level, but is used to develop transaction managers.

- *Java Transaction API*. The JTA defines a high-level transaction management specification intended for multi-vendor resource managers and for transactional applications in distributed transaction systems. JTA includes a Java mapping of the industry standard X/Open XA protocol that allows a transactional resource manager to participate in a global transaction controlled by an external transaction manager. (See Section 12.10.)

- *JavaMail*. The JavaMail API provides a set of abstract classes that models a mail system. The API is meant to provide a platform-independent and protocol-independent framework to build Java-based mail and messaging applications.

- *RMI-IIOP.* RMI-IIOP combines the programming ease of RMI with CORBA's Internet Inter-ORB Protocol (IIOP) for easier integration of J2EE applications with non-Java applications, meaning that remote non-Java components can be used transparently like Java classes. (See Section 12.7.)

Extensions

Java platforms can be easily extended with additional library packaging. The following is a selection of relevant packages:

- *Java Media API.* The Java Media Framework (JMF) defines a unified architecture for media playback and capture, such as audio, video, midi, telephony, etc.
- *Java 3D.* The Java 3D API provides functionality for creating and manipulating 3D geometry, and for rendering the virtual worlds created with Java 3D.
- *Java Commerce API.* This API includes functions to conduct secure payment and financial management across the web. The API includes Java Wallet, which defines and implements a client-side framework for conducting network-based commerce.
- *Java Cryptography Extension.* JCE provides a framework and implementations for encryption, key generation and key agreement, and Message Authentication Code (MAC) algorithms.
- *JavaHelp.* JavaHelp is the Help system for the Java platform.
- *Java Authentication and Authorization Service.* JAAS is a framework that provides user-based authentication and access control capabilities. It includes an implementation of the standard Pluggable Authentication Module (PAM) architecture, and provides support for user-based, group-based or role-based access controls.
- *InfoBus.* InfoBus enables dynamic data exchange between JavaBeans components.

12.4   RMI and distributed objects

Compiled Java applications are not deployed as large monolithic modules. Java does not use the static linking process after compilation as traditional languages do, but links small compiled modules dynamically to the application when the application is executed (late binding). This technique had been successfully used with 4GL systems, where large-scale applications consist of several tens of thousands of modules. Java-based applications consisting of more than 250,000 classes have been reported.

Remote method invocation explained

   Java technology goes a step beyond late binding. Because the JVM is Internet enabled it can load modules not only locally but also across the net. A client application, such as an applet in a web page, can load classes from a remote server, e.g. from its home base (the server that it was loaded from). This ensures that the latest version of an applet is used.

However, in a client–server or multi-tier application, application logic is located on both client and server. Communication with remote objects becomes necessary. The Java remote method invocation (RMI), which was introduced with Java 1.1, supports the invocation of methods of a remote object in a transparent fashion. For the client, remote method invocation is transparent – a remote object is treated just like a local object. The only requirements are that the remote class implements a subtype of the `Remote` interface and that objects that are passed as parameters or are returned as return values implement the `Serializable` interface.

All methods of the remote object that belong to a remote interface are available as local methods on the client side. A stub (proxy) replicates the remote methods locally (Figure 12.4).

Normally, when an object on the client side invokes a method of another object, and this object's class byte code is not available, the JVM will load the class byte code dynamically. Not so with a remote object. In this case the JVM only loads the stub byte code. The stub accepts the method calls for the remote object and forwards them through the Remote Reference Layer and the Transport Layer to the server. A corresponding skeleton issues the corresponding method call to the remote object. After method execution the return value is passed back similarly.

All this is invisible to the programmer who calls the remote methods just as he or she would call local methods. Stubs and skeletons are automatically generated by the Java `rmic` compiler.

Latency

Although the invocation of remote methods via RMI is transparent, programmers should not ignore the physical location of objects. Invocation of remote methods can raise new types of exceptions (due to possible communication problems), and latency becomes a topic. When communicating with remote objects it may become necessary to implement performance improving techniques, such as *latency hiding* or caching.

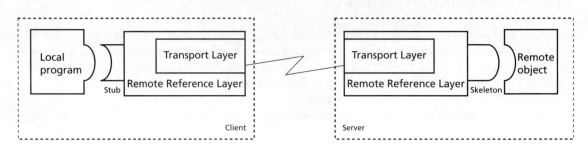

Figure 12.4 The RMI extension cord: stub, wire, skeleton.

RMI can pass objects as method parameters. This implies that the internal state of an object is passed:

- Local objects are passed
  - to a local destination by copying the object;
  - to a remote destination by serializing the object. If these objects do not implement the `Serializable` interface an exception is raised.
- Remote objects are passed by reference. This means that state changes of the object do affect the original, instead of affecting only the copy, as with local objects.

Because objects can be passed as parameters it is possible that the client introduces new behaviour into the RMI server. Several scenarios are possible with varying degrees of security:

- *Closed-system*. The RMI server is configured to load no classes at all. The services provided are defined exclusively by the remote interfaces which are all local to the server. This server does not need an RMI security manager (because it does not import code). When clients send remote objects for which the server does not have stub code, an exception is raised.

- *Open-system*. An open server will define a `java.rmi.server.codebase` from which class code can be loaded. This server needs to install an `RMISecurityManager`. It is possible to set the property `java.rmi.server.useCodebaseOnly` (command line) to disable class loading from client-supplied URLs.
- *RMI in the sandbox*. An untrusted applet is by default allowed to establish a connection only with the host from which it was loaded (home base). That means that all resources relevant to applet execution are available on the server. It is therefore not required to load class code from other network connections – this setup is very secure because no code is imported.
- *Beyond the sandbox*. Applications and applets can – depending on security policies – establish a connection to any network address. If an application is loaded locally, the classes used directly in the application must be available locally. The only classes that can be downloaded from a network source are the classes of remote interfaces, stub classes, and the extended classes of parameters and return values for remote method invocations.

  If an application is loaded from a network source (using a bootstrapping mechanism), all classes used by the application can be downloaded from the same network source.
- *Firewalls*. By default RMI uses direct socket connections for transmissions. Many intranets, however, have firewalls which do not allow this. RMI can switch to a firewall-trusted HTTP protocol (HTTP tunnelling), but at the cost of performance – HTTP-based transmission is at least one order of magnitude slower than direct socket connection.

● *SSL (Secure Sockets Layer)*. With Java 2 it has become possible to use RMI together with SSL. However, this requires modifications in the program logic: customized sockets are created on a per object basis by using a Socket Factory.

Registry

Remote objects can register with a server-based RMI registry. This enables a client application to look up the name of a remote object. The registry returns a reference to the remote object to the client. Usually, the client uses this facility only once for a root object, and obtains references for other remote objects as the result of method calls. Alternatively, the Java Naming and Directory Interface (JNDI) may be used as a more abstract interface to the RMI registry.

Distributed garbage collection

RMI implements Distributed Garbage Collection. A server object that is no longer referenced by a client is automatically detected and its memory can be reclaimed.

Protocol

For transport, RMI uses JRMP (Java Remote Method Protocol) as its native protocol. Optionally in J2EE, the IIOP protocol can be used. IIOP is part of the Object Management Group's Common Object Request Broker Architecture (CORBA) for distributed computing (see Section 12.7).

12.5 Threads

The first rule of using threads is this: avoid them if you can.

From a Java tutorial

One of the outstanding features of Java is the integration of a programming construct providing support for concurrent execution of multiple instruction sequences – *threads* (Lea 2000). Runtime multi-threading support is provided by the Java Virtual Machine (JVM).

Why do we need multi-threading? Used properly, multi-threading enhances the throughput and responsiveness of an application. In particular, an electronic business application should implement the user interface and the business logic in different threads. Otherwise, the processing of a business task would block the user interface – there would be delayed reactions to the mouse, to keyboard events, or to navigation actions. This is especially true when the business task has to wait, e.g. on a database operation or on a remote method invocation. In fact, graphical user interfaces themselves often consist of several threads, for example one for rendering and one for event handling. Otherwise, mouse and keyboard would freeze during a complex rendering task.

In contrast to multi-tasking, multi-threading is a lightweight technique for concurrency. We speak of multi-tasking if a processor (or a group of processors) is shared among various jobs or applications. Each executing application gets a time slice of the processor. After the time slice has expired, the application has to wait until the other applications have been served before it can have another slice of processor time (simplified). Because this happens very quickly the user has the impression that applications run in parallel. On hardware with multiple processors tasks can truly execute in parallel (when supported by the operating system).

Multi-tasking vs. multi-threading

Because each application has its own address space, multi-tasking has a relatively high overhead. Synchronization and communication between tasks require the use of operating system functions. Multi-tasking is organized by the operating system, i.e. multi-tasking support is platform dependent.

Multi-threading is similar to multi-tasking but happens within an application and within the same address space. Synchronization and communication do not require operating system functions, but can be achieved with relatively small effort. In Java, multi-threading is organized by the JVM, so most features of multi-threading are platform independent. Some features, however, depend on the underlying hardware architecture. We will discuss this later. On some platforms (e.g. Sun Solaris or Windows NT), Java threads can utilize multiple processors simultaneously.

In Java, a thread is set up either

Creating a thread in Java

- by creating a new instance of the library class `Thread` and passing an object as parameter to the new thread (the object must implement the interface `Runnable` and provide a method `run`), or

- by extending the class `Thread` and overriding the inherited `run` method. A thread can then be set up by creating an instance of the new class.

Once a thread instance has been created, it can be started by calling its `start()` method. This will cause the invocation of the thread instance's `run()` method. In addition, threads can be stopped, suspended and resumed.

Starting and stopping

The overhead of creating and destroying threads can be significant if threads are used for very short tasks and a process requires many threads. A common technique to reduce this overhead is to use a *thread manager* with a *thread pool*. Threads that are no longer used are returned to the thread pool and are reused for the next request. The thread manager creates new threads when a new thread is required with no more idle threads left in the pool.

Thread pools

In principle, two concurrent threads can access the same object. However, this can cause havoc. Let us consider the following example:

Concurrent threads

```
class CustomerAccount {
    private double Balance;
    public method Deposit(double Amount) {
        Balance = Balance + Amount;
    }
}
```

While this little program looks quite innocent, two competing threads can cause considerable trouble – basically the same sort of trouble that two competing database updates would cause if the database management system did not support a locking concept. In Chapter 7 we have already shown an example of what can happen when two concurrent processes access the same object. Unsynchronized access of two competing threads to `CustomerAccount` can lead to the situation that one deposit to the account is lost.

32-bit vs. 64-bit!

To make things worse, the `Balance` field is of type `double`, meaning it is 64 bits long. When running on a computer with a 32-bit architecture such as a PC, a 64-bit number is stored in two steps. When Thread 1 is interrupted between these steps, the high-order part for the `Balance` field will result from the Thread-1 operation, but the low-order part will result from the Thread-2 operation (Figure 12.5). This is a good random number generator but inappropriate for business arithmetic. This specific problem applies to the Java primitives `double` and `long`, and only on 32-bit machines.

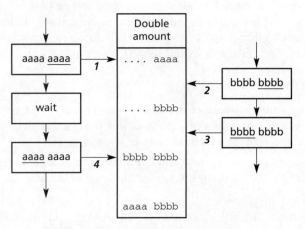

Figure 12.5   Two concurrent processes trying to assign a number of type double. After storing the low-order word, process 1 is interrupted. After the process resumes it overwrites the high-order word of the value that was stored by process 2.

Locks

The solution is to lock the object `CustomerAccount` while the method `Deposit` is executed, and to unlock the object again when the method is finished. However, an explicit lock/unlock mechanism requires very great discipline from the programmer. The unlocking is often forgotten, especially in the case of an exception. Forgotten locks usually lead to thread starvation and finally to deadlocks.

Monitors

Java, therefore, combines lock and unlock into one keyword with which a method or a statement block can be attributed. The keyword is `synchronized`.

Java's thread model follows C.A.R. Hoare's monitor model (Hoare 1974), discussed in Chapter 7. When a synchronized method is executed, the object is locked for other threads. Another or the same synchronized method of this object cannot be executed by other threads. Non-synchronized methods can still be executed.

```
class CustomerAccount {
     private double Balance;
     public synchronized method Deposit(double Amount) {
          Balance = Balance + Amount;
     }
}
```

To synchronize with other threads, Java uses the methods wait(), notify(), and notifyAll(). The wait method places a thread into the wait set, the notify method notifies an arbitrary waiting thread in the wait set, and the notifyAll method notifies all waiting threads in the wait set (see Chapter 7).

Perils

Writing and testing multi-threaded applications is hard. It is necessary to fully understand the synchronization mechanisms. Because the Java language does not define how threads are implemented, thread behaviour can differ from platform to platform. On some platforms, for example, multi-threading can take advantage of multiprocessor architectures, on others it can't. No assumptions can be made about which thread of a waiting set is picked for reactivation. Timing conditions in a test environment and in a production environment will vary, so that problems are hard or impossible to reproduce. Some bugs may show up soon, others only after weeks of operation.

Separation of concerns

In Chapter 7 we discussed the problems that exist when concurrency is introduced to object-oriented programming. We came to the conclusion that the separation of synchronization logic into separate objects leads to a relatively clean architecture:

Control objects

- A simple solution is to implement control objects. A control object implements the same set of methods as the original business object. The synchronization logic is removed from the business object and moved into the control object (Figure 12.6). Clients now call the methods of the control object which in turn call the methods of the business object. Now business objects can be extended easily, because they no longer contain synchronization logic (see Chapter 7).

- CSP (communicating sequential processes) (see Chapter 7) has recently been applied to Java programming (Welch 1998), (Hilderink 1997).

CSP

  A separate *channel object* is implemented with read and write methods. A sender thread writes messages to the channel, while a receiver thread reads messages from the channel. Because the channel is the only link between the two threads, no synchronization logic is required within the threads, and the channel handles all the synchronization issues (Figure 12.7).

  The simplest case is a one-to-one channel where one writer sends messages to one reader. However, one-to-many, many-to-one and many-to-many channels are possible. Channels can optionally queue messages and can use different drivers to establish communication locally or transparently over networks. Channels involve some overhead in the application: the reading thread must implement a dispatcher to distribute incoming messages to the appropriate methods.

```
class CustomerAccountSync {
    private CustomerAccount c;
    public synchronized CustomerAccountSync
    {
        c = new CustomerAccount;
    }
    public synchronized Deposit(double Amount)
    {
        c.Deposit(Amount);
    }
}

class CustomerAccount {
    private double Balance;
    public Deposit(double Amount)
    {
        Balance = Balance + Amount;
    }
}
```

Figure 12.6 Synchronization logic moved to a separate class. Clients now call CustomerAccountSync.Deposit, and developers can safely extend CustomerAccount.

```
Class CustomerAccount extends Thread
{
  public Channel ch = new Channel;
  private CustomerAccount ca = new CustomerAccount;
  . . .
  public method run() {
    while (true) {
        Message m = ch.read();
        if m.method = "Deposit" {
            ca.Deposit (m.Amount)
        }
      }
    }
}
```

Figure 12.7 The CustomerAccountThread object reads messages from the Channel object and forwards them to the business object. Clients now send messages to the Channel object instead of calling the method Deposit directly.

● Other researchers in the area of parallel computing developed the concept of tuple spaces (see Section 9.3). The Linda system is a well-known example (Gelernter and Carriero 1989). Tuple spaces were later ported to the Java environment: JavaSpaces is Sun Microsystems' concept (contained in the Jini architecture), while T Spaces is the IBM version.

Tuple spaces

Both implementations, JavaSpaces and T Spaces, provide tuple spaces that are persistent, can work across distributed environments, and offer a transaction concept. The comfort, however, comes at a price. The pattern matching between stored tuples and queries involves some overhead, and additional overhead is caused by the serialization and deserialization of objects written to and read from the tuple space.

12.6 Messages

Message-oriented Middleware (MoM) is conceptually close to the previously discussed CSP (communicating sequential processes). MoM products establish channels between client processes that transport messages from one client to another. The middleware manages all synchronization issues. Typical products in this area are IBM's MQSeries or Software AG's EntireX.

Message-oriented Middleware

Middleware services connect applications or business components with each other. They are not designed for small-scale messaging like the transportation of mouse events. MoM systems deal with business events and business messages.

The Java Message Service (JMS) API – which is part of the Java 2 Enterprise Edition (J2EE) – provides a common way for Java programs to create, send, receive, select and read an enterprise messaging system's messages. JMS does not provide this service itself; it acts purely as a common API for heterogeneous messaging systems from different vendors.

JMS explained

JMS (Sun 1998-1) supports two types of messaging:

● **Point-to-point**. Here a client sends messages to a specified queue (a channel). The receiver of the message is able to select messages by specified criteria, or to browse messages within queues without removing them from the queue.

● **Publish-and-subscribe**. Here clients can either publish or subscribe to a content *topic*. Subscribers receive a message when a topic they have subscribed to has changed. JMS supports a hierarchical structure of topics – each topic is an element within a content tree (Figure 12.8). This closely resembles the structure of an XML document, and in fact XML is adopted by MoM producers as a messaging format.

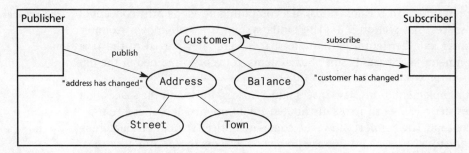

Figure 12.8   The publish-and-subscribe mechanism in a hierarchical content structure. The subscriber has subscribed to the `Customer` topic. When the Publisher publishes a new `Address`, the subscriber is notified upon an update of the `Customer` topic, because the `Address` topic is a subtopic of the `Customer` topic.

In addition, JMS supports the following messaging facilities:

- **Connection management** includes the creation of a connection from client to messaging service, authentication, pausing a connection and closing a connection.

- **Session management** includes opening and closing of sessions. Each session can create several `MessageProducers`, `MessageConsumers` and `MessageListeners`.

  Sessions may optionally support transactions (transacted session). Series of messages (both incoming and outgoing) within a transaction are treated as a single atomic unit. When a transaction is rolled back, the outgoing messages of the transaction are destroyed, and the already consumed incoming messages of the transaction are recovered. JMS session transactions can be combined with transactions on other resources (DBMS, other JMS sessions, etc.) via JTS (Java Transaction Services) or some other transaction monitor facility (see Section 12.10).

- **Delivery services** support synchronous and asynchronous delivery:
  - A client that chooses to receive messages synchronously has to *request* a message. The client has the option to *poll* or to *wait* for the next message.
  - A client that chooses to receive messages asynchronously has to register a `MessageConsumer` object that implements the `MessageListener` interface with the provider. When a message arrives the `onMessage` method of the `MessageListener` interface is called.

- **Message acknowledgment**. In transacted sessions messages are automatically acknowledged (a receipt message is returned to the sender). In other sessions, JMS supports three acknowledgment modes:
  - Lazy acknowledgment. The method with the least overhead, but can lead to duplicate messages.
  - Automatic acknowledgment. The session object acknowledges the message when it is delivered to the `MessageConsumer`.

– Client acknowledgment. The client explicitly calls the message's
`acknowledge` method.

● **Message selection**. Depending on the underlying messaging system,
receivers can specify filters to select only messages they are interested in.
Selection is based on a message's header information. The syntax of filter
expressions is based on SQL '92.

● **Quality of service**. Messages can be either persistent or non-persistent. Non-
persistent messages require less overhead, but cannot be guaranteed to be
delivered (for example, when the server crashes).

With these services JMS provides a portable programming interface for messaging services from different vendors. JMS, however, concentrates on the aspects of
those systems related to clients and messages. It does not provide an API for
other aspects, such as administration, load balancing, fault tolerance or security.

12.7 Component support

JavaBeans

The Java programming language already offers many features that are typical of
component systems.

● The late binding technique allows a compiled object to be added to an
already deployed application without an explicit linking process.

● The Java runtime system can load missing classes over remote connections as
they are needed.

● Java reflection allows an object to be interrogated about its features.

An explicit component model, JavaBeans, was introduced in 1997 (Sun 1997).   *Beans explained*
Like Java classes, JavaBeans are platform independent and can run anywhere
that a Java Virtual Machine exists. JavaBeans were designed to cover small to
medium-sized components, similar to ActiveX controls.

The JavaBeans model is closely related to the Java programming language. A
JavaBean is a Java class or a collection of Java classes that provide support for:

● **Introspection**. A client can find out which properties, events and methods
the bean supports. A builder tool, for example, can analyze how a bean
works. The programmer can supply with the bean a `BeanInfo` class that
describes the published features. Alternatively, the Java runtime environment
can use the Java reflection mechanism and extract the required information
from the bean's code.

● **Customization**. At 'plug'-time, for example, when using a GUI-builder, a user
can customize the appearance and behaviour of a bean. The bean must be able
to make the customized state persistent and reload it later. Therefore all beans
must support either serialization or externalization, in order to export and
import a bean's state either in Java internal format or in a user-defined format.

- **Events** as a simple communication metaphor can be used to connect up beans. Events provide a notification mechanism between components. An event listener object can be registered with an event source. When the event source has something to tell, it notifies registered event listener objects by calling the appropriate methods.

- **Properties**, both for customization and for programmatic use. Properties are accessed through special `get...` and `set...` methods. This implies that properties may represent computed values.

Bean communication   JavaBeans can communicate with remote components via:

- **Java RMI**. The Java Remote Method Invocation (see Section 12.4) is used to invoke methods of remote JavaBeans.

- **Java IDL**. Java IDL implements the CORBA distributed object model (see Section 12.7). Component interfaces are described in the Java CORBA IDL (Interface Definition Language). Java stubs are generated from these descriptions, allowing method calls between JavaBean components and CORBA components in both directions. This API is part of the Java 2 Standard Edition and Enterprise Edition.

- **RMI-IIOP**. RMI-IIOP allows beans to access remote CORBA-based components (see Section 12.3) via the CORBA protocol IIOP (Internet Inter-ORB Protocol). RMI-IIOP works transparently: remote CORBA components can be used just like remote Java components; the use of IDL by the programmer is not required. RMI-IIOP is part of the Java 2 Enterprise Edition.

- **Infobus**. Infobus implements a bus-like local (within the same JVM) information infrastructure. Beans can join the bus, and can either produce or consume data items, or they can act as data controllers (Colan 1999).

- **Java Message Service API**. JMS allows JavaBeans to communicate with enterprise components through Message-oriented Middleware (MoM) (see Section 12.6).

COM/DCOM

Microsoft's component model has evolved from the OLE (Object Linking and Embedding) architecture (Brockschmidt). COM (Component Object Model) was introduced in 1993 (Box). DCOM (Distributed COM) was introduced with Windows NT 4.0 and was later ported to UNIX and mainframe platforms by Software AG in cooperation with Microsoft.

In Java the support for DCOM varies depending on the JVM and the application server used. Not surprisingly, Microsoft's JVM features strong DCOM integration, treating Java classes as COM objects (Hightower 1999).

DCOM explained   Because DCOM is an integrated part of the Windows operating system it is relatively cheap. Because of the omnipresence of the Windows platform, DCOM is today's most used component model. It is also the standard way to integrate standard Windows applications like Microsoft Office or programming systems like Visual Basic into applications.

OLE defined not a component architecture but an architecture for compound documents, for example a spreadsheet embedded into a Word document. These roots are still visible in DCOM.

Each DCOM component is defined as a *class*, which implements one or several *interfaces*. This feature (supporting multiple interfaces) is similar to Java which also allows one class to implement multiple interfaces.

Classes and interfaces are identified by GUIDs (global unique identifiers): class identifiers (CLSIDs) and interface identifiers (IIDs). DCOM interfaces are defined with the DCOM-IDL (interface definition language), not to be mistaken for the CORBA IDL. DCOM does not support multiple inheritance of types and does not encourage single inheritance. Complex components are therefore constructed not by inheritance but by delegation and aggregation. Variability is introduced not via inheritance but via parameterization, generation and aggregation (Udell 1994).

For communication with remote components, DCOM uses a version of DCE RPC (Distributed Computing Environment Remote Procedure Call) (OSF 1995).

DCOM components must be registered on each network node (on Windows platforms the Windows registry is used for this purpose). That rules out manual deployment of components in a large network but requires deployment tools.

DCOM supports both static and dynamic invocation. It utilizes Windows NT wire-level security and transport neutrality, supporting TCP/IP, UDP/IP, IPX/SPX, AppleTalk and HTTP.

Originally the languages to implement DCOM components were C++ or Visual Basic. Because of the popularity of DCOM and the complexity of DCOM programming, other languages now support DCOM, too.

Enterprise JavaBeans

Enterprise JavaBeans (EJB) are intended as non-visual components on the server side. The EJB architecture supports transactional semantics.

EJBs explained

EJBs require an extra infrastructure which is provided by an EJB server. A CORBA-compliant EJB server is contained in the Java 2 SDK, but can also be provided by other CORBA ORBs (Object Request Brokers), such as Iona's Orbix, IBM's CICS, or Inprises' VisiBroker.

EJB server

EJB servers provide the necessary services through an EJB container. EJB containers provide a scalable, secure, thread-safe and transactional environment in which beans can operate. The container handles a bean's life cycle, including creation and deletion. When a bean is installed in a container, the container provides two interface implementations: an implementation of the bean's Home interface (features published to the server), and the bean's Remote interface (features published to the client). Access to a bean always goes through the bean container and always uses remote protocols (like RMI), with the container acting as a skeleton.

Enterprise JavaBeans can be either transient (session bean) or persistent (entity bean):

Session beans

- A session bean typically represents a conversation with a client. It may execute database accesses for the client in the context of a transaction. The transient nature of a session bean means that in the case of a crash of either the server or the client the bean is gone. Session beans are typically used to implement business tasks.

Entity beans

- An entity bean represents data in the database. Entity beans are persistent, survive crashes, and are transactional. Each instance of an entity bean is identified by a primary key by which it can be addressed. Entity beans are typically used to implement business objects.

The transaction model of entity beans does not require explicit transaction demarcation. Instead transactions can be attributed with six different transaction rules:

Six transaction rules

- BEAN_MANAGED. The bean manages its own transaction control. Client applications can create transactions by calling transaction interfaces (like JTA) directly.
- NOT_SUPPORTED. The enterprise bean cannot execute within the context of a transaction. If a client has a transaction when it calls the enterprise bean, the transaction server suspends the transaction for the duration of the method call.

In all other cases the EJB *server* has to manage transaction control.

- SUPPORTS. The enterprise bean can run with or without a transaction context. If a client has a transaction when it calls the enterprise bean, the method call will use the client's transaction context. If the client does not have a transaction, the method call will run without a transaction.
- REQUIRES. The enterprise bean must execute within the context of a transaction. If a client has a transaction when it calls the enterprise bean, the method call will use the client's transaction context. If the client does not have a transaction, the transaction server automatically starts a new transaction for the method call.
- REQUIRES_NEW. The enterprise bean must execute within the context of a new transaction. The transaction server always starts a new transaction for the method call. If the client has a transaction when it calls the enterprise bean, the transaction server suspends the client's transaction for the duration of the method call.
- MANDATORY. The enterprise bean must always execute within the context of the client's transaction. If the client does not have a transaction context when it calls the enterprise bean, the transaction server throws the `TransactionRequired` exception and the request fails.

The implementation of entity beans is optional in the EJB specification V1.0 but mandatory with version 2.0.

The EJB architecture is communication protocol neutral. This means that a server can support multiple protocols like RMI, IIOP (CORBA) and DCOM. An ORB manufacturer supporting EJBs might only implement IIOP while a UNIX system provider might implement RMI and IIOP. The protocol used is transparent to the bean developer who writes only to the Java platform.

The EJB architecture defines an own security concept. Bean-related security settings are contained in the EJB deployment descriptor.

EJB security

The concept is based on principals, resources, roles and permissions. A *principal* represents a real-world object like a person or a group of persons. A *resource* is any item that needs to be secured against unauthorized use. In the context of EJB, the Home and Remote interfaces are the only resources that can be secured. A *permission* is, alas, a permission to use a resource. A *role* is a set of permissions that a principal must have.

The EJB deployment descriptor allows permissions and roles to be defined in a declarative way. Permissions to use different methods can be assigned to the same role, and more than one role can be assigned to a permission.

The relationship between roles and principals is defined outside the EJB deployment descriptor. At runtime, it is the EJB container's task to check the access rights to a resource. The principal must have at least one role that has permission to invoke the method in question.

With adequate programming, a bean, in addition, can perform its own security checks.

At deployment time the security information found in the deployment descriptor is mapped to the security mechanisms available in the operation environment.

CORBA

The Common Object Request Broker Architecture was introduced in 1991 by the OMG (Object Management Group), a consortium of manufacturers of object technology.

CORBA explained

CORBA is in widespread use in heterogeneous computer worlds. The CORBA Interface Definition Language (IDL) is used for the formal specification of components. IDL-bindings into many languages exist, so that CORBA components can be implemented in almost any language. CORBA works over the Internet through the Internet-Inter-ORB Protocol (IIOP), which defines the way CORBA objects communicate over a TCP/IP network. CORBA IDL supports multiple inheritance for types. Inheritance can therefore be used to construct complex component interfaces from smaller specialized interface definitions. Inheritance together with aggregation provides the necessary variability mechanisms.

CORBA is strong in connecting enterprise components, but is not really a choice on the desktop. This is partly due to the fact that the desktop is dominated by DCOM, but also that CORBA is a heavyweight. The Linux community, which had used CORBA to connect desktop components (because of the lack of DCOM on this platform), has now introduced its own communication method which is aptly named DCOP (Desktop Communication Protocol).

Invocation interface

CORBA supports a static invocation interface (SII) where access to a remote component is directly defined by the program and can be checked by the compiler. Alternatively, CORBA supports the dynamic invocation interface (DII) which allows components that are not known at compilation time but are determined at runtime to be accessed.

Object request broker (ORB)

CORBA components require an infrastructure – ORBs (object request brokers). Because ORBs must be purchased separately, CORBA is not automatically available on the majority of client platforms. This rules out CORBA for most Internet clients. CORBA components, however, can communicate with DCOM components via a CORBA–DCOM bridge.

Proxies and skeletons

Similar to Java RMI (see Section 12.4), CORBA-compliant ORBs construct proxy objects (derived from the IDL specification) on the client side and skeletons on the server side for remote component access. The client talks to the local proxy which forwards requests to the remote skeleton. The skeleton then forwards the requests to the addressed component.

Persistence and transactions

CORBA supports the distributed registration of components in an interface repository, which simplifies deployment and administration. CORBA defines a relatively powerful infrastructure, supporting persistent components and transactions. The main drawback of the CORBA technology is that components may not be portable across heterogeneous systems. Depending on the implementation language, a component must be recompiled when migrating to another host system.

Enterprise JavaBeans and CORBA

Enterprise JavaBeans and CORBA were seen initially as competitors, but it soon became obvious that both technologies complement each other well. While Enterprise JavaBeans provides a component technology that is portable across virtually all platforms, the extensive language support in CORBA is well suited to integrating legacy applications into the component world.

The industry has therefore moved quickly to integrate both technologies. Through RMI-IIOP, Enterprise JavaBeans can interoperate with non-Java CORBA components. EJBs are becoming the prime component model within the CORBA architecture.

12.8　Serialization

Java serialization (Sun 1996) is a base technology for many other features connected with Java. Serialization is used, for example, in remote method invocation (RMI) (see Section 12.4) to transmit parameters to remote methods, or in JavaBeans (see Section 12.7) to make property settings persistent.

Serialization explained

Serialization is a way to convert the data structures of object hierarchies into a flat data stream that can be stored on a hard disk or transmitted over a wire. The serialization format is specific to Java – it was not designed as a format for data interchange with other applications.

Serialization can be used to make an object persistent. The technique is quite simple: one object, one file. The file name identifies the object. A condition is that the object's class definition implements the `Serializable` interface. This sounds more difficult than it is: all that is required is to specify 'implements `Serializable`'.

To store an object, the application has to open an output stream to a specified file, then use the `writeObject(Object)` method to store the object. If the object is an aggregate (i.e. contains other objects), Java will also store the sub-objects to the same file. If a sub-object is referenced multiple times, Java will store only one copy of the object, and include an object handle for each reference. This technique saves space and allows cyclic object structures to be stored.

Serialization writes non-static and non-transient fields to the stream (including private fields). Fields that must not be exported should be declared as `private` and `transient`. It is also possible to exclude whole classes from serialization by implementing the `writeObject` method to throw an exception when the method is called.

Reading an object works just the other way around. An input stream to the file containing the serialization string is opened, and a `readObject()` method is used to read the object. The `readObject()` method delivers an object of type `Object`, so it is necessary for the client to know the type of the object and to *cast* the result to that type.

Within the serialization stream, field values are identified with the symbolic names of fields. This allows objects to be deserialized even if the class definition has changed since serialization.

Classes are identified with a `serialVersionUID` (SUID), which is normally computed automatically, but can also be supplied explicitly. By supplying identical SUIDs to different versions of a class, a programmer can enforce cross-version compatibility for a given class (Kurotsuchi 1999).

Java also offers an externalization interface which allows objects to perform serialization under their own control. When an object is being serialized and the object implements the externalization interface, control is completely transferred to the object's externalization methods.

12.9   Database interface

In an enterprise application, however, serialization would be hardly used to make business objects persistent. Instead, business data is stored in a database, mostly relational databases. Any relevant development system for commercial programming must therefore offer support for relational database systems (RDBMSs), such as Oracle, DB2, Sybase or Adabas. Java supports RDBMS with a standard interface: JDBC.

RDBMS and OODBMS

Object-oriented database management systems (OODBMSs) may be better suited to storing object-oriented data in a pure OO environment, but are seldom found in enterprise situations. Java support for OODBMS is provided by the makers of these systems.

Relational data structures

The design principles for relational data storage were outlined by E.F. Codd in 1970 (Codd 1970).

A relational database consists of a set of tables. Each table consists of a set of rows (records), each row consists of a set of columns (fields). Each row consequently establishes a *relation* between the fields of a record. This is why these databases are called *relational*.

Codd's theory postulates that each field must contain only atomic values, such as integer or string (First Normal Form, 1NF). To achieve 1NF it is often required to decompose complex data structures into a set of tables (Figure 12.9).

There are additional normal forms (2NF, 3NF, ...) which can cause further decomposition into even more tables. This can lead to a high fragmentation of data. The design of database schemata is therefore a trade-off between normalization and efficiency.

Records within a table are identified by *primary keys*, which can be a single column or any combination of columns. Other columns or column combinations may be defined as *foreign keys* to match with primary keys of other tables. This matching operation – called JOIN – is one of the most used operations with relational database systems, because the fragmented data must be reconstructed into the original data structure when retrieved.

SQL:1999

The problems with the storage of complex objects have been addressed with SQL:1999 (formerly called SQL-3) (Eisenberg and Melton 1999). Among other things, SQL:1999 adds the following new features to SQL:

- New data types, like Boolean and Large Objects (LOB).
- Support for collections in the form of ARRAYs.
- Storage and retrieval of structured data in the form of ROWs – this allows data that has not been decomposed into 1NF to be stored.
- Structured user-defined data types. These can be arbitrarily (but not recursively) nested data structures, consisting of primitive data types or other user-defined data types.

  Access to the attributes of these data structures is via `get...` and `set...` methods or user-defined functions, procedures and methods. These data structures can be part of an inheritance hierarchy (`CREATE TYPE employee UNDER person`), and polymorphism is supported. Comparison between such data structures must be exclusively facilitated through user-supplied functions.
- Recursive queries (`WITH RECURSIVE`), to support applications that rely on recursive data structures, such as a bill-of-material list.

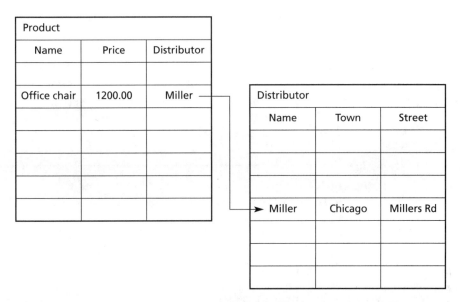

Figure 12.9 Decomposing a complex object. Objects of class `Product` contain objects of class `Distributor` which are not atomic. To achieve 1NF it is necessary to store `Distributor` objects in a separate table.

JDBC

Java Database Connectivity (JDBC) provides a database interface that is independent of the underlying relational database management system (RDBMS). JDBC-compliant drivers need to support at least the ANSI SQL-2 entry-level API. Support for SQL:1999 on the client side is provided with JDBC 2.0 in Java SDK 1.2.

JDBC API is part of the standard edition of Java (J2SE). A JDBC-ODBC bridge allows all ODBC-compliant database systems to be accessed through JDBC. Some database systems also offer native JDBC drivers for better performance.

JDBC consists of the following parts:

JDBC ingredients

`java.sql.Driver.Manager` is responsible for the loading of drivers and provides support for new database connections.

`java.sql.Connection` represents a connection to a particular database. A `Connection` defines a session with a specific database. Within a session, SQL statements are executed and results are returned. Transactions can be committed explicitly, or automatically after each statement execution, which is the default mode.

`java.sql.Statement` acts as a container for executing a static SQL statement on a given connection.

Note that an SQL query is just an object of type `String`. The syntax of an SQL statement is not checked by Java compilers (some Java IDEs do) – mistakes in the SQL syntax are detected at runtime only.

java.sql.PreparedStatement acts as a container for compiled SQL statements. With the PreparedStatement construct, JDBC allows the compilation and the execution of an SQL statement to be split into two steps. If the query is executed many times, this can result in better performance – the SQL string is only compiled once by the database.

java.sql.CallableStatement provides a way to execute SQL stored procedures. Stored procedures are queries or update procedures that are stored in the database and can be executed by referencing them.

```
// loading driver
Class.forName("sun.jdbc.odbc.JdbcOdbcDriver");
// setting up connection
Connection con = DriverManager.getConnection(url,
"myLogin", "myPassword");
// set SQL query string
String queryString =
     "select p.name, p.price" +
          "from Product p, Distributor d" +
     "where p.distributor = d.name" +
          "and d.town = ?"
// prepare query (just to demonstrate this feature)
PreparedStatement ps =
con.preparedStatement(queryString);
// set query parameter value
ps.setString(1,"Paris");
// execute query
Resultset rs = ps.executeQuery();
// check query
if (!rs.wasNull) {
   {
// create new instance for each record in result set
     Product prod = new Product();
// get first field
     prod.name = rs.getString(1);
// get second field
     prod.price = rs.getFloat(2);
// continue with next record
   } while rs.next()
}
```

Figure 12.10   Example program to retrieve the Product object. Because Product contains a sub-object Distributor, a join is necessary.

`java.sql.ResultSet` provides access to the result table of an executed SQL statement. `ResultSet` contains an SQL cursor which points to a single row of data in the result table. It can be positioned to other rows using the `next()` method. In addition, `ResultSet` provides methods to retrieve table columns by name or by number.

JDBC works like ODBC APIs in other programming languages: an SQL query is passed as a string to the database. The database evaluates the SQL query and executes it. The DBMS keeps a result set, which can then be retrieved field by field, using methods of the JDBC API, like `getString()`, `getFloat()`, etc. (Figure 12.10).

How JDBC works

12.10 Transactions

Updates to the database are formulated similarly by passing an SQL statement to the database. Here we use a `Statement` object instead of a `PreparedStatement` for simplicity (Figure 12.11).

By default, JDBC is in *auto-commit mode*. This means that whenever a statement is completed it is automatically committed. If we want to change other records in the same transaction, as in the next example, we need full control over transaction logic. This requires us to switch auto-commit mode off. We now can (and must) explicitly commit the transaction.

Transactions in JDBC

```
// loading driver
Class.forName("sun.jdbc.odbc.JdbcOdbcDriver");
// setting up connection
Connection con = DriverManager.getConnection(url,
"myLogin", "myPassword");
// create statement object
Statement stmt = con.createStatement();
// set SQL update string
String updateString = "update Product " +
    "set Price = Price * " + eFactor +
    " where Distributor like 'Dupont'";
// execute update using statement in updateString.
stmt.executeUpdate(updateString);
```

Figure 12.11 Updating a database table. Please note that the arithmetic operation to compute a new price is not done here by Java but by the DBMS.

```
// loading driver
Class.forName("sun.jdbc.odbc.JdbcOdbcDriver");
// setting up connection
Connection con = DriverManager.getConnection(url, "myLogin",
"myPassword");
// switch auto-commit off
con.setAutoCommit(false);
// create statement object
Statement stmt = con.createStatement();
// set SQL update string
String updateString = "update Product " +
    "set Price = Price * " + eFactor +
    " where Distributor like 'Dupont'";
// execute update using statement in updateString.
stmt.executeUpdate(updateString);
// set SQL update string for next operation
updateString = "update Distributor " +
    "set Town = 'St.Petersburg'" +
    " where Name like 'Dupont'";
// execute update using statement in updateString.
stmt.executeUpdate(updateString);
// commit transaction
con.commit();
// reset auto-commit to default
con.setAutoCommit(true);
```

Using a transaction manager

But what if our data is distributed, if we store, for example, Product on database A and Distributor on database B? We need a transaction mechanism that spans across multiple databases, possibly heterogeneous database systems from different vendors. Such a mechanism is a transaction manager, middleware that provides the services and management functions required to support transaction demarcation, transactional resource management, synchronization and transaction context propagation.

The infrastructure to process distributed transaction involves (Figure 12.12):

- Application.
- Application server, for example an EJB server or a TP monitor.
- Transaction manager, which implements a two-phase commit to provide transaction integrity over multiple heterogenous and distributed resources.
- Resource managers, for example relational database servers. Resource managers are connnected to the application server through resource adaptors (for example, a JDBC driver).
- Transactional messaging services (optional) as discussed in Section 12.6.

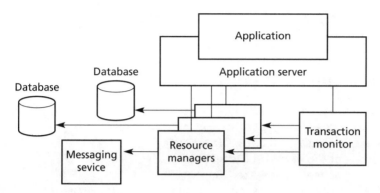

Figure 12.12 Infrastructure for a distributed transaction.

Instead of sending transaction demarcation commands (COMMIT, ROLLBACK) to resource managers, an application (or an application server) now sends equivalent commands to the transaction manager.

Java 2 Enterprise Edition (J2EE) comes with the Java Transaction API (JTA) which provides portable access to external transaction managers. The client is not only required to demarcate the end of a transaction (COMMIT, ROLLBACK) but also to demarcate the beginning of a transaction (BEGIN).

Java Transaction API

```
// get the system property value configured by administrator
String utxPropVal =
        System.getProperty("jta.UserTransaction");
// use JNDI (Java Naming and Directory Interface)
//      to locate the UserTransaction object
Context ctx = new InitialContext();
UserTransaction utx =
        (UserTransaction)ctx.lookup(utxPropVal);
// loading driver
Class.forName("sun.jdbc.odbc.JdbcOdbcDriver");
// setting up connections
Connection con1 = DriverManager.getConnection(url1,
"myLogin", "myPassword");
Connection con2 = DriverManager.getConnection(url2,
"myLogin", "myPassword");
// switch auto-commit off
con1.setAutoCommit(false);
con2.setAutoCommit(false);
// mark transaction begin
utx.begin();
// create statement objects
Statement stmt1 = con1.createStatement();
```

```
Statement stmt2 = con2.createStatement();
// set SQL update string
String updateString = "update Product " +
    "set Price = Price * " + eFactor +
    " where Distributor like 'Dupont'";
// execute update using statement in updateString.
stmt1.executeUpdate(updateString);
// set SQL update string for next operation
updateString = "update Distributor " +
    "set Town = 'St.Petersburg'" +
    " where Name like 'Dupont'";
// execute update using statement in updateString.
stmt2.executeUpdate(updateString);
// commit transaction via Transaction Manager
utx.commit();
// reset auto-commit to default
con1.setAutoCommit(true);
con2.setAutoCommit(true);
```

Portability?

This example also shows one of the problems of JTA: the use of a transaction manager is not transparent. This restricts the portability of the program: when we want to port it from an environment with a transaction manager to an environment without one, or vice versa, we have to modify the program code.

Enterprise JavaBeans are a better choice in this case. Because the code for setting up database connections and for demarcating transactions is contained in the EJB container, EJBs themselves are easier to move to different environments (provided the transaction policy BEAN MANAGED is not used).

In Section 15.6 we will discuss how Software AG's Bolero solves this problem.

From applet to servlet 13

13.1 Applets

Applets made Java famous. The motto of Java, 'Develop once, run anywhere', makes sense in such a diverse environment as Internet client computing. Different machines (PC, Macintosh, workstations), different operating systems (Windows, Macintosh, UNIX, Linux, etc.), different browsers (Microsoft Internet Explorer, Netscape, etc.) in different versions, have made the idea of the virtual machine a very appealing one (see Chapter 12).

However, after a first generation of electronic business applications that utilized applet technology, enterprise computing has moved towards server-centric solutions. There are still many problems left open by applet technology:

- The first applet generation (Java 1) used a strict security concept of all or nothing. An applet was either trusted and had full access to all resources, or it was untrusted and had to play in the sandbox: no access to resources, not even the printer. *Applets in real life*

- One of the consequences of this security concept was that applet components could not be stored on the client's computer, requiring an applet to be downloaded from the server with each new session. This wastes bandwidth and – except on LAN-based Intranets – requires users to wait.

- Because of security concerns some users have disabled Java in their browser security settings.

- Browsers may not support Java at all, for example browsers on palmtop computers, PDAs, or web-enabled mobile phones and pagers.

- Version problems. Incompatibilities between Sun's and Microsoft's Java versions have drawn a lot of attention. Netscape on Macintosh seems to lag behind a bit in new versions, and the same applies for the Linux platform.

- While RMI support for applets is a bit 'patchy' for Microsoft Internet Explorer (clients have to apply a patch), no RMI support exists at the time of writing for Netscape on Macintosh.

- Java 2 has introduced a sophisticated security concept which gives users a fine-grained control over security policies. This concept also allows applet components to be stored on the client's machine, avoiding repeated downloads of the applet.

  However, most browsers do not yet support Java 2. Sun has therefore introduced a Java 2 plug-in for popular web browsers. Once downloaded and installed, the plug-in provides the necessary runtime environment for Java *Java 2 applets*

2-based applets. The problem is that web pages that want to run an applet via the plug-in require a different HTML syntax. The `<applet>` tag is replaced by an `<object>` tag on Internet Explorer and by an `<embed>` tag on Netscape Communicator, requiring different versions of web pages for the two popular browsers.

In intranet/extranet solutions most of these problems can easily be solved by restricting the variety in client platforms. Download times for applets are short, because LAN networks usually feature a high bandwidth.

In an open Internet situation, however, it is often better to restrict the functionality of web pages to the lowest common denominator and to implement business logic and parts of the presentation logic on the server.

Java has finally grown up. With servlet technology, Enterprise JavaBeans and CORBA support it provides a solid basis for server-centric electronic business applications. Let us now take a look at some server issues.

13.2   Electronic business and transactions

By 'electronic business' we understand business conducted by electronic means without direct participation of a human agent.

What separates electronic business applications from other Internet-based applications is the fact that electronic business applications are transactional. Transactions are an elementary part of electronic business, in fact of any business. Without transactions there is no business.

Traditional business transactions comprise an exchange operation, whether that be material or immaterial goods, services, money, or some kind of information token that acts as a substitute for goods, services or money.

This sounds quite simple, but actually is not. Court proceedings all over the world provide a rich record of business transactions that have failed because of plain misunderstanding, misconception or fraud.

In an electronic business scenario things can become even more complex. Let us consider the simple case of a soft drink vending machine – in its present form not really an electronic business application but an early example of conducting business by a machine.

A sales agent

The business transaction starts when I put a coin into the slot. It ends when I receive the bottle. In between anything can go wrong. The coin may get stuck. The bottle may get stuck. The bottle may break. The machine may be empty. The bottle may be empty. There may not be enough small change for the money to be returned. The customer may fraudulently use some substitute for a coin of the proper value. The electric power may fail while the transaction is in process, etc.

Other than our vending machine, an electronic business application does not exchange tangible goods but information tokens. In some cases the information tokens are identical with the goods delivered, for example a piece of software, an electronic book, a musical record, a video, a copyrighted article, patent rights, services, etc. In other cases the information tokens exchanged act as vouchers for goods and services to be received or for money being paid. However, the possibilities that something can go wrong during a transaction are just as numerous as in the example above.

13.3   Sessions

Intrinsically linked to the concept of transactions is the concept of the session. In our vending machine example, a session starts when I drop a coin into the slot and it ends when I pick up the bottle and collect the returned money.

In this example the session acts as a container for a single transaction. However, multi-transaction sessions are possible in electronic business, just like multi-session transactions. Transactions that span several sessions, possibly with different end users, are typical for a workflow scenario.

Session and transaction

In an Internet-based electronic business scenario, a session starts when a customer enters a web site. It ends when he or she leaves the site. However, determining the boundaries of a session is not as easy as it seems, especially determining the end of a session.

Session defined

In traditional computer applications, for example in a spreadsheet application, a session is started when the application is started, and the session ends when the application is exited. The end is clearly defined by the user closing the application window, or using the `Exit` menu function, or when the application is forcibly closed by the operating system.

In an electronic business application we can use the same criteria when the client is 'fat' – a stand-alone application that requests services from a remote server. The fat client determines the start and end of a session, just like a typical desktop application.

With a thin client (typically a browser) things are not that easy. Business logic resides on the server. The client's web browser receives web pages from the server. These web pages may contain active elements such as scripts or applets, but these elements usually deal with presentation issues, not with the application's control flow. It is therefore the server that has to determine the start and end of a session.

The easier part is to find out when a session begins. When we keep track of all customers entering the site, we can easily detect a new customer and assign a new session to the customer. The tricky part is to detect when the session ends. When the customer has explicitly committed a transaction or has made clear that he or she does not want to continue the transaction, we can confidently regard the session as finished. But when the customer simply leaves the site, we don't really know what is going on. Has the customer left the site only for a while to compare prices? If so, will he or she come back? We don't know. But if the customer does not return, the session remains in limbo.

Determining session boundaries

This of course is not acceptable. Open sessions allocate computer resources. Thousands or even millions of open sessions would soon bring the server down. But not only is the server affected – the warehouse could be affected, too.

Competing clients

In online shops we often find a familiar metaphor from traditional shopping: the shopping cart. We browse around, collect items into the shopping cart, and finally proceed to the cashier where the transaction is completed. But what would we think of a shop where the shop assistant removes items from our shopping cart and sells them to another customer? We would probably leave the shop angrily and never come back. At least, we would like to speak to the manager.

> *Yet, these things happen. In an online shop for electronics I had filled my shopping cart with several items. The online catalogue indicated that all of them were in stock. When I later received the goods by mail, two items were missing: out of stock.*
>
> *What had happened was this: when I put these items in my shopping cart, they were probably the last items in stock. Placing them into my shopping cart did not change the availability status in the warehouse database. Another customer selected the same items after me – they were still marked as in stock – but checked out earlier than I did. So he won the race for the day's special.*

It would be easy to solve this sort of problem. The system must simulate the process of shopping completely: if an item is placed into the shopping cart, the stock count for this article must be decremented. If the transaction is aborted, the stock count of the article must be incremented again – the item is returned from the shopping cart to the warehouse. The virtual warehouse must always represent the true state of the stock.

Abandoned sessions

However, with the unruly behaviour of online customers who just leave the shop without a word, leaving the shopping cart somewhere in cyberspace, the place would soon be littered with abandoned but filled shopping carts, and the warehouse would be empty. Sales would come to an end.

It is therefore crucial to detect cases of open but abandoned sessions. This is far from simple, because the HTTP protocol is stateless. With plain HTML, leaving a page is a non-event. While scripts can help to detect when a displayed page on the browser is closed (unloaded), the leaving of a site – in our case a shop – is harder to decide. When a session is aborted for some reason, it is hardly probable that the client's browser is able to run a script to notify the server.

Detecting session end

Some techniques have been developed to decide the end of a session:

- *Check-out by the customer*. The customer confirms or explicitly cancels a transaction.

- *Time window closed*. When entering a site the customer is given a certain time interval in which to conduct business. This is a technique often used by online banks to limit security risks.

- *Non-activity time-out*. After a certain period of non-activity by the client the session is closed by the server.

- The client application *notifies* the server of the end of the session (fat client).

Even with logic in place to detect session end, most electronic business systems prefer an 'optimistic' approach to stock management: the warehouse's stock count is not decreased when the customer puts an item into the shopping cart, but when the customer checks out and pays. Well-designed systems will check the status of the warehouse at this time and warn the customer when an item has become unavailable.

13.4   Session state

Session control includes the management of state information for the session.

On a fat client, where the client controls the session's control flow, state information is managed by the client, and is usually stored in the client's application data areas or in a client-side database or file system.

With a thin client solution several options exist. State information can be stored on the client computer in form of a *cookie*, in the server application or in a server database.

As already stated, HTTP is a stateless protocol. Each request is intended to be independent of previous requests. An HTTP server typically has no memory of previous requests made by the same client – it has no idea of a session. If the connection to the client is lost the application server doesn't even notice.

Several techniques have been evolved to bind requests to a session:

Keeping session state

- *Authentication mechanisms*, such as basic authentication or client certificates, identify the user to the server on each request. The user identification from the authentication can be used by the server to look up the state information for each request.

  For example, Secure Sockets Layer (SSL), the encryption technology used in the HTTPS protocol, can identify client requests unambiguously as being part of an accepted session.

- *Dynamic URLs.* Servers that create HTML pages dynamically (server pages) can embed a user ID or other information into the query part of a URL. All outgoing links of an HTML page are prepared in this way (URL rewriting). When the user clicks on the link, the URL and the information embedded in it are sent back to the server. The server extracts this information and can identify user and session. When security is important, the information embedded in the URL must be protected using cryptographic methods.

- *Hidden fields in forms.* A similar technique is possible with hidden fields in HTML forms. Hidden fields are not displayed to the user but their content travels back to the server when the user posts the form. Again, information stored in hidden fields should be protected against tampering.

● *Cookies*. Originally introduced by Netscape, most browsers today support the concept of cookies. A cookie is a small data record that is transmitted from the server to the client and is stored by the client's web browser on the local hard disk. With each subsequent request the cookie is sent to the server. Cookies can be made persistent across browser sessions and can have an expiry date. Cookies can store session state information or session identifiers, but they are not really appropriate for storing user profiles: cookies do not travel well with a user that moves between different client machines (nomadic computing).

Some browsers do not support cookies, and users may choose not to accept cookies because of privacy concerns. Cookies are also accessible to savvy users, so they should be protected against tampering (encoding, checksum).

13.5   Server-side logic

On most servers we find a mixture of competing and cooperating technologies, such as Perl, CGI, server APIs, server-side scripts, and servlets. In large sites such a mixture can cause problems in system maintenance and change management.

CGI

The Common Gateway Interface was the first facility to implement server-side logic. Originally it was created to couple existing 'legacy' applications with a web front-end. However, it is not really suited to implementing mission-critical applications – it does not scale well. The CGI scripting language, designed for relatively small interfaces, does not lend itself well to software engineering practices known from large IT applications.

In terms of performance, CGI suffers from the fact that the application must be launched with each request for a URL and is exited after the page has been sent. The application is required to store session information on a persistent medium and retrieve it again with the next request. For each request the server has to start the Perl interpreter (most CGI interpreters are written in Perl), load the required modules, establish a connection to the database, and return the required information to the client. It then has to close the database connection and exit the Perl process.

FastCGI

FastCGI improves the situation by running CGI programs as independent processes, abolishing the time-consuming start and stop operation. However, existing CGI scripts must be modified to run under FastCGI (the program must not exit, but run in a loop). This restricts portability because FastCGI is not available for every server platform.

Server APIs

Server Application Programming Interfaces, such as Netscape's NSAPI or Microsoft's ISAPI, allow an application to be integrated directly with the web server. This approach yields high performance, but applications are no longer portable. Also, the application is not well isolated from the server – a faulty application can bring the server down, and it is not possible to hot-swap new application versions.

Server-side scripting

Microsoft Active Server Pages (ASP) are an example of server-side scripting. Web pages contain scripts written in JavaScript or VBScript combined with ActiveX controls. When a page is requested the server executes the scripts and sends the resulting page to the client. Because ASP can only run on IIS under Microsoft Windows, portability is limited.

Java servlets

Java servlets are small, platform-independent Java programs running on a web server or application server. Servlets interact with web clients via a request–response paradigm implemented by the servlet container. This request–response model is based on the behaviour of the Hypertext Transfer Protocol (HTTP).

The servlet container provides the runtime environment (Java Virtual Machine and other resources) for servlets. It manages servlets throughout their life cycle and handles, in conjunction with a web server or application server, requests and responses from and to web clients on behalf of the servlet. Servlet containers decouple the servlet from the web server, leading to increased stability in the operation of the web server. *Servlet container explained*

Because servlets are not loaded with each request, they provide far better performance than CGI. The servlet engine is responsible for servlet loading. Servlets can scale with the traffic: new instances of the same servlet can be loaded when the traffic increases, and servlet instances can be destroyed when the traffic decreases.

Each servlet can own a `ServletContext` object. This object defines the servlet's view of the web application it is running in. By using a `ServletContext`, servlets can log events and obtain objects and URL references to resources from the servlet container. Each servlet can run in only one servlet context, but different servlets can own different contexts providing different views of the same application. *ServletContext explained*

The servlet container also handles session logic, by providing a session object (`HttpSession`) with the servlet context. This session object can be used to store state information, so the servlet programmer does not have to deal with cookies or URL query strings. The session object can be accessed from every servlet that processes requests from the current session. The servlet container can use either cookies, URL rewriting or SSL session control for session identification. *Session object explained*

Java Server Pages (JSP)

JSP (Pelegrí-Llopart et al 1999) is Sun Microsystems' answer to Microsoft's Active Server Pages. JSP is based on Java servlet technology and is therefore portable to all servers that support Java servlets. JSP supports the JavaBean component model. Beans can be accessed directly from a Java Server Page:

```
<html>
<jsp:useBean id="clock"
            class="calendar.jspCalendar" />
<ul>
<li>Day: <%=clock.getDayOfMonth() %>
<li>Year: <%=clock.getYear() %>
</ul>
</html>
```

In addition, JSP allows script elements to be embedded into pages. The scripting language currently used is Java, but the specification is open to other scripting languages. The script elements – called scriptlets – are Java code fragments enclosed in `<%...%>` and can occur in combination with HTML elements:

```
<% if (Calendar.getInstance().get(Calendar.AM_PM) ==
Calendar.AM) {%>
Good Morning
<% } else { %>
Good Afternoon
<% } %>
```

13.6   The Java Enterprise Application Model

The Java Enterprise Application Model introduced with Java 2 Enterprise Edition (J2EE) features a four-tier architecture (Figure 13.1):

Four-tier architecture

- APIs such as JTA or JMS, which are part of J2EE, provide access to the enterprise's information systems, such as databases or other data sources. These data sources form the first tier.

- The second tier contains the business logic which is modelled using Enterprise JavaBeans.

- The third tier handles server-side presentation logic, such as navigation. Java Server Pages are used to produce dynamically generated HTML pages. Alternatively Java servlets offer a more generic approach for communication with client-side logic.

- Finally, the fourth tier deals with client-side presentation. Clients can be web browsers (either pure HTML or Java enabled). Desktop applications or other servers can also establish a connection with the server and communicate with a Java servlet.

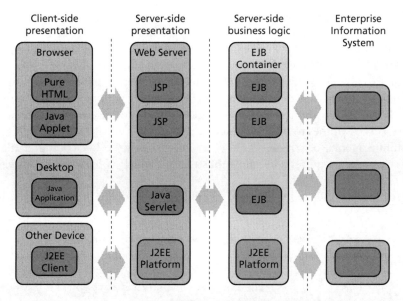

Figure 13.1   The Java Enterprise Application Model. (Source: Sun Microsystems)

13.7   Agents

In the 1962 science fiction novel *A for Andromeda*, astronomers pick up an interstellar message. They decipher it as a construction plan for a large computer. The computer is built and instructs the scientist to create artificial life: an agent is born (Hoyle and Elliot 1962).

Autonomous behaviour is the feature that best describes agents. Other than normal components that provide functions which can be invoked from a client, agents are deployed with a mission or an agenda. Once deployed, an agent continues to live outside the client's session, develops its own initiative, can learn, and can use other software components, usually through agent servers. Mobile agents can travel within networks, provided the network nodes are equipped with agent servers. Typically, an agent autonomously selects the travel destinations. Like the famous Chinese monkey king Sun Wu, agents are able to clone themselves and travel to several destinations simultaneously. When an agent has finished its mission or is recalled, it returns to its home base (or commits suicide). Agents may report the progress of the mission periodically or on demand, e.g. by sending mail to the home base.

Autonomous behaviour

However, the mobile and autonomous character of agents can make it difficult to predict the behaviour of a large agent-based system. During the American SDI 'Starwars' programme in the 1980s, David L. Parnas took a strict position against the proposal to implement the Starwars' software as independent agents communicating with each other, because he feared that systems with so many degrees of freedom could display chaotic behaviour.

Chaotic behaviour

Nevertheless, there are many situations where agents can prove beneficial. To evaluate, for example, massive remote databases, an agent could be deployed to the database server, read the data locally and return with the result, instead of reading all data over a remote connection.

Agents can act as buyers and sellers in an electronic market environment. IBM Japan's *aglets* (the word aglet is a blend of applet with agent), for example, have been used in the travel market. Aglets travel (no pun intended) between the servers of airlines to find the best offer for an air fare.

Agent server

Mobile agents, of course, cannot just move to any other computer like a virus. An agent requires a certain infrastructure which is provided by an *agent server* or agent container.

Within a Java RMI environment, an agent server could implement the following interface:

```
public interface AgentServer extends java.rmi.Remote
{
    void accept(Agent a)
                throws InvalidAgentException,
                java.rmi.RemoteException;
.}
```

An agent would have to implement the following interface:

```
public interface Agent extends java.io.Serializable
{
    void run();
}
```

An agent is deployed by calling the `accept` method on the `AgentServer` with the agent as parameter. RMI downloads the agent's implementation and its state to the server. The server's `accept` method starts up a new thread for the agent, invokes the agent's `run` method, and returns. The agent's `run` method now takes over the new thread. Later, the agent could migrate to another host by invoking `accept(this)` on the new host, passing itself to the new server, and killing the thread on the original host.

Agents can meet

An agent that just moves from server to server and does nothing is useless. An agent must rendezvous and communicate with other agents, or with server components. One possibility is that the agent server arranges such meetings. Another possibility is that agents post their wishes to meet somebody (tall, well groomed and honest) on a server-based whiteboard, such as a tuple space (see Section 12.5). Once in contact two agents can communicate. To communicate, agents usually register each other as an `eventListener`.

When the agent moves on, partners would be left with an invalid address for event delivery. A common technique to overcome this problem is to leave a proxy behind which accepts these messages and forwards them to the new address.

When agents communicate with each other they should use the same language. Dialects are possible and agents must be flexible enough to handle variations in their partners (for instance, when a new version of a partner agent is introduced). Java reflection can be used to find out the partner's capabilities. Java serialization and deserialization can be used to communicate complex data objects. Another option is to use XML for communication between agents. XML offers the possibility of transferring highly structured information while providing almost the flexibility of unstructured text (see Section 14.2). *Agent communications*

There are security concerns, too. For example, agents must protect their identity against impostors, who could take their identity and cause havoc. Agents must therefore identify themselves when they enter new server regions. In some cases, highly reliable, cryptographic forms of proof may be required. Another option is that an agent does not travel by itself but asks the server to transport it in a trusted message. *Agent security*

Agents are only allowed to interact with the host system via the agent server, similar to a Java applet which can run only in the context of a browser and does not have access to system resources. This, as a matter of fact, restricts the functionality of agents. IBM's aglets, for example, follow the security restrictions for Java applets. This implies that an aglet cannot communicate directly with other aglets, but only with its home base. A router, installed at the home base server, forwards messages sent between aglets (at least the first message – once the connection is trusted, direct communication is possible).

Java 2 environments, with finer-grained security architecture, could offer more sophisticated security policies for agents. However, agents should not rely on special security settings on the hosts visited.

Persistence of data is another problem. Agents are not usually allowed to create persistent data structures on the current host. Instead the agent has to carry all the data with it, or forward it to the home base. *Persistent agents*

On some systems it is possible to make the whole agent persistent. The agent's state is serialized and stored on a persistent medium by the agent server, while the agent is deactivated (sleeps). At a later time the agent is reactivated. This is a useful technique for agents with a periodic agenda, for example an agent that creates a financial report on the first of each month.

The robustness of agents against system crashes is still an area for research. In the case of a crash of the host system, the agent dies. In the best case, the agent is restored to its initial state when the system is restarted. On the other hand, because of the autonomous character of agents, reliability is an issue, more than for traditional applications. Agent servers should support not only the persistence of an agent's state during 'sleep' periods, but also during activity periods (synchronization points, transaction concept) and should support forward recovery in the event of a crash. *Robust agents*

13.8   Application servers

With servlets, agents and Enterprise JavaBeans (see Section 12.7) requiring application services from their container applications, application servers have started to emerge from the classical web server. Typical products in this area are: IBM WebSphere, IBM CICS TS, BEA WebLogic, ATG Dynamo, Allaire Jrun, Apache Jserv.

While the development of application servers is still in flux, the following characteristics can already be identified:

- **Client connectivity.** This includes interfaces for different client types to interact with server components, such as HTML clients, XML clients, Java clients, Windows clients.
- **State management.** The server manages a user context as the session state across several HTTP requests. For example, all of the application servers mentioned above implement the Java Servlet API which covers state management.
- **Transaction processing.** The server provides services for transaction demarcation, including distributed processing (two-phase commit), for example by implementing the Java Transaction API (JTA) and the Java Messaging Service (JMS).
- **Resource adapters.** These services include access to databases (for example, through JDBC), legacy applications and packaged applications. Design-time services help to construct integration logic.
- **Development tools.** These include various tools, such as GUI-builders, HTML-editors, report writers, program editors, compilers, debuggers, etc.
- **Runtime management.** This includes facilities for improved quality of service, such as reliability and availability (e.g. failover), scalability and performance (e.g. load balancing), security (e.g. authentication, access control, encryption), monitoring and configuration (e.g. availability).

As we can see, many of these features are covered by the Java 2 Enterprise Edition (J2EE) specifications (see Section 12.3). At the time of writing, most products cover only the services for client connectivity and state management. Complete support for all services is expected by 2003.

From HTML to XML 14

The HyperText Markup Language, HTML, is one force behind the massive growth of the World Wide Web. Providing means for the definition of hyperlinks and for device-independent layout, it allowed the Internet to grow into a web of interrelated and compelling information items.

But the success of HTML has also exposed its shortcomings. Designed for content presentation and for manual browsing (surfing), it is not well suited for automated information processing. Representational markup, such as in HTML, does not inform processors about the context in which content must be interpreted. Electronic business such as advanced searching, data mining on the Internet or information exchange between global partners requires semantic markup instead of presentational markup. Semantic markup, however, is only possible with a markup language that supports the extension of the language with user (or industry) defined tags. The eXtensible Markup Language (XML) is such a language.

14.1 HTML

HTML is the standard presentation language for the web and this will not change in the short term. Fragmentary XML support is present in version 5 browsers, but full XML support is expected from version 6 browsers onwards. Until these browsers become a standard for web clients, HTML is the only choice for web pages published on the Internet.

HTML for content presentation

The next generation of HTML, XHTML (XHTML 1999-6), is based on XML, requiring HTML pages to be well formed, i.e. to consist of syntactically correct XML.

Because HTML pages are static, non-HTML technology was added over time to make pages more dynamic:

Dynamic presentation

- **Images** are supported in GIF, JPEG and PNG formats; GIF allows animated images. Support for image formats across platforms is fairly consistent.

- **Multimedia.** Plug-ins for web browsers exist for many other image formats, including vector graphics formats such as CGM. Other plug-ins support multimedia (sound, movies, animated vector graphics), or 3D worlds, often in proprietary formats. Using plug-ins requires the user to download the plug-in module – not all plug-ins are available for all platforms.

- **JavaScript** allows the elements of a web page to be modified dynamically and to react to events.

- **Java applets**. Applets are small applications that are embedded in a web page. Java 1 applets can be embedded directly into web pages. Java 2 applets require the Java 2 plug-in (see Section 13.1).

- **ActiveX controls** (Chappell) are Microsoft's answer to Java applets. ActiveX controls are basically DCOM components that can be embedded into a web page. ActiveX controls can interoperate with Visual Basic Script – the language can also interoperate with JavaBeans. ActiveX controls can easily communicate with each other using DCOM.

Which technologies are used should be decided based on the IT environment.

- In a closed system (intranet) the environment is controlled: it is known which web browser versions are used, etc. A closed system therefore allows for more advanced or even proprietary features.

- Web pages to be used in an open system (Internet) should be designed for the lowest common denominator. Another option is to use features conditionally, depending on the client's browser. However, this increases the complexity of web pages.

  Also, end users may have disabled active elements like Java applets, JavaScript or ActiveX because of security concerns, and may allow only plain HTML.

14.2   Why XML?

When Tim Berners-Lee designed HTML in 1990 he was able to base his design on an already existing standard for the electronic representation of documents: SGML, the Standard Generalized Markup Language, which was standardized by the ISO in 1986 (ISO 1986).

SGML identifies document elements such as titles, tables, chapters and paragraphs as distinct items. These elements are identified by *tags* embedded in the document. The tags make the document, to a certain extent, self-describing. In a product catalogue, for example, elements can be tagged as an article number, a price, or a product description. The tag set and the relationships between document elements are defined in the Document Type Definition (DTD).

HTML, however, utilizes only a small fixed tag subset of SGML. This allowed the quick implementation of HTML browsers and made HTML very popular – it is easy to learn. The basic HTML concepts can be understood and applied within a few hours. But the strength of HTML is also its weakness: most tags are purely representational, like <B> for bold type style, or <H1> for a header. (There are some rudimentary exceptions such as <TITLE> or <ADDRESS> .) Because the set of tags is fixed, the application domain of HTML is limited: the browser defines which tags are recognized and how they are processed. The browser war between Microsoft and Netscape further complicated the situation: proprietary tags were introduced while basic features were interpreted differently.

While HTML is designed for the representation of information and for navigation between information entities, it does not provide a solid foundation for automated information processing. The expression `<H1>12.45</H1>`, for example, indicates only that the number 12.45 is displayed as a headline, but it does not indicate what the number means: a version number, a chapter number, a time of day, or a price.

Applications such as advanced search engines, smart agents or data mining on the Internet require a more structured approach. Instead of representational markup, automated information processing requires semantic markup relating content to context.

Advanced electronic business applications require a semantic markup language such as XML

It became necessary to reconsider the virtues of SGML:

- *Extensibility*: New tags and attributes can be introduced without changing the standard.
- *Structure*: Document elements can be nested. Standard paragraphs (elements) can be reused between documents.
- *Validation*: If desired, a document can be checked for structural integrity.

In 1996, a new team of experts led by Jon Bosak of Sun Microsystems and backed by the World Wide Web Consortium (W3C) began to work on a new standard. The new standard had to be simple, extensible and readable for both humans and computers. Finalized in February 1998, it was called XML (eXtensible Markup Language). Within the same year the commercial world started to use XML. The new standard was quickly adopted by industry leaders such as Sun, Microsoft, DataChannel, NetScape, IBM, SAP, Adobe and Software AG. Dozens of vertical standards, such as CDF (Channel Definition Format) or OSD (Open Software Description), were based on XML.

The design of XML is also based on SGML. XML maintains the SGML features of validation, structure and extensibility, while being simple to use, to learn and to implement. XML is, like SGML, a meta-language for defining the markup of different types of documents. However, the XML specification has a length of only 26 pages, compared to the 500 pages of the SGML specification. XML also avoids some SGML features that work against portability, such as compulsory Document Type Definitions (DTDs) or complex linking conventions.

- XML is **simple**. XML is extremely legible. Creating an XML document is much simpler than creating an HTML document, where the author has to be aware of how different browsers react to different tags. In fact the author must ignore display issues altogether, and leave representational aspects to the style sheet.

XML basic features

- XML is **open**. XML is a W3C standard, not a proprietary format. It is endorsed by software industry market leaders, such as Sun, Microsoft, DataChannel, NetScape, IBM, SAP, Adobe and Software AG.
- XML is **extensible**. There is no fixed set of tags. New tags can be created when they are needed. The creation of new tags does not require the deployment of new software versions.

- XML is **self-describing**. The tags contained in an XML document augment the interpretation of the document content in a standard way. Content elements can be clearly identified with an element name and additional attributes.

- XML is **human readable**. The tags can be defined in such a way that they are meaningful to human readers.

- XML provides **machine-readable** context information. Tags, attributes and element structure provide context information that can be used to interpret the meaning of content. This is a major advantage over HTML or plain text, where context information is difficult or impossible to evaluate. The structured approach to context enables new possibilities for highly efficient search engines, intelligent data mining, artificial intelligence, machine-based document translation, etc.

- XML facilitates the **comparison** and **aggregation** of data. The tree structure of XML documents allows processors to efficiently compare and aggregate documents element by element.

- XML provides a basis for author **identification** and **versioning** at element level. Any XML tag can possess an unlimited number of attributes such as author or version.

- XML supports **multilingual** documents and **Unicode**, which is important for globalized web-based applications.

- XML can embed **multiple data types**. XML documents can contain any possible data type: from multimedia content (image, sound, video) to active components (Java applets, ActiveX).

- XML separates **content** from **presentation**. XML tags describe meaning, not presentation (Figures 14.1 and 14.2). The motto of HTML is: 'I know how it looks', but the motto of XML is: 'I know what it means'. The look and feel of an XML document is controlled by XSL style sheets (see Section 14.4). This allows the look of a document (or of a complete web site) to be changed without touching the document.

Will XML bury HTML?

XML will certainly not replace HTML in all areas. There is still a rationale for hand-crafted, individually designed pages. (At the time of writing, a new HTML standard is being discussed: XHTML is proposed as a successor for HTML 4.0 and is based on XML.)

XML, however, flourishes in areas where machine-generated data dominates. To display, for example, product data sheets from a product catalogue, all that is required is an XML database server that stores XML-product descriptions, and an XSL style sheet that describes how the product sheets should look on the screen or on the printer. The XML pages can then be displayed on an XML-enabled browser, or a server-based XSL processor can convert XML pages into HTML pages.

Main application areas of XML

The main application of XML, however, will happen in areas not visible to the average web user.

```
<?xml version="1.0" encoding="UTF-8"?>
<PRODUCT>                      <!-- root element -->
    <NAME>Walkman</NAME>   <!-- elements -->
    <DESCRIPTION>Elegant Long-Play Walkman in new
design</DESCRIPTION>
    <SPECIFICATION>Mega Bass Dolby B, Auto Reverse</SPECIFICATION>
    <PRODUCT_DETAIL>               <!-- nested elements -->
        <COLOR>silver</COLOR>
        <ORDER-NO>34 97 11-65</ORDER-NO>
        <PRICE CURRENCY="EUR">54.90</PRICE>
                               <!-- elements with attributes -->
        <PRICE CURRENCY="USD">59.90</PRICE>
    </PRODUCT_DETAIL>
    <PRODUCT_DETAIL>
        <COLOR>black</COLOR>
        <ORDER-NO>34 97 11-66</ORDER-NO>
        <PRICE CURRENCY="EUR">49.90</PRICE>
        <PRICE CURRENCY="USD">55.90</PRICE>
    </PRODUCT_DETAIL>
</PRODUCT>
```

Figure 14.1 XML document for a product catalogue. Each document contains the general product data, but also lists several product colours with order number and price. The prices are given in US dollars and Euro. The currency is specified via element attributes.

Electronic data interchange (EDI), pioneered by the car industry, is now used in several industries for the exchange of business data between large corporations and suppliers. The origin of EDI has deeply influenced its architecture – EDI was designed to exchange data on a one-to-one basis. Any connection between two partners requires the definition of a fixed transaction set (Figure 14.3). Transaction sets define the fields of a data record according to their order and length. In addition, transaction sets contain business rules ('implementation guidelines'). Since these rules usually differ between companies, a special solution is required for each new combination of client and supplier.

Setting up a connection between client and supplier is a costly exercise. Because the transaction sets are fixed, change management is costly, too – each change has to go through a development–revision cycle. The cost is carried by the (usually) smaller supplier. In many cases, therefore, suppliers do not implement an integrated solution but use methods of manual data transfer (retyping or cut-and-paste).

EDI means costly supply chains

```
<?xml version="1.0" encoding="UTF-8"?>
-<PRODUCT>
  <!-- root element -->
  <NAME>Walkman</NAME>
  <!-- elements -->
  <DESCRIPTION>Elegant Long-Play Walkman in new design</DESCRIPTION>
  <SPECIFICATION>Mega Bass Dolby B, Auto Reverse</SPECIFICATION>
-<PRODUCT_DETAIL>
    <!-- nested elements -->
    <COLOR>silver</COLOR>
    <ORDER-NO>34 97 11-65</ORDER-NO>
    <PRICE CURRENCY="EUR">54.90</PRICE>
    <!-- elements with attributes -->
    <PRICE CURRENCY="USD">59.90</PRICE>
  </PRODUCT_DETAIL>
-<PRODUCT_DETAIL>
    <COLOR>black</COLOR>
    <ORDER-NO>34 97 11-66</ORDER-NO>
    <PRICE CURRENCY="EUR">49.90</PRICE>
    <PRICE CURRENCY="USD">55.90</PRICE>
  </PRODUCT_DETAIL>
</PRODUCT>
```

Figure 14.2   The same document as Figure 14.1, displayed in a web browser without using a style sheet.

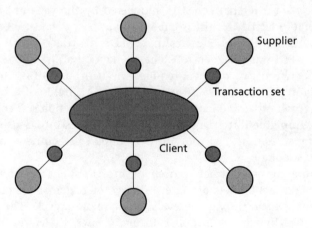

Figure 14.3   The typical EDI configuration: suppliers serve one large client, and separate transactions sets are defined for each supplier.

It comes as no surprise that EDI was slow to take off. Originally introduced in the 1970s, EDI now serves only 2 per cent of enterprises (80,000) in the United States and about 125,000 organizations worldwide.

EDI through XML, or XML/EDI, sets out to deliver what traditional EDI had always promised. XML allows a flexibility in data transmission that should turn the one-to-one client–supplier relation of traditional EDI into a many-to-many network of supply chains. The separation of business rules from content and the extensibility of XML should ease change management considerably (Vijghen 1997).

XML/EDI means cheap supply chains

Transfer and storage of business data (financial data, orders, invoices, part lists, legal documents, etc.) between business partners is fertile ground for XML. As a meta-language, however, XML does not offer a universal communication method without the active participation of user groups. Nevertheless, as it is a new standard, it provides an opportunity for a fresh start. Many business association bodies have adopted XML/EDI and are currently working on XML/EDI standards for their specific industries (Figure 14.4). The International XML/EDI Group is at work on an electronic business framework based on XML and the ISO Open-edi standard (see Section 15.11).

One example is the health industry. The transfer of patient records between health institutions is a crucial task, but there is also the processing of claims, controlling, etc.

In the past, paper-based records were used. As more and more hospitals, practitioners and insurers were equipped with information systems, records became computer-based. Yet, as different institutions use different systems from different suppliers, the format of health records varies from one institution to the next. It is therefore common practice to re-enter data into the local information system manually. Mistakes are made, and patients are possibly either treated for diseases they don't have or not treated for diseases they do have, and they end up paying huge bills because of the administration overhead.

The introduction of chip cards has improved this situation, but these cards also have drawbacks. Health cards can store only a limited amount of data, they can get lost, and political or legal changes are expensive to implement. Sending out new health cards to all patients could incur costs to the tune of $50 million according to a large German health insurer (AOK). What is required is a unified computer network spanning practitioners, hospitals, insurers and other health institutions.

A common XML-based format for health records could improve this situation. Owing to the size of the health sector and the complexity of health records, a one-fits-all solution is unlikely. Instead, agreement on core components and the ability for amendments by individual sectors of the health system is a more realistic approach. Adopted by the HL-7 standardization body (Kona Proposal), XML supports existing transaction standards such as NSG, ANSI-X12 and ASTM, and provides a common basis for further standardization efforts.

aecXML for Architecture, Engineering and Construction
Artificial Intelligence Markup Language (AIML)
Bean Markup Language (BML)
Bioinformatic Sequence Markup Language (BSML)
Call Policy Markup Language (CPML)
Call Processing Language (CPL)
Cold Fusion Markup Language (CFML)
Common Rules and Business Rules Markup Language (BRML)
DTD for patent documents – ST32 US Patent Grant
Electronic Component Manufacturer Data Sheet Library Specification (ECMdata)
Encoded Archival Description (EAD)
Extensible Financial Reporting Markup Language (XFRML)
Financial Product Markup Language (FpML)
FinXML – XML for Capital Markets
Formal Language for Business Communication (FLBC)
Information and Content Exchange (ICE)
Internet Content Exchange (ICE)
Internet Open Trading Protocol (IOTP)
Java Speech Markup Language (JSML)
Koala Bean Markup Language (KBML)
Liturgical Markup Language (LitML)
Mathematical Markup Language
Media Object Communications Protocol (MOS-X)
Molecular Dynamics Language (MoDL)
NAA Standard for Classified Advertising Data
Navigation Markup Language (NVML)
Open Trading Protocol (OTP)
Predictive Model Markup Language (PMML)
Procedural Markup Language (PML)
Product Definition Exchange (PDX)
Resource Description Framework (RDF)
Scalable Vector Graphics (SVG)
Synchronized Multimedia Integration Language (SMIL)
Translation Memory Exchange (TMX)
Tutorial Markup Language (TML)
Voice Recognition ML (VoxML)
Web Interface Definition Language (WIDL)
Wireless Markup Language (WML)
XML Bookmark Exchange Language (XBEL)
XML Metadata Interchange (XMI)

Figure 14.4   Many industries have defined specific XML-based languages. The selection given here is based on the announcements made under www.xm1.com.

We can find similar examples in most industries. Initially introduced to solve the problems with HTML, XML has found its own domain: not so much as a replacement for HTML, but as a generic document description language, a *lingua franca*, for the storage and interchange of any type of information.

14.3   Mobile computing with WAP

The Wireless Application Protocol (WAP) enables wireless devices such as mobile phones to surf the web. WAP was released in June 1999 and soon afterwards the first WAP-enabled devices appeared on the market.

WML is XML

WML (Wireless Markup Language) (WAP Forum 1999) acts as a page description language within WAP. WML is based on XML and is a good example of what can be achieved by using XML. It is not compatible with HTML, although it uses many tags known from that language. WML is specialized for the small display sizes usually found in mobile phones, and the limited input capabilities of these devices.

Conceptually, WML uses a navigation metaphor known from HyperCard, which is a popular hypermedia system for the Apple Macintosh. In HyperCard the content is separated into single *cards*, which usually but not necessarily matched the small screen of the first Mac (tombstone). Semantically related cards within the stack are grouped into card *stacks*. Each stack contains several cards and a *background*. Background elements are displayed with each card. The sequence of the cards within the stack defines a natural browsing direction. To navigate forwards and backwards between the cards of a stack, it is not necessary to link each card with its predecessor and successor. Each card has a name. Links to other cards are possible (also into other stacks).

HyperCard revisited

WML uses a similar concept (Figure 14.5). Each card deck (stack in HyperCard) forms a single XML file and can contain several cards. Because of the limited resources on a mobile device, a deck is restricted to a size of 1.5 kB.

WML explained

WML knows several tags for text representation, including tags for simple tables. It supports links to other cards, and allows input fields and selection lists in cards. In contrast to HTML, a WML session has a state: card elements can define variables and assign values to them. References to these variables in cards are replaced at runtime with the content of the variable. This improves the reuse and caching of cards. It also allows input operations for one transaction to be distributed over several cards.

The WML specification also specifies a simplified version of JavaScript: WMLScript. Some mobile phone-specific functions have been added: the script language can dial, send SMS messages, or add phone numbers to the address book.

WMLScript

```
<?xml version="1.0"?>
<!DOCTYPE wml PUBLIC "-//WAPFORUM//DTD WML 1.1//EN"
          "hhtp://www.wapforum.org/DTD/wml_1.1.xml">
<wml>
  <template>
      <onevent type="ontimer">
        <go href="/next"/>
      </onevent>
      <timer value="30"/>
  </template>
  <card id="london" title="weather - London">
    <p>
      <b>9-12</b>
    </p>
    <p>
      foggy
    </p>
  </card>
  <card id="paris" title="weather - Paris">
    <p>
      <b>14-18</b>
    </p>
    <p>
      sunny
    </p>
  </card>
  <card id="rome" title="weather - Rome">
    <p>
      <b>12-16</b>
    </p>
    <p>
      cloudy
    </p>
  </card>
</wml>
```

Figure 14.5 This WML deck contains three cards. The template section (similar to the HyperCard background) is inherited by each card and defines a timer event – after three seconds the next card is displayed.

14.4   The XML framework: XSL, XQL, DOM, …

The XML 1.0 Recommendation covers only syntactic and structural aspects of
XML documents and Document Type Definitions (DTDs):

- A **DTD** defines a class of valid XML documents (XML 1998-3), i.e. it defines
  which tags, attributes and elements are valid. DTDs are the main instrument
  for defining common vocabularies within industries. DTDs are only required
  to establish a common vocabulary, to support authoring tools in the creation
  of valid XML documents or to check the validity of an XML document. They
  are not required for accessing, displaying, processing or searching XML documents. An XML processor must be able to process any well-formed
  (syntactically correct) XML document, even if a DTD does not exist or is
  inaccessible. Figure 14.6 shows an example of a DTD.

  Schema definition

- **XML Schema** is an alternative way to describe valid XML documents. The current XML Schema Working Draft (W3C 1999-9) introduces data types into
  XML and supports inheritance between document archetypes. XML Schema
  definitions are – unlike DTDs – well-formed XML documents themselves,
  allowing the processing of XML Schema definitions with XML tools.

```
        <!--   A Sample Product DTD -->
        <!--   Defining the root element -->
<!ELEMENT  PRODUCT
(NAME,DESCRIPTION,SPECIFICATION,PRODUCT_DETAIL+)>
        <!--   Defining the leaf elements -->
<!ELEMENT  NAME (#PCDATA)>
<!ELEMENT  DESCRIPTION (#PCDATA)>
<!ELEMENT  SPECIFICATION (#PCDATA)>
        <!--   Defining a subnode -->
<!ELEMENT  PRODUCT_DETAIL (COLOR,ORDER-NR,PRICE)>
        <!--   Defining an attribute with valid values
               and default value -->
<!ATTLIST  PRICE Currency (EUR | USD | YEN)"EUR">
        <!--   Defining inner elements -->
<!ELEMENT  COLOR (#PCDATA)>
<!ELEMENT  ORDER-NR (#PCDATA)>
<!ELEMENT  PRICE (#PCDATA)>
```

Figure 14.6 An optional DTD for the XML example shown in Figure 14.1, defining the
valid document structure.

Additional standards are necessary to define topics not dealt with in the XML recommendation, topics like linking, presentation, namespaces, APIs and databases:

Presentation

- **XSL** (eXtensible Style Language) (W3C 1999-1) defines an extensible style sheet language for the presentation of XML documents. A style sheet can control the look and feel of a single document or of a whole web site. An example is shown in Figure 14.7. XSL consists of three parts:

Access to elements

  - **XPath** (also known as XML Pattern Language) (W3C 1999-7) defines how to address a node (element, attribute, etc.) within an XML object. XPath is a common basis for XSL, XQL and XPointer.
    Example: The XPath expression

    ```
    customer//street
    ```

    selects any <street> element that is a descendant of a <customer> element. (A descendant is either a child of an element or a descendant of a child.)

  - **XSLT** (XSL Transformations) (W3C 1999-10) supports rule-based translation of XML documents into documents of a different grammar, such as HTML documents, or XML documents of a different structure. Each template rule consists of a head element and a body. The head element (`match=`) specifies an XPath pattern-matching expression. When the head of a rule matches the current document node, the processing instructions in the rule body are executed: either text is written to the output stream, or further rules can be applied. (If several rules match the current node, the rule with the most specific header is selected.) Matching expressions can refer to the content of elements. This allows content aware formatting to be defined (e.g. display negative amounts in red).

  - **XFO** (XML formatting objects) (W3C 1999-1) provides a rich set of layout options. Different and personalized style sheets can be applied to the same XML document for different purposes and different output media, such as display, print, hand-held devices, etc. XFO is completely internationalized – left-to-right, right-to-left and top-to-bottom scripts can occur mixed in the same document – and is equipped with professional page layout facilities such as multiple column sets, rotated text areas, float zones, pagination, hyphenation, aural rendition for speech processors, etc.

In Figure 14.8 we use an alternative style sheet producing a different layout. We also sort the elements by colour and display the price in Euro.

XSL style sheets are XML documents themselves. This allows processors to transform XSL style sheets by means of XSL. In the example shown in Figure 14.8, this technique could easily be used to replace EUR by USD, resulting in a style sheet that displays all prices in US dollars.

```
<?xml version='1.0'?>
<xsl:stylesheet xmlns:xsl="http://www.w3.org/TR/WD-xsl">
        <!-- Defining XSL namespace ID -->
<xsl:template match="/">
        <!-- Selects root element -->
<HTML>          <!-- Here starts the generated output -->
  <BODY>
    <TABLE BORDER="2" CELLPADDING="6">
        <TR>
        <TH>Name</TH>
  <TH>Color</TH>
  <TH>Order-No</TH>
        </TR>
        <xsl:for-each select="PRODUCT/PRODUCT_DETAIL">
          <!-- loops over subnodes -->
        <TR>
  <TD><xsl:value-of select="/PRODUCT/NAME"/></TD>
          <!-- inserts name -->
        <TD><xsl:value-of select="COLOR"/></TD>
          <!-- inserts color -->
        <TD><xsl:value-of select="ORDER-NO"/></TD>
          <!-- inserts order-no -->
        </TR>
        </xsl:for-each>
          <!-- ends loop -->
    </TABLE>
  </BODY>
</HTML>
</xsl:template>
</xsl:stylesheet>
```

Name	Color	Order-No
Walkman	silver	34 97 11-65
Walkman	black	34 97 11-66

Figure 14.7   (Above) A style sheet for the XML example shown in Figure 14.1. The style sheet creates an HTML table from the XML document. (Below) The resulting display is also shown.

```
<?xml version='1.0'?>
<xsl:stylesheet xmlns:xsl="http://www.w3.org/TR/WD-xsl">
          <!-- Defining XSL namespace ID -->
<xsl:template match="/">
          <!-- Selects the root element -->
<HTML>      <!-- Here starts the generated output -->
  <BODY>
  <xsl:for-each select="PRODUCT/PRODUCT_DETAIL"
                                  order-by="COLOR">
          <!-- Loop over subnodes and sort by color -->
      <P>
      <H3>
      <xsl:value-of select="/PRODUCT/NAME"/>
      <xsl:value-of select="COLOR"/>
      </H3>
              <!-- Create header from name and color -->
      <I>Description:</I>
      <xsl:value-of select="/PRODUCT/DESCRIPTION"/>
      <BR/>
      <I>Specification:</I>
      <xsl:value-of select="/PRODUCT/SPECIFICATION"/>
      <BR/>
      <I>Order Number:</I> <xsl:value-of
                                  select="ORDER-NO"/>
      <BR/>
      <xsl:for-each select="PRICE">
          <!-- loops over all PRICE elements -->
          <xsl:if test="@CURRENCY(.='EUR')">
          <!-- but only the ones with currency=EUR -->
          <I>Price:</I> <xsl:value-of select="."/>
          </xsl:if>
      </xsl:for-each>
      </P>
  </xsl:for-each>
  </BODY>
</HTML>
```

Figure 14.8 Alternative style sheet (above) and the resulting output (below). Note that the SORT instruction has inverted the order of the product entries.

```
Walkman black

Description: Elegant Long-Play Walkman in new design
Specification: Mega Bass Dolby B, Auto Reverse
Order Number: 34 97  11-66
Price: 49.90

Walkman silver

Description: Elegant Long-Play Walkman in new design
Specification: Mega Bass Dolby B, Auto Reverse
Order Number: 34 97  11-65
Price: 54.90
```

Figure 14.8 continued

- **XQL** (XML Query Language) (W3C 1999-8) is defined as an extension of the XPath pattern language and defines additional access and retrieval methods for document elements. Instead of applying pattern expressions to a single document, XQL allows patterns to be specified as a query to XML data sources (Software AG 1999-4). The result contains all documents (or elements) that match the query. In addition to the operators contained in XPath, XQL contains special operations for multi-document processing: the JOIN operation allows two documents to be matched and combined by content, while the Dereferencing operation allows a reference (URL) to be replaced by its target document. *(Queries)*

- **XLink** (XML Link Language) (W3C 1998-4) defines the conventions of linking Internet objects to XML documents. XLink extends the linking capabilities considerably compared to HTML. XLink allows bi-directional links and enables the user to initiate a traversal of two linked documents from either direction, or to define one-to-many links. This makes it possible, for example, to direct a link to both a document and to a review of that document. *(Links)*

  XLink can also provide a 'one server' view for distributed data. Linked external elements can be dynamically embedded into XML documents.

- **XCatalog** (XML Catalogue Language). When the location of a web page is changed, the result is either an unresolved link or it is necessary to update all links to that page manually. XLink allows the redirection of links through a separate intermediate link catalogue. When the location of a document changes, only the document entry in this catalogue need be changed. XCatalog defines the language to describe the mapping between XML public identifiers and XML system identifiers. *(Link redirection)*

- **XPointer** (XML Pointer Language) (W3C 1998-5) extends the capabilities of the Universal Resource Locator (URL). By using the XPath pattern language, XPointer can address individual elements within a target XML document. *(Location)*

So it is possible to point to the third paragraph in the second element of the target document. This is useful with read-only or remote documents where it is impossible to insert anchor points.

- **XML Namespaces** (W3C 1999-3) solve the problem of name clashes. Name clashes occur when identical tags are used for different purposes. This can happen between documents, when applications have to process documents from different sources. But it can also happen within a single document when the same tags are used in different document elements with different meanings.

  XML Namespaces solve this problem. Tags and attributes are made unique by prefixing them with a unique namespace identifier. Each namespace identifier relates to a domain-based URL, which, like any URL, is unique. To solve the problem of name clashes within a document, XML Namespaces are organized in global and element-specific partitions.

- **DOM** (Document Object Model) (W3C 1998-2) is the application programming interface (API) for HTML and XML documents. It defines the logical structure of documents and the way a document is accessed and manipulated. With DOM, programmers can create documents, navigate their structure, and retrieve, add, modify or delete elements and content. DOM is designed to be used with any programming language. To provide a language-independent specification, DOM uses the OMG IDL (Object Management Group Interface Description Language) as defined in the CORBA 2.2 specification. Bindings to other programming languages, for example Java, exist.

- **SAX** (Simple API for XML) (SAX 1998) is a standard API for event-based XML parsing. SAX is not a W3C standard but was jointly developed by the members of the XML-DEV mailing list. Because SAX has a small memory footprint (due to event-based parsing) it is a popular de-facto standard for machine-based *reading* of XML documents.

14.5   XML and databases

XML documents are nested structures of tagged elements (Figure 14.9). Concepts such as XPointer, XSL and XQL support access to inner elements of documents. Therefore, efficient storage and retrieval of XML documents requires the DBMS to know about the structure of the documents. The structure of document classes is described in the Document Type Definition. But, like any XML processor, a DBMS must be able to process XML documents that do not have a DTD or where the DTD is not available. It must be possible to add new attributes or elements at any time without disrupting the existing database structure and without breaking existing application code, a requirement that current DBMSs with their static schema definitions can hardly satisfy:

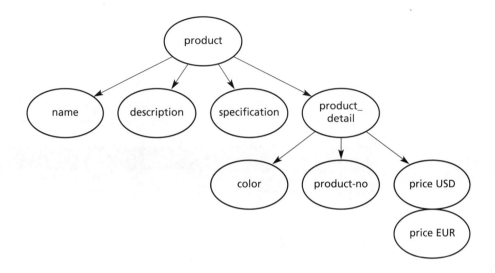

Figure 14.9 Hierarchy of elements in an XML document. All information about the data structure is contained within the document – the document is self-contained.

- *Relational database management systems (RDBMS)*. Relational databases consist of multiple independent tables, each containing 'atomic', unstructured data. Complex structures are not visible in the database but are established in applications by joining tables via keys (Figure 14.10).

  Storing an XML document in a relational database would require the use of a preprocessor that decomposes the document into single elements and stores each element in a separate table. A query against this database could result in many relational retrieval and join operations, degrading performance considerably.

  Locking is another problem. RDBMSs cannot lock at document level: the document is split into tables and is not known as an entity to the DBMS. Most RDBMSs lock at table row level. Updating an XML document would require the RDBMS to set many locks because a complex document is split into many tables, and to reset as many locks at the end of the transaction. This results in further performance degradation.

  Finally, in RDBMSs the table setup is described by SQL schemata. A given class of XML documents with a known DTD can be mapped onto an SQL schema. But, how do we store a document with an unknown DTD in an RDBMS? Do we dynamically create new SQL schemata, or do we store the document simply as a text file?

- *Object-oriented database management systems (OODBMS)*. OODBMSs can store and retrieve persistent data objects and can handle aggregations of objects. An XML document looks in many ways like a hierarchical aggregation of objects. Each element in the document can be mapped to an individual

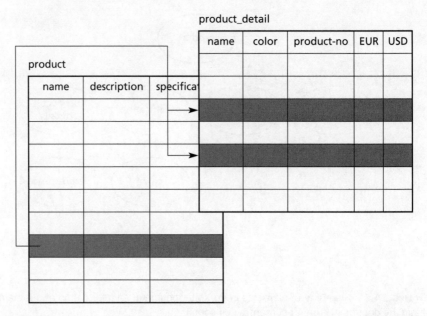

Figure 14.10 The same data structure as in Figure 14.9 mapped on relational tables. The JOIN between the two tables is not defined in the data, but is defined in the application (SQL statement).

object. However, there are differences: in XML the sequence of elements within a document counts; in object-oriented structures sub-objects are not ordered by sequence.

OODBMSs experience similar performance problems as RDBMSs when storing XML documents. Each document is stored in multiple objects: one object for each document element. In addition, sequence relations must be stored in auxiliary fields or objects. During retrieval, many objects must be read and composed into the resulting document.

● *Native XML database management systems (XDBMS)*. With XML gaining momentum we expect to see a whole new generation of database management systems evolve, DBMSs that can store XML documents natively. Such DBMSs would provide high-performance storage, retrieval and access at the document level, while indexing (providing search capabilities) at element level. One of the first native XML DBMSs is Software AG's Tamino Information Server (Software AG 1999-4). Tamino combines a high performance XML engine and an SQL database in one architecture. While providing native storage for both XML documents and relational data, it also allows relational data to be mapped to XML: native relational data can be viewed as an XML document. The system also provides a 'single document' view of data from distributed and heterogeneous data sources. Tamino can process both known and unknown tags in a document by combining traditional indexing methods with advanced text retrieval techniques.

From Java to Bolero   **15**

15.1   Bolero for business

The significance of Java lies not so much in providing a new language, even if it does away with some of the not so nice constructs of C++. The real progress achieved with Java is a consistent programming platform that abstracts from the underlying hardware and operating system. Integrated support for Internet-based, multi-tier computing, concurrent programming, an integrated component model, and an ever-increasing number of standard libraries that cover almost every aspect of computing have attracted enterprises to adopt Java as a strategic platform.

The wide span of applications covered by Java, from embedded systems to enterprise applications, requires the Java language to be very generic. The Java core language is a lean language, with a syntax close to C++.

Portability with Java

With the release of the specification for Java 2 Enterprise Edition, Sun Microsystems has defined a programming framework that supports the information infrastructure within enterprises, such as directory services, message systems, and transaction and resource managers. With Enterprise JavaBeans (EJB) a component model is provided that is both portable and can interoperate with CORBA.

Traditionally, the corporate world had always used business programming languages: COBOL and fourth-generation languages (4GLs), such as Software AG's Natural, dominate the field. These languages and systems are better tuned to the requirements of enterprise computing than general-purpose languages. 4GLs (a term coined by James Martin) in particular provide direct language support for transaction and I/O control.

Business orientation

By providing high-level language constructs for tasks typical in commercial programming, 4GLs have made commercial programmers more productive and programs more robust. For example, a database operation that is handled via a statement can be checked by the compiler for correctness. This is not possible with an equivalent library call. Here the moment of truth comes when the program is executed for the first time.

In this chapter we introduce Software AG's Bolero (Software AG 1999-1). Introduced in 1998, Bolero is best described by the term Java-based 4GL:

The best of both worlds

- Bolero features its own object-oriented language with high-level support for persistent objects, and transaction control. Bolero supports a programming model that is closely oriented at the business model by providing adequate language constructs for entities such as business processes, business tasks and business objects. Bolero adds language features for safety and productivity, such as contracts and design patterns.

A J4GL?

- Bolero supports multiple component models, such as Enterprise JavaBeans, CORBA and DCOM, recognizing the fact that many IT landscapes utilize all of them.

- With the Bolero Component Studio, Bolero has its own IDE (Interactive Development Environment), comprising for example language-specific editors, and a remote debugger.

- Bolero's architecture is extensible. CLIPs (Component Library Integration Packages) allow support to be added for Software AG's Tamino XML Information Server, Software AG's high performance DBMS Adabas C, SAP R/3, and so on.

- Nevertheless, the Bolero compiler produces Java byte code, allowing Bolero classes to be executed on platforms equipped with Java Virtual Machines (Figure 15.1). Bolero is interoperable with Java to a high degree: it can use Java libraries (including J2EE libraries) and vice versa. In addition, the Bolero compiler can optionally produce Java source code.

Enterprise-level applications are supported by the Bolero Application Server, a collection of Java classes that provide the necessary runtime support for constructs such as long transactions, persistency, transaction control, etc. The application server is completely written in Java (except for the DCOM support).

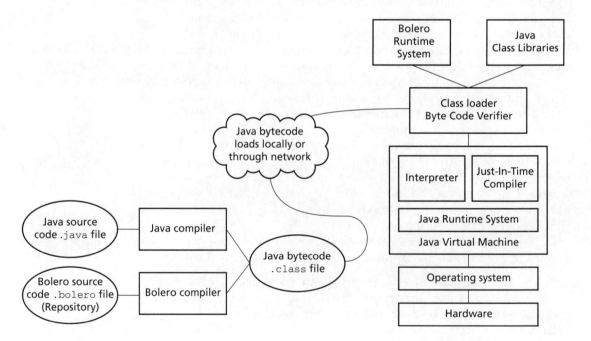

Figure 15.1   The Bolero compiler produces Java byte code (.class files) that can be deployed on Java platforms. The Bolero Application Server (also a Java application) provides the necessary runtime environment.

All Bolero components, such as the compiler, the IDE with editors, GUI-builder and report writer, and the Bolero runtime system, are written in Java.

Because the Bolero compiler produces Java byte code, Bolero applications can in principle run on any platform that is equipped with a Java Virtual Machine (JVM). However, as there are differences in the practical implementations of Java Virtual Machines, Java class libraries and database drivers, Software AG has certified popular enterprise platforms from desktop to mainframe for the deployment of Bolero applications.

Certifications for application deployment exist at the time of writing for: Windows NT, Linux, Sun Solaris, IBM AIX, HP-UX, Compaq TRU64 UNIX (Alpha server) and IBM OS/390. The Bolero development platform is available for Windows NT 4.0 and Linux.

15.2   Where did all the curly brackets go?

When we compare the Bolero language with the Java language, the immediate impression is that Bolero is more verbose and less cryptic (Figure 15.2 (a) and (b)). This results in program sources that are easier to read and to understand.

But when we look closer at the object-oriented principles, we find that both languages have much in common.

In the following we will discuss how Bolero utilizes the advantages of Java, and which programming concepts have been added. We will also discuss the interoperability of Bolero with Java.

Similarities between Bolero and Java

The similarities between Bolero and Java are due to the fact that Bolero produces Java byte code. Bolero is therefore constrained by the functionality of the Java Virtual Machine.

Object-oriented programming

Bolero's object-oriented concepts are closer to Java than to any other object-oriented language:

- **Separation of behaviour and type.** *Interfaces* define the type of an object. *Classes* define the behaviour of an object. Each class definition also acts as an implicit default interface, defining the default type (Budd 1997).
- **Static typing**. Both Bolero and Java feature static typing. Each variable is defined with a fixed type. This allows the compiler to check the compatibility of types during assignments, method calls and operations.

  In contrast, a language like Smalltalk detects incompatible types at runtime.

```
/**
 * Instances of this class represent numbers
 * that print themselves as Roman numerals.
 **/
public class RomanNumeralJava {

    static String[][] r_digits;

    ...

    /**
     * Returns the numeral's value as a sequence of roman
digits.
     **/
    public String toString() {
        String result = "";
        int i = 0;
        int a = i_value;
        while (a != 0) {
            try {
                result = r_digits[i][a % 10] + result;
                a /= 10;
                i++;
            }
            catch (Exception e) {
                return "Out of range: " + i_value;
            }
        }
        return result;
    }

    ...

}
```

Figure 15.2 (a)   Java code for the RomanNumeral class.

- **Polymorphism**. In Java and Bolero variables are polymorphic. A variable defined as being of a certain type can hold values not only of this type but also of subtypes.
- **Reverse polymorphism** (assigning the value of a given type to a variable of a subtype) is possible through explicit typecasting. However, we will find that in almost every case this functionality in Bolero is replaced by the safer type parameters (see below).

```
    class RomanNumeral is public
        doc "Instances of this class represent numbers"
            "that print themselves as Roman numerals."

class field r_digits type Array{Array{String}}

    ...

    instance method toString is public and overrides
        doc "Returns the numeral's value"
            "as a sequence of Roman digits."
        result type String

        implementation
            field i type Integer value 0
            field a type Integer value i_value

            loop
              exit loop when a = 0
              result := r_digits[i, a mod 10] + result
              a := a / 10
              i := i + 1
            end loop

            on exception e
                exit method with result := "Out of range: " +
i_value
            end exception

        end implementation
    end method toString

    ...

end class RomanNumeral
```

Figure 15.2 (b)   The class RomanNumeral in Bolero. Only the code in bold face has to be written by the programmer, the rest is generated by the Bolero Component Studio. (Source: Software AG)

- **Dynamic binding**. Both Bolero and Java feature dynamic method binding. Each variable knows the dynamic type of its content. This implies that a method call like `variable.method()` calls the method associated with the content of `variable`, not the method associated with the type definition of variable. The two may be different, because of polymorphism.

- **Single inheritance from classes**. In Java and Bolero classes can inherit only from a single parent class. This is in contrast to languages such as C++ and Eiffel, which support multiple inheritance.

  From a conceptual view it seems to be desirable to mix the implementations of two parent classes. But in reality, multiple inheritance tends to be tricky. What happens if methods from the parent classes have the same names? Which ones are used? Or, are they merged? In which sequence? (Sakkinen 1988).

- **Multiple inheritance from interfaces**. Instead, Java and Bolero allow multiple inheritance from interfaces. Interfaces do not contain implementations (they are abstract). So, only method signatures and field names are inherited, and clashes between implementations cannot occur. (A signature consists of the method name and the type definitions of the method parameters.)

  There is one exception: an interface can implement constants (`final static` in Java, `final class field` in Bolero). Clashes are possible, but are detected by the compiler when a field with ambiguous content is used.

- **Method overloading**. Both Java and Bolero can overload method names. Overloading means that the same method name can be defined in different classes with different semantics. (This is different from method *overriding* where an inherited method from a parent class is replaced by a new implementation.) Parametric overloading is also possible: the same method name is used for different method implementations but with different parameter sets (different signatures). For example, `print()` and `print(range)` identify different methods. In OO-related literature, method overloading is sometimes called *operator overloading* for historic reasons.

Simplicity and robustness

- **Garbage collection**. Both languages support garbage collection. It is not necessary to destroy objects explicitly when they are no longer needed. Instead the system keeps track of the references to an object. When an object is no longer referenced it becomes a candidate for garbage collection.

  In contrast, languages such as C++ or Delphi do not feature garbage collection but make the programmer responsible for memory management.

- **No pointers**. C++ inherited pointers from C – baggage from the past not required for object-oriented languages and the source of many problems. Java and Bolero abolish explicit pointers altogether.

- **No globals**. C++ allows functions to modify the global environment. This limits the reusability of software because objects have to be context aware. Java and Bolero do not use globals.

Portability

Java was first designed as a language for creating software for consumer electronics. In such an environment different processor architectures may be used, depending on price and availability. Java offers high portability for applications between different hardware platforms and operating systems:

- **Architecture-neutral** interpreted byte code.

  Java and Bolero programs are compiled to Java byte code. This code is platform independent – the Java Virtual Machine executes the code and abstracts from the underlying hardware and the operating system.

- **Standard class libraries** abstract from operating system and enterprise services.

  The Java Virtual Machine is accompanied by a set of Java standard class libraries that abstract from the host operating system, and in the case of J2EE also from existing enterprise IT services, such as middleware products. It is not possible to access operating system functionality from a Java or Bolero program directly (except through a wrapped C program or the Java Native Interface (JNI) classes).

Performance

Java and Bolero are interpreted languages. Java byte code is interpreted by the JVM. Compared to native machine code (executables), byte code modules load faster (because they are smaller) but execute slower (because of interpretation). Several compilation techniques have been developed that convert Java byte code into the target platform's native machine code to enhance performance while maintaining portability, such as JIT compilers HotSpot compilers and High Performance Compilers (see Section 12.2). All these compilers rely only on Java byte code, so Bolero-created Java byte code can also be subject to optimization.

Internet-based computing

The JVM integrates TCP/IP, the Internet Transport Protocol. This enables the JVM to load modules dynamically over the Internet as they are needed.

- **Applets**. Both Java and Bolero can be used to author applets (see Section 13.1).
- **Servlets**. There are many reasons to use servlets instead of applets for business logic (see Section 13.1). Particularly for enterprise computing, Java has moved towards the server, by providing servlets which enable a portable and efficient infrastructure for electronic business applications (see Section 13.5).
- **Remote method invocation (RMI)**. Both Java and Bolero support RMI – calling a method from an object residing on another network node. This allows for distributed object-oriented applications (see Section 12.4).

Section 15.3 discusses Internet-based computing with Bolero in more detail.

Internationalization

- **Unicode**. Both Bolero and Java support Unicode. Unicode is the two-byte fixed width character set maintained by the Unicode consortium, and standardized by ISO with ISO standard 10646. Unicode includes character sets of most of the languages in the world. It also includes special symbols, such as those for mathematics or medical science. Unicode is currently supported by Microsoft Windows NT, Java, Bolero, XML, etc.

- **Locales**. Both languages support the concept of *locales*. A locale represents a cultural region and comprises a country code and a language code.

- **Calendar systems**. Both languages contain support for different calendar systems, which can differ from country to country.

Internationalization is discussed in detail later in this section.

Multi-threading

The multi-threading functionality of Bolero and Java is identical. Both systems can run concurrent threads and synchronize them (see Section 12.5).

The JVM integrates a set of synchronization primitives that are based on the concepts developed in (Hoare 1974). Bolero implements the same synchronization primitives as Java, but integrates them fully into the language as statements. (In Java `wait()`, `notify()` and `notifyAll()` are methods, not statements.)

Differences between Bolero and Java

There are only a few differences between Bolero and Java in the basic concepts of object-oriented programming.

Object-oriented programming

- **Primitive data types**. Java normally operates with primitive data types (`int`, `long`, `double`, ...). In addition it offers class definitions (`Integer`, `Long`, `Double`, ...) that wrap these primitive data types.

  Bolero does not allow explicit primitive data types to be used but always treats data types as first-class citizens. In this regard Bolero takes a similar approach to Smalltalk. The Bolero compiler takes care of mapping these data objects to internal Java primitives.

  Because all data items in Bolero are first-class citizens, Bolero can support a consistent concept for null values (see below). This is important for processing data coming from relational databases where data fields may have the value `null`.

- **Null values**. Java does not have pointers but it is still possible to get a null-pointer exception. This can happen when a variable that has not been properly initialized is used.

  To minimize this risk, Bolero requires the programmer to specify *nullable* fields. A non-nullable field must either have an initial value or be initialized by a class constructor. This is checked by the compiler.

Null values as in SQL

  For nullable fields the null value can be carried through arithmetic and Boolean operations. Bolero uses the same processing rules for null values as SQL.

- **Overloading of infix operators**. This means that infix operators can use the same overloading techniques as methods. Java does this only on a predefined basis: the operator '+' can be used for numbers and strings; other numeric operators can be used for numeric primitives independent of the type (`int`, `double`, ...).

  Bolero also allows infix operators to be used for methods defined by the user. This can lead to more consistency in program code: why should we write a + b when the operands are integers, but a.add(b) when the operands are of type `BigDecimal`?

- **Instance fields in interfaces**. While Java only allows for the definition of class fields (`static`) in interfaces, Bolero also allows the definition of instance fields. A Bolero interface definition is therefore a more powerful concept than a Java interface, and is closer to the concept of abstract data types (ADTs) than to a mere interface. Because Bolero supports multiple inheritance for interfaces, this feature allows multiple inheritance for instance fields, too.

- **Visibility**. Java and Bolero know the modifiers shown in Table 15.1 to control visibility.

- **Override protection**. In Bolero and Java classes that are specified as `final` cannot be extended and methods that are specified as `final` cannot be overridden.

  In addition, Bolero requires method overriding to be made explicit by using the keyword `override` to prevent accidental overriding.

- **Field access control**. In Java, fields can be protected from modification by specifying them with the keyword `final`.

  Bolero follows a different concept: references to objects (fields, return values and parameters) can be marked as `non-modifiable`, `modifiable` or `unchecked`.

  - The `non-modifiable` modifier has a similar effect to Java's `final` – the field may not be modified. This is checked by the compiler.   *Modifiable vs. non-modifiable*

  - The `modifiable` keyword marks a field whose content is *intended* to be modified. If a method parameter is defined as `modifiable`, the compiler rejects any non-modifiable value for that parameter in a method call.

  - The `unchecked` modifier signals to the compiler that no control of access rights is required.

Table 15.1

Java	Bolero	Visibility
public	public	All packages
private	private	Current class definition
package	{no modifier}	Current package
{not supported}	protected	Current package and all derived subclasses

- **Implicit parameters**. Both Java and Bolero methods use implicit parameters that are normally not visible to the programmer. Such parameters transport necessary references through a method call. One example is the value `this`, the reference to the current object. Other implicit parameters are generated when class features (static fields or methods) are used, such as `System.out`. In this case the client object must be provided with a reference to the class object (e.g. `System`), and this is done with an implicit parameter.

  In Bolero implicit parameters can be made visible to control the access rights of these parameters – they can be marked, too, as `non-modifiable`, as `modifiable`, or as `unchecked`.

Simplicity and robustness

- **Syntax**. The Java syntax is close to the C syntax. This makes it easy for C programmers to learn the language but poses a problem in the commercial world. Bolero therefore features a more verbose and readable syntax.

  Along with the curly brackets, the semicolons have also vanished. The Bolero syntax does not need an explicit end token for statements like the semicolon in Java. Block structures in programs are expressed not by curly brackets but through an opening keyword and a closing keyword that clearly indicate what kind of structure is opened and closed.

  Some control structures and operators are named differently, for instance the '%' operator in Java is called `mod` in Bolero, because it could be mistaken for a percentage operation. The '==' operator in Java is called `isSameInstance()` in Bolero, the `equals()` method known from Java is always expressed as '=' in Bolero. Assignments are expressed with ':=' as known from Pascal. There are more differences but the idea should be clear: Bolero is syntactically closer to commercial programming.

- **Generic types**. A concept developed in the context of functional programming – generic types – has been adopted in some object-oriented languages, such as Eiffel (Meyer 1997) and Bolero. Similar techniques are found with templates in C++. This feature as yet has no equivalent in Java (except for arrays), but is among the top requests in the wish list of Java programmers (Sun 1999). James Gosling has indicated that parameterized types will be supported in future Java versions.

  Genericity means that some aspects of a software unit are not specified when the software unit is defined. Instead the missing specification is supplied when the software unit is used (referred to), depending on the context in which the unit is used.

  A typical example is the class `List` (see below), a collection class. Like all collection classes, `List` implements methods to access elements, such as `add(Element)` or `removeElementAt(Index)`. All these methods are neutral to the type of the element because they only deal with the membership issue.

In many object-oriented languages, including Java, collection classes are implemented in such a way that elements are of the most general type (Object). This is unfortunate because it prevents the compiler type-checking. First, we can add anything to the list, for instance add a Customer object to a list of Product objects, without getting a compiler error. Secondly, if we take something from the list, the static result type of the get method would be Object. If we want to assign this to a field of type Product, we must explicitly *cast* the element to type Product. If the list, however, contains a Customer object, we will get an exception at runtime.

A safer construction is to implement a special class ProductList where all elements have the static type Product. But we would have to implement a new list class for each element type we are going to use in lists, such as CustomerList, SupplierList, a task we would prefer not to do manually in the age of computing.

With generic types (or *parameterized types* as they are called in Bolero),   *Wishes fulfilled* however, we can define a generic List class, where the parameter type of the add() method and the result type of the get() method are not defined as a fixed type but as a *type variable*, for example, as ElementType (Figures 15.3 and 15.4). When we use the List class for an actual implementation, we simply specify a concrete type like Product for ElementType. The compiler can now check that a parameter supplied with the add() method is in fact of type Product (or a subtype). Neither do we need to cast the result of the get() method, because the result of get is already of type Product.

```
class List is public

   method add
      type parameter ElementType extends Object
      parameter Element type ElementType
      ....
   end method add

   method get
      type parameter ElementType extends Object
      parameter Index type Integer
      result type ElementType
      ....
   end method get
   ....

end class List
```

Figure 15.3 Definition of a class with with methods using a generic type as parameter and as a result. Note that a generic type definition can be constrained by making it a subtype of an existing type (here the most general type Object).

```
instance field custList type List{Customer}
instance field myCust type Customer

custList := List{Customer}()
myCust := Customer()
...
custList.add(myCust)
...
myCust := custList.get(1)
```

Figure 15.4   Using a class with generic types in field declaration and operation. And yes, this is where the curly brackets went: they are used to demarcate type parameters.

Parameterized types are of course not restricted to collection classes but can be used in Bolero as a general concept.

Contracts

● **Programming by contract.** The concept of programming by contract is as old as computing. The concept of checking a program routine by using assertions was first postulated by Alan Turing in 1950 (Hoare 1981). However, only a few programming languages have provided constructs for assertions. C++ supports a limited form of assertions for debugging. In Java assertions are not available, probably because Java was not initially designed for large projects. Programming by contract in the present form was pioneered by Eiffel, and was adopted by Bolero. Contracts are – like generic types – at the top of the wish list (Sun 1999) of programmers participating in the Java Community Process.

The basic idea of programming by contract is to establish a client–supplier contract between the object (as the supplier) and the object's user (as the client). Methods or fields of the object are equipped with pre-conditions and post-conditions.

   ● **Pre-conditions** apply before a method is called or before a field is modified. Pre-conditions can check the parameters of methods or the new value for a field, and can check the state of the object before a method is started or an assignment is made.

   ● **Post-conditions** apply when a method returns, or when a field value is retrieved. Post-conditions can describe the state of an object after method execution and can make assertions about the return value.

A client that wants to use the services of an object must therefore adhere to the criteria laid down in the pre-conditions. On the other hand, it can be sure that it will not obtain return values that do not satisfy the post-conditions.

In the following example, the method getVAT() computes the value added tax for a product price, depending on the tax rate. The pre-condition rejects any negative tax rate. (To be open to further developments in tax rates we deliberately do not check for a maximum rate.) The post-condition rejects any negative return value.

```
class Product
   is public and is persistence capable with population

instance field Name type String is public

instance field Price type BigDecimal is public
   contract
      precondition newValue >= 0
      postcondition result >= 0
   end contract
value 0

instance method getVAT is public
   parameter Rate type Decimal
   result type BigDecimal
   throws VatError, VatRateError, PriceError
   contract
      precondition Rate >= 0 else throw VatRateError()
      precondition Price >= 0 else throw PriceError()
      postcondition result >= 0 else throw VatError()
   end contract

   implementation
      result := Price*Rate/100
   end implementation

end method getVAT
end class Product
```

As we can see, contracts can be applied directly to fields. Pre-conditions are executed as the first action when a value is assigned to a field, while post-conditions are executed as the last action when the value of a field is retrieved.

Thus, it is possible to safeguard read and write accesses to an object's state by using contracts. Readers versed in relational database systems might find similarities to SQL integrity constraints.

In the above example, the post-conditions for Price and getVAT() seem to be unnecessary: if the rate is not negative and the price is not negative, then the resulting tax is certainly not negative, true? But can we be sure that the price is not negative? The class Product is persistence-capable – its fields may be stored in a database (see Section 15.6). Another (legacy) application that does not use integrity constraints may access the same database and write an (illegal) negative value into the Price field!

In some cases it might be sufficient to use contracts only in the test phase of an application. Bolero therefore provides a compiler option to switch off contracts.

Multiple component model technology

Bolero supports multiple component models. In an enterprise scenario there are usually several component models working in cooperation. While DCOM is almost omnipresent on desktops, CORBA has a strong position in the middleware area. Enterprise JavaBeans is the preferred component model of Java 2 Enterprise Edition.

We have already discussed the various component models in the context of Java in Section 12.7. Because Bolero incorporates Java, all these component models are supported by Bolero too. Bolero, however, provides support for these component models transparently and on a higher level. Bolero classes can be easily deployed in different component models, and external components can be imported into the Bolero Component Studio and can then be handled like Bolero classes.

We discuss Bolero's component support in detail in Section 15.4.

Database support

Java supports access to relational databases via the JDBC interface. Transaction control is achieved through native SQL, or, in the context of J2EE, via the Java Transaction API (JTA) (see Section 12.3).

Bolero supports persistent data on a more abstract level:

- **Persistent objects**. In Bolero each class can be defined as persistence-capable. Such a class can have both persistent and non-persistent (transient) instances. Persistent objects live beyond the boundaries of a Bolero session until they are explicitly deleted (see Section 15.6).

- **Object–relational mapping**. Because persistent objects are stored in relational databases their fields must be mapped on columns in database tables. This is done through Bolero's object–relational mapping, which can also handle object aggregations (see Section 15.6).

- **Relational–object mapping**. Vice versa, Bolero allows relational schemata to be imported from relational databases and class definitions to be generated from these schemata (see Section 15.6).

- **Object Query Language**. Bolero implements a subset of the Object Query Language (OQL), an SQL-style query language that conforms closely to the ODMG (Object Data Management Group) query language specification for object-oriented database systems. In contrast to the SQL support in Java, where an SQL expression is just a string, OQL is an integral part of the Bolero programming language – the compiler can check for syntactic and semantic correctness of OQL expressions (see Section 15.6).

- **Transaction control objects**. Bolero separates transaction logic from persistency. Transaction-control classes and persistence-capable classes are mutually exclusive, thus ensuring the separation of business logic and transaction control.

  The start and end of a transaction-control method also demarcates the start and end of a database transaction. Within the course of a transaction-control method, one or more persistent objects can be modified.

  We will discuss transaction-control classes in more detail in Section 15.7.

Advanced concepts

- **Long transactions**. The concept of database (ACID) transactions is not sufficient for modelling electronic business processes. An electronic business process can involve many database transactions and can run over a long time. This requires features such as partial and complete rollback, semantic undo and forward recovery.

  Bolero provides the concept of *long transactions*. A long transaction consists of several business tasks – implemented as transaction-control objects. Each business task represents one step in a long transaction and can command a single database transaction where one or several business objects may be involved.

  - Long transactions are persistent and can recover from failure, continuing a business process at the point of interruption.

  - Long transactions allow single steps or the whole transaction to be undone by executing semantic *undo tasks*.

  - Long transactions can run in a distributed environment and several long transactions can cooperate in one application.

  Long transactions, transaction control objects and persistent objects are the three pillars of application design in Bolero. They closely match the business model consisting of business processes, business tasks and business objects.

  Long transactions, loosely related to the command objects found in IBM's San Francisco framework and in (Jacobson 1992), thus provide a blueprint for implementing complex business processes.

  We will discuss long transactions in detail in Section 15.9.

- **Patterns** provide a method of knowledge transfer. A solution found in one problem domain can be transferred (cloned) to another problem domain. First developed for urban planning (Alexander et al 1977), patterns were later introduced into software development (Gamma et al 1994), a fact that proved the very concept of patterns (transfer of knowledge).

  In Bolero, patterns are implemented in such a way that a pattern can be executed before and after the transfer process, allowing rapid application development (RAD). Patterns are discussed in detail in Section 16.7.

Foundation classes

Because Bolero incorporates Java, it contains all foundation classes found in Java (see Section 12.1).

It adds packages with business-specific foundation classes:

Business arithmetic

`Decimal`, `BigDecimal` and `BigInteger` classes provide more accurate results than floating point numbers do.   *Precise arithmetic*

Since COBOL was introduced (even since programming in assembler) business arithmetic has been done in decimal number format. For good reasons: in contrast to floating point number format, decimal number format can represent decimal numbers accurately.

The floating point format is based on the hexadecimal number system. Storing a decimal number such as 48.10 as a floating point number results in an infinite sequence of hexadecimal digits: 0x33.19999999... Of course, no computer can store an infinite sequence, so the sequence is truncated, let us assume to 0x33.1999. Converting the value back to decimal format results in 48.09999084472656. A small error, but an error, nevertheless.

Another problem with floating point arithmetic is platform dependency. Usually, floating point arithmetic is executed by special-purpose hardware: floating point processors are either external or integrated with the CPU. These floating point processors can differ slightly from platform to platform.

Java defines the storage format for floating point numbers (IEEE 754). But the storage format does not define the accuracy of operations, so results of floating point operations – especially when truncations like the above occur – may differ from platform to platform.

In order to support accurate number formats for business arithmetic, Bolero implements the following data types:

- **Integer**. This class is equivalent to the Java `Integer` class and wraps the Java primitive data type `int`. An object of the `Integer` class represents a 32-bit signed two's complement `integer` in a range from –2,147,483,648 to 2,147,483,647 inclusive.

- **BigInteger**. This class defines an arbitrary-precision signed two's complement integer. `BigIntegers` support all of Java's integer operators, and all relevant methods from `java.lang.Math`. In addition, `BigIntegers` implement modular arithmetic, greatest common divisor (GCD) calculation, primality testing, prime generation, single-bit manipulation, etc.

- **Decimal**. A `Decimal` number object comprises an `Integer` for the significant digits of the value, and an integer scaling factor in the range 0..17 specifying the number of decimal digits after the decimal point. The total number of significant digits is restricted to 18.

- **BigDecimal**. A `BigDecimal` number object consists of a `BigInteger` for the significant digits of the value, and a non-negative integer scaling factor. `BigDecimals` provide operations for basic arithmetic, scale manipulation, comparison, format conversion and hashing. The `BigDecimal` class provides the user with eight different rounding options for operations where potentially precision may be lost (`divide` and `setScale`).

Amounts

The classes `Amount` and `BigAmount` implement a unit-related value system. These classes can be extended by the programmer to implement, for example, a multi-currency monetary class, or to implement dimensions that can be represented both in the metric and in the imperial system, etc.

● **Unit**. Units relate the numeric value of an amount to a system of measurement, for example metric or imperial systems or currency systems. Each Unit consists of a unique string ID, a name and an integer scale (number of decimal places).

● **Amount**. The Amount class comprises a Decimal and a Unit. In order to convert amounts from one unit to another, it is possible to register converters with the class Unit:

```
field fahrenheit type Unit
   value Unit("fahrenheit","°F",1)
field celsius type Unit
   value Unit("celsius","°C")
field temperature type Amount
   value Amount(25.5, celsius)
...
Unit.registerConversion("celsius","fahrenheit",
                    FactorConverter(1.8,32))
...
System.out.println(temperature.convert(fahrenheit))
```

The class FactorConverter shown here is a standard implementation of the UnitConverter interface. It automatically provides an inverse conversion. The UnitConverter interface allows more general conversions to be implemented, for example logarithmic or exponential conversions.

Conversions are executed automatically when arithmetic operations combine amounts of different units. Both the Unit and the Amount class are persistence-capable. This allows Amount fields to be used in persistent objects, too.

Automatic unit conversion

Using plain numbers instead of proper amounts with a specified unit of measurement can prove disastrous. One of the most expensive cases to date is that of NASA's Mars Climate Orbiter (MCO):

> *The MCO Mission objective was to orbit Mars as the first interplanetary weather satellite and provide a communications relay for the MPL which is due to reach Mars in December 1999. The MCO was launched on December 11, 1998, and was lost sometime following the spacecraft's entry into Mars occultation during the Mars Orbit Insertion (MOI) maneuver. The spacecraft's carrier signal was last seen at approximately 09:04:52UTC on Thursday, September 23, 1999.*
>
> *The MCO MIB (Mars Climate Orbiter Mishap Investigation Board) has determined that the root cause for the loss of the MCO spacecraft was the failure to use metric units in the coding of a ground software file, 'Small Forces,' used in trajectory models. Specifically, thruster performance data in English units instead of metric units was used in the software application code titled SM_FORCES (small forces). ...* (NASA 1999)

● **BigAmount**. The BigAmount class has similar functionality to the Amount class, except that BigAmount values are BigDecimals.

Arrays

Compared to Java arrays, Bolero allows true multi-dimensional arrays. It also implements an `Iterator` method.

A loop across array elements in Java looks like:

```
for (int i = 0; i < arr.length; i++)
    sum += arr(i);
```

An equivalent Bolero expression looks like:

```
for v in arr do
    sum := sum + v
end for
```

The `Iterator` construct is a general construct in Bolero which is also found in the `Range` type and the collection types discussed below, or in result sets of OQL queries. It provides a consistent way to iterate across ranges and sets of data objects.

Collection classes

The Bolero standard libraries define a set a predefined collection classes. Because Bolero supports parameterized type definition, the implementation of collection classes in Bolero is type safe.

All collection classes are extensions of the `AbstractCollection` class. Programmers can implement their own specific collection classes by extending the `AbstractCollection` class. All collection classes implement an `Iterator` that allows iteration over the elements of a collection.

The following concrete collection class implementations are available in the Bolero collection class library:

- **Lists**

  - **ArrayList**. A list that is internally implemented as an `Array`. This is similar to the Java `Vector` class, but is not thread synchronized for better performance.

  - **LinkedList**. The classical double-linked list. `LinkedList` is not thread synchronized.

  - **PersistentList**. Recursive data structures like `LinkedLists` are difficult to map onto relational data structures. Therefore a special `PersistentList` class has been made available.

- **Maps**

  - **HashMap**. Maps keys to values by using a hash method defined by the key object class. `HashMap` is similar to the Java `HashTable` class but is not synchronized and can contain the `null` value as a key value. `HashMap` provides constant access time to map elements.

– **SortedMap**. Key values in this map are kept in ascending sorted order. This sequence is reflected when iterating across a sorted map. It implies that key object classes must implement the `Comparable` interface.

– **TreeMap**. A sorted map that is organized internally as a tree. The algorithm used guarantees a log(n) access time to map elements.

● **Sets**

Sets provide similar functionality to maps but do not allow duplicate elements. (Two elements are considered to be duplicate when they satisfy the `equals()` method.) The following classes are available:

– **HashSet**. See HashMap.

– **SortedSet**. See SortedMap.

– **TreeSet**. See TreeMap.

Range

The `Range` interface defines a minimum value and a maximum value of a parameterized type. It defines a type-dependent `Iterator` method. A concrete implementation of the `Range` interface is the `IntegerRange` class:

```
Field iRange type IntegerRange value 1..10
    ...
For i type Integer In iRange Do
    System.out.println(i)
End For
```

Internationalization

In a global marketplace the internationalization of electronic business   *Think global...*
applications is an important issue. Internationalization can affect many areas in the development of an electronic business application, from user interface to business logic.

An application can be called internationalized when:

● It can run worldwide (by adding the necessary localized data).

● Texts presented to the end user are not hard-coded into the application but are stored as external resources.

● Other culture-dependent data, such as calendars, currency amounts, date and time appear in formats that conform to the end user's region and language.

● Support for new languages does not require recompilation.

In addition, further localization may be necessary:

● Support for local business rules (for example, different tax laws).

● Local versions of culturally sensitive pictorial and sound material.

- Layout and graphic design elements depending on the cultural context.
- Different navigation methods depending on the cultural context.

From the technical viewpoint the following areas are affected:

... act local

- **Messages**, **Labels**, **Help texts**. The text should be displayed in the user language. Variable data inserted into running text should appear in the right position. Plurals should be treated correctly.
- Special text **fonts** may be necessary (for example, for Greek or Russian).
- **Writing direction** (left-to-right, right-to-left, top-to-bottom) and **cursor movement** (for example, for Hebrew and Arabic, Chinese or Thai).
- **Text length** of messages. The same message displays in different width depending on the language. Page layout has to consider this. Fortunately, neither Java nor Bolero know `String` objects of fixed length, solving the all too familiar 'String too long' problem in internationalized applications.
- **Case conversion**. Obviously, which characters are fit for upper/lower case conversion depends on a language's alphabet.
- **Collation sequence**. Depending on the alphabet of a language, the collation sequence for the same binary sequence may be different for different languages. Language-specific rules are, for example, the treatment of umlauts ä, ü, ö in German, the accents in French or the sorting of Chinese ideographs according to pronunciation. String collation sequences determine how string comparisons and the sorting of strings are processed.
- **Phonetic comparison**. Some applications use phonetic comparison algorithms to find an item in a database even if the search key is spelt differently but pronounced in the same way. These algorithms are language dependent.
- **Honorifics** and **personal titles** are country dependent.
- **Postal address**. The format of postal addresses differs from country to country.
- **Rounding** of numeric values. Different countries have different rounding conventions.
- **Date arithmetic** (calendar). Calendar systems include the base calendar (Gregorian, Hebrew, Islamic, Buddhist, Japanese), day encoding, week start, workdays, public holidays, daylight savings switch-over.
- Formatting of **date** and **time**.
- Formatting of **amounts** (currency, measurements, etc.).
- Formatting of **numbers** and **percentage values** (the decimal point or thousand separator can differ).
- Formatting of **phone numbers**.
- **Number spell-out** in words.
- **Colour usage**. Colours mean different things in different cultures.
- **Symbols**, **icons**, **graphics**, **images**, **sound**. It may be necessary to use different versions in different cultural contexts.

- **Position** of GUI elements such as buttons, scrollbars and the **page layout**. For instance, if the writing direction is left-to-write, users scroll mostly vertically. If the writing direction is top-to-bottom, scrolling horizontally would be the preferred action to navigate in a text.

- **Shortcuts**. Key shortcuts (CTRL-key) can be language dependent.

- **Accelerators** (ALT-key sequences) can be language dependent.

- **Navigation** (a site may include sections that are specific to certain regions).

- **Business rules** (tax rates, different laws, etc.).

- **Character encoding**. The need for using different character encoding is greatly reduced with Unicode, but when reading from and writing to legacy files, it may be necessary to handle different character encoding. `java.io.InputStreamReader` and `java.io.OutputStreamWriter` are classes that allow different character encoding to be specified.

Bolero builds on the internationalization support found in Java (Unicode, locales, calendars). In addition, Bolero provides classes, like the above mentioned `Amount` class, or the `LocalString` class, to support a more productive environment when writing internationalized applications:

- **Unicode** is the standard character set. Unicode is the two-byte fixed width character set maintained by the Unicode consortium. It is standardized by ISO with ISO standard 10646 and includes most of the languages worldwide.

- A **locale** comprises a language and a country code. These two elements together represent a cultural region. For example, language `fr` (French) and country `CA` (Canada) represents the francophone part of Canada. Two-letter strings for language and country as defined by ISO 3166 are valid. An optional user-defined third parameter allows further differentiation.

  Each Bolero application runs under a separate default locale. The scope of the default locale is application-wide – concurrent threads run under the same default locale. However, it is possible to switch locales dynamically. This allows for collaborative applications where users come from different regions.

- A **resource bundle** is a file that maps keys to values: for example, logical names for labels and the text equivalents that are actually to be displayed. A separate resource bundle can be provided for each locale.

- The `DateTime` class is used to handle dates, times and timestamps with nanosecond precision. The class can perform date and time arithmetic and comparisons, and can convert date and time values to strings (and vice versa) depending on the current locale. To interpret a `DateTime` value according to the locale-specific rules, a concrete calendar must be used.

- The `Calendar` class is an abstract class for converting between a `DateTime` object and a set of `Integer` fields such as YEAR, MONTH, DAY, HOUR, etc. A concrete `Calendar` is used to interpret a `DateTime` value and implements a specific calendar system.

For example:

```
Calendar.getCalendar(Locale("fr","CA"))
```

constructs a calendar for the French-speaking part of Canada.

It is possible to create specific business calendars by extending existing calendars.

- The class **LocalString** is a subtype of the String class. LocalString objects contain a value and a locale. For example:

```
field ls type LocalString
    value LocalString ("It's a nice day.", Locale.US)
```

sets both the value and the locale of the new string.

Another way is to create a LocalString by specifying a key that points into a resource bundle:

```
field ls type LocalString
    value LocalString.lookup("NICEDAY")
```

The key is automatically looked up in the resource bundle. When the default locale changes, the value of the LocalString does, too, because a different resource is used.

The class LocalString also handles locale-dependent collations for comparisons and sorting.

```
LocalString.getCollationMode(Locale lc)
```

LocalString can format messages, such as

```
Please call {0} until {1} o'clock.
```

where the position and sequence of the parameters can depend on the locale.

When objects are inserted in or appended to a LocalString, the objects are formatted according to the rules of the locale of the LocalString for which the inserting or appending method was invoked.

- The **Amount** class (see above) allows programmers to store an amount in a given measurement unit and retrieve it later in another measurement unit. For example, is it possible to convert between the metric and imperial systems, or to use the Amount class for currency conversions.

- The Java class **NumberFormat** in the java.text class library can format numbers and currencies depending on the locale. For example, NumberFormat may return a number as:

  - 71 323,50 (France)

  - 71.323,50 (Germany)

  - 71,323.50 (Australia).

Depending on the scale and scope of a project, different internationalization strategies can be adopted. Applications can be localized on all levels, whether these are simply texts, complete GUIs or even user interaction, navigation and business logic. By using the programming concepts provided with Java or Bolero, programmers can keep the program code simple, allowing easier development and maintenance.

Interoperability between Java and Bolero

Java and Bolero classes can be used within the same applications.

- **Importing Java classes and packages**. Java classes can be imported into the Bolero Component Studio and can be viewed like Bolero classes – all features are visible but not the source code. The Java source code is not required for the import process – only the Java byte code is required.

- **Accessing Java features from Bolero**. Bolero objects can call methods from Java classes. This allows all Java class libraries to be used in Bolero, too. It is not required to import a Java class to call its methods. Remote method invocation (RMI) is also possible.

    Bolero objects can access instance or class fields defined in Java classes.

- **Bolero class adapters**. Adapters allow predefined Java (and Bolero) classes to be accessed, fields, methods and parameters to be renamed and the type of parameters (within limits) or the visibility of features to be changed. It is also possible to add new methods.

- **Calling Bolero methods from Java**. Java objects can call methods from Bolero classes.

    Because all Bolero fields are mapped internally to `private` Java fields, Bolero fields cannot be accessed directly by a Java object. Instead `get-` and `set-` methods must be used by Java programmers to access public Bolero fields. Bolero generates these methods automatically.

- **Inheriting from Java classes and interfaces**. Bolero can extend Java classes and implement Java interfaces.

- **Inheriting from Bolero classes and interfaces**. Java classes can extend Bolero classes and implement Bolero interfaces.

- **Visual JavaBeans** can be imported into the Bolero GUI-builder as new visual components.

- **JavaBeans** can be imported into the Bolero Component Studio.
    Bolero can export classes as JavaBeans.

- **Enterprise JavaBeans (EJB)** can be imported into the Bolero Component Studio.
    Bolero can export classes as Enterprise JavaBeans.

- **Source-to-source conversion**. Because Bolero is a proprietary technology it offers users a migration path to mainstream technology. Bolero does so by supporting the conversion of Bolero classes into Java source code.

- **Two-language debugging**. The Bolero debugger can step through both Bolero and Java source code.

15.3   Bolero and the web

Applets

Bolero applets can be created with the Bolero GUI-builder, saving a GUI as an applet. The applet can then be called in the usual way from any HTML page:

```
<APPLET   CODE="BoleroApplet.class" WIDTH="200" HEIGHT="150"
          CODEBASE="classes/"
          ARCHIVE="my.jar">
...
</APPLET>
```

or, when using the Java plug-in:

```
<EMBED code="BoleroApplet.class"
        codebase="classes/"
        width="200"
        height="150"
        pluginspage=
    "http://java.sun.com/products/plugin/1.2/plugin-install.html"
        type="application/x-java-applet;version=1.2"
        archive="my.jar">
...
<NOEMBED>
```

This is for Netscape Communicator. Here is the 'Redmond' version for Microsoft Internet Explorer:

```
<OBJECT
   classid="clsid:8AD9C840-044E-11D1-B3E9-00805F499D93"
   width="200"
   height="150"
   codebase="http://java.sun.com/products/plugin/1.2/
             jinstall-12-win32.cab#Version=1,2,0,0">
<PARAM NAME="code" VALUE="BoleroApplet.class">
<PARAM NAME="codebase" VALUE="classes/">
<PARAM NAME="type" VALUE="application/x-java-applet;version=1.2">
<PARAM NAME="archive" VALUE="my.jar">
...
</OBJECT>
```

The main class of the applet is specified under the CODE attribute. On the client side the Java class loader loads classes from the specified archive file. If no such file is specified or if a class is not found in the specified archive, the class loader loads classes from the location specified with CODEBASE.

Which method is preferable depends on the environment. Loading class by class may shorten the initialization time in an Internet environment, because the applet can start running as soon as the first class is loaded.

Archive files or single class loading?

However, if the initialization of an applet requires the majority of classes to be present it is better to use archive files. These can be downloaded in one operation. Archive files are compressed, too, so download of a whole archive is faster then a class-by-class download.

Additional compression is possible with a tool provided by IBM's Alphaworks: JAX can shrink `jar`-files substantially, by applying advanced techniques like constant pooling and name obfuscation. However, the latter can cause problems with debugging: in the case of an error only the obfuscated (and shorter) method name appears on the Java console.

JAX compression

Servlets, Bolero style

While the attraction of applet technology has faded a bit for electronic business applications, Java server technology delivers (see also Chapter 13).

Java servlets are small applications that run on the server. They are used to generate dynamic HTML pages. Sun's Java Server Pages (JSP) technology is based on Java servlets.

While Bolero implements Java servlet technology, it goes its own way in terms of server pages. In Bolero the creation of a server page starts with the design of an HTML prototype. This can be done with a visual editor such as Microsoft FrontPage, NetObjects Fusion or Macromedia Dreamweaver. HTML-diehards use Notepad.

Creating servlets visually

Using the *Build Servlet* function in the Bolero Component Studio, an HTML page is converted into two Bolero classes:

Separating presentation from business logic

- A servlet class, implementing the Java Servlet API. This class is to contain the program logic, for instance extracting data from a relational database, or other business logic.

- A layout class, containing Bolero WebAPI (see below) method calls to generate a dynamic HTML page, which corresponds to the original HTML page.

What remains for the programmer to do is to add business logic to the servlet class. If business rules change at a later time, changes are applied here while the layout class stays unchanged.

Vice versa, layout changes can be made with a visual HTML editor. The *Build Servlet* function is then applied again. Now, only the layout class is regenerated and the servlet class (containing business logic) is left untouched.

The generation of servlet and layout classes from the HTML prototype pages, and vice versa, the generation of HTML by the layout class, utilise the methods of the Bolero WebAPI.

WebAPI

The Bolero WebAPI implements several classes that facilitate the construction of HTML pages. A subset of HTML 4.0 and above is supported, but extensions (support for additional tags) can be added by the programmer.

Toolbox

The WebAPI also implements a `BServletToolbox` class. This class enables programmers to load existing HTML pages dynamically, to locate elements within a page, and to add more elements. For example, database records could be added as rows to a table.

Session pool

Establishing a connection to a database is a task that incurs some overhead. Repeatedly connecting and disconnecting to a database for each server request incurs much overhead for the server.

Bolero therefore offers a utility class `BSessionPool`, a pool for database connections. This class holds a number of open database connections. Servlet instances can take open connections from the pool, use them for database access, and return them to the pool before they finish the client's request. `BSessionPool` can hold connections for several databases and database users. It scales automatically – if the pool of connections is exhausted `BSessionPool` will automatically open new connections. So, frequent connection and disconnection to databases is avoided and performance is improved.

Runtime scenario

A servlet is invoked by the Java Servlet container (like the Apache Jserv Servlet Engine), when a client requests a URL that identifies the servlet:

Figure 15.5 A web page designed using a visual HTML editor (Microsoft FrontPage).

1. The servlet container creates a new instance of the Bolero servlet class.
2. The client's request (including the query string) is passed to the servlet object as a parameter via the doGet or doPost method.
3. The servlet object creates a new instance of the Bolero layout class and passes control to this new instance via the method generateDocument.
4. The generated document is then passed from the layout object to the client via the servlet object and the servlet container.

An example servlet

First we design a web page using a visual HTML editor (here Microsoft's FrontPage) (Figure 15.5).

Code examples

The page contains a GIF image, nested tables and form elements for input. The resulting HTML code looks like this:

```html
<html>
<head>
  <meta http-equiv="Content-Type"
    content="text/html; charset=iso-8859-1">
  <meta name="GENERATOR" content="Microsoft FrontPage Express 2.0">
  <title>Invitation</title>
</head>

<body bgcolor="#FFFFFF">
  <h1>
  <font color="#008000">Welcome</font>
  <font color="#FF0000">to</font>
  <font color="#808000">the</font>
  <font color="#FF00FF">party</font>
  <font color="#008080">!</font>
  </h1>
  <table border="1" cellspacing="0" width="100%"
    bordercolor="#C0C0C0">
   <tr>
    <td>
        <img
            src="Pierot.gif"
            alt="party" align="baseline" width="320" height="226">
    </td>
    <td valign="top" bgcolor="#F8B889">
        <table border="0" id="guests">
            <tr>
                <td><strong>Already attending:</strong></td>
            </tr>
        </table>
```

```
            </td>
        </tr>
        <tr>
            <td bgcolor="#008080">
                <font color="#FFFFFF">
                    <strong>To reserve your ticket to the </strong></font>
                <font color="#FFFFFF" size="5">
                    <strong>big</strong></font>
                <font color="#FFFFFF"><strong>
                    party please register here!</strong></font>
                <font color="#008080">
                    <strong>!</strong></font><p>
                <font color="#000000" face="Times New Roman">
                    <strong><tt>Your Name</tt></strong></font>
                <input type="text" size="50" maxlength="50" name="T1">
                </p>
                <p>
                <font color="#000000" face="Times New Roman">
                    <strong><tt>How many persons </tt></strong></font>
                <font color="#FFFFFF">
                    <select name="D1" size="1">
                        <option>1</option>
                        <option selected>2</option>
                        <option>3</option>
                        <option>a lot</option>
                    </select>
                <input type="submit" name="B1" value="Submit"></font>
                </p>
            </td>
            <td bgcolor="#800000">
                <font color="#FFFFFF">
                    ...and a mystery guest!</font>
            </td>
        </tr>
    </table>

    <hr color="#008000">
    </body>
    </html>
```

Note the second table definition

```
<table border="0" id="guests">
```

The attribute id identifies this table as a target for the Bolero servlet logic. Identifying elements with an id attribute has become a standard technique when processing HTML and XML documents.

The following two classes are generated by the Bolero Component Studio from the above HTML source:

1. The layout class `invitatiServletGen`
   This class recreates the HTML page. Programmers should not modify this class – after a design change of the original HTML page this class is overwritten by the regeneration process. Here we have shortened the program text somewhat.

2. The servlet class `invitati`
   This class is to contain the servlet's application logic. On regeneration it is *not* overwritten.

```
class party.invitatiServletGen
   extends com.softwareag.bolero.language.standard.Object is public
   doc
      "This class is simply used to create the HTML tags"
      "that were originally in the HTML page. You can later"
      "make changes to the HTML page and just regenerate"
      "this class and maintain all your business logic."
   import java.io,
      com.softwareag.bolero.webapi.util,
      com.softwareag.bolero.webapi.dom,
      com.softwareag.bolero.webapi.html
class constructor is public
   implementation

   end implementation
end constructor

instance method generateDocument is public
   doc
      "The method generateDocument is called by the servlet "
      "to generate the HTML tags."
   parameter tool type BServletToolbox
   parameter servlet type party.invitati
   result type BHTMLDocument
   implementation
Field head type BHTMLHead Value Null
   Field body type BHTMLBody Value Null
   Field myDoc Type BHTMLDocument
   Field fldMETA1 Type BHTMLMeta
   Field fldMETA2 Type BHTMLMeta
   Field fldTITLE1 Type BHTMLTitle
   Field fldHEADER1_1 Type BHTMLH1
   Field fldFONT1 Type BHTMLFont

      ....
```

```
    ....
    Field fldOPTION4 Type BHTMLOption
    Field fldINPUT2 Type BHTMLInput
    Field fldTD5 Type BHTMLTableCell
    Field fldFONT13 Type BHTMLFont
    Field fldHRULE1 Type BHTMLHR

// fields created within the HTML page
    myDoc := BHTMLDocument ()

    Decide On First type of x := myDoc.getBody ()
      Case BHTMLBody
        body := x
    End Decide
    Decide On First type of x := myDoc.getHead ()
      Case BHTMLHead
        head := x
    End Decide

....
....
body.setBgColor ("#FFFFFF")
// creating fldHEADER1_1 in class BHTMLH1
        fldHEADER1_1 := BHTMLH1 ()
        body.#add (fldHEADER1_1)
// creating fldFONT1 in class BHTMLFont
          fldFONT1 := BHTMLFont ()
          fldHEADER1_1.#add (fldFONT1)
          fldFONT1.setColor ("#008000")
          fldFONT1.#add (BHTMLAnyText ("Welcome"))
....
....
// creating fldTABLE1 in class BHTMLTable
        fldTABLE1 := BHTMLTable ()
        body.#add (fldTABLE1)
        fldTABLE1.setBorder ("1")
        fldTABLE1.setCellSpacing ("0")
        fldTABLE1.setWidth ("100%")
        fldTABLE1.setAttribute ("bordercolor", "#C0C0C0")
          // attribute not recognized, generic method used !!
// creating fldTR1 in class BHTMLTableRow
          fldTR1 := BHTMLTableRow ()
          fldTABLE1.#add (fldTR1)
// creating fldTD1 in class BHTMLTableCell
            fldTD1 := BHTMLTableCell ()
```

```
                    fldTR1.#add (fldTD1)
// creating fldIMAGE1 in class BHTMLImage
               fldIMAGE1 := BHTMLImage ()
               fldTD1.#add (fldIMAGE1)
               fldIMAGE1.setSrc ("Pierot.gif")
               fldIMAGE1.setAlt ("party")
               fldIMAGE1.setAlign ("baseline")
               fldIMAGE1.setWidth ("320")
               fldIMAGE1.setHeight ("226")
// creating fldTD2 in class BHTMLTableCell
               fldTD2 := BHTMLTableCell ()
               fldTR1.#add (fldTD2)
               fldTD2.setVAlign ("top")
               fldTD2.setBgColor ("#F8B889")
// creating fldTABLE2 in class BHTMLTable
               fldTABLE2 := BHTMLTable ()
               fldTD2.#add (fldTABLE2)
               fldTABLE2.setBorder ("0")
               fldTABLE2.setId ("guests")
// creating fldTR2 in class BHTMLTableRow
               fldTR2 := BHTMLTableRow ()
               fldTABLE2.#add (fldTR2)
// creating fldTD3 in class BHTMLTableCell
                fldTD3 := BHTMLTableCell ()
                fldTR2.#add (fldTD3)
//**** tag not recognized...generic object will be generated ***
// creating fldSTRONG1 in class BHTMLGenericTag
                fldSTRONG1 := BHTMLGenericTag ()
                fldTD3.#add (fldSTRONG1)
                fldSTRONG1.setTagName ("strong")
                fldSTRONG1.#add (BHTMLAnyText
                        ("Already attending:"))
....
....
....
// creating fldFORM1 in class BHTMLForm
               fldFORM1 := BHTMLForm ()
               fldTD4.#add (fldFORM1)
               fldFORM1.setAction ("mailto:party@where.com")
               fldFORM1.setMethod ("POST")
               fldFORM1.setName ("F1")
...
...
// creating fldINPUT1 in class BHTMLInput
               fldINPUT1 := BHTMLInput ()
               fldTD4.#add (fldINPUT1)
```

```
                              fldINPUT1.setType ("text")
                              fldINPUT1.setSize ("50")
                              fldINPUT1.setMaxLength (50)
                              fldINPUT1.setName ("T1")
....
....
....
....
// creating fldINPUT2 in class BHTMLInput
                    fldINPUT2 := BHTMLInput ()
                    fldFONT12.#add (fldINPUT2)
                    fldINPUT2.setType ("submit")
                    fldINPUT2.setName ("B1")
                    fldINPUT2.setValue ("Submit")
....
....
// creating fldHRULE1 in class BHTMLHR
        fldHRULE1 := BHTMLHR ()
        body.#add (fldHRULE1)
        fldHRULE1.setAttribute ("color", "#008000")
            // attribute not recognized, generic method used !!

   Result := myDoc
       end implementation
end method generateDocument

instance constructor is public
     implementation

     end implementation
end constructor
end class invitatiServletGen
```

We see that the Bolero generator does not recognize some tags (STRONG) and attributes (COLOR, BORDERCOLOR) but treats them as generic tags and attributes. If we want to, we could create our own tag and attribute classes, but this is not necessary.

The following servlet class was generated, too, but was then modified by the programmer. We have highlighted the modified parts.

```
class party.invitati
   extends javax.servlet.http.HttpServlet
     is public and controls transaction
   doc
      "This is a generated class from Bolero. It is invoked "
      "within a HTTP-Server and creates one HTML-page"
   import java.io,
```

```
        javax.servlet,
        javax.servlet.http,
        com.softwareag.bolero.webapi.util,
        com.softwareag.bolero.language.standard. #transaction,
        com.softwareag.bolero.webapi.dom,
        com.softwareag.bolero.webapi.html,
        com.softwareag.bolero. #transaction

class constructor is public
    implementation
    end implementation
end constructor

instance method doPost overrides and is public
    doc
        "The doPost method is called for a POST request from "
        "a browser. By default we call the doGet method so "
        "that POST and GET requests are handled identically."
    parameter req type javax.servlet.http.HttpServletRequest
    parameter res type javax.servlet.http.HttpServletResponse
    throws java.io.IOException
    implementation
// call doGet so that this servlet can process GET and POST requests
        doGet (req, res)
    end implementation
end method doPost

instance constructor is public
    implementation
    end implementation
end constructor

instance field myPool type BSessionPool is nullable

instance method doGet overrides and is public
    doc
        "The doGet method calls the generateDocument method"
        "to fill in the pure HTML tag classes. After that"
        "you can put your business logic and calls"
        "to persistent objects or DCOM objects into this class"
        "or into a class that is called from this class"
    parameter req type javax.servlet.http.HttpServletRequest
    parameter res type javax.servlet.http.HttpServletResponse
    throws java.io.IOException
    implementation
Field tool Type BServletToolbox
```

```
Field myDoc Type BHTMLDocument
Field body Type BHTMLBody Value Null
Field head Type BHTMLHead Value Null
Field servletGen Type party.invitatiServletGen
Field mySession Type com.softwareag.bolero.#transaction.Session


//** Enable the following statements if you use persistent objects
//** and want to use the same database frequently. The BSessionPool
//** will assign your thread a database connection. This will happen
//** instantly in most cases because the BSessionPool keeps a pool of
//** connected database connections. For more details about limitations
//** refer to the documentation.
//** Also don't forget to have a class that controls the transaction.
//** Enter the correct userid, databasename and password in the
//    second statement.
//** start
//    myPool:=BSessionPool.getPool()
//    mySession:=myPool.join("TestDB","Fred","Wilma")
//** end (make sure you also call BSessionPool.leave()
//    at the end of the servlet !!!)

    tool := BServletToolbox (req, res)

//** If you need to check incoming parameters do it here !!!!
//
// your code......
//
//
//
// These two lines call the class that generates the
//    static part of the HTML page
    servletGen := party.invitatiServletGen ()
    myDoc := servletGen.generateDocument (tool, This)

// As an alternative you can load the HTML page dynamically
// with this statement.
// You need to import java.net and
// put the lines above (....generateDocument(tool....etc.) in comments.
// myDoc := tool.loadHTMLPage(URL("http://<your-
//       webhostaddress>/<htmldir+file.htm>"));

// This line passes the generated doc to the toolbox,
// no matter how it was created.
    tool.setDocument (myDoc)

    Decide On First type of x := myDoc.getBody ()
```

```
      Case BHTMLBody
         body := x
   End Decide
   Decide On First type of x := myDoc.getHead ()
      Case BHTMLHead
         head := x
   End Decide

//** If you want to make modifications to the generated HTML page,
//** here is a good place to put them. If you regenerate this class
//** only invitatiServletGen will be overwritten.
//** Modifications in this class will not be overwritten.
//
//
// your code......
//
// ... my code
// Connect to database
   connect user "MyUserID" to "PromoDB" using password "MyPass1"
//
// list all registered guests
   buildTable (tool)
//
// Disconnect from database
   disconnect
// ... end of my code
//
//** Also enable the next line if you want to make use
//** of the BSessionPool (see above).
//** Don't forget to modify databasename, userid and password.
// myPool.leave(mySession,"TestDB","Fred","Wilma")

   tool.sendPage ()
   end implementation
end method doGet
```

```
instance method buildTable controls transaction and is private
   parameter tool type BServletToolbox
      implicit parameters unchecked
   implementation
Field   selection Type collections.Iterator{String}
Field   findElement Type BHTMLElement
Field   fldTABLE1 Type BHTMLElement
Field   fldTR1 Type BHTMLTableRow
```

```
Field   fldTD1 Type BHTMLTableCell
Field   valuedGuest Type String
Field   earlyBirds Type Array{String}
   value Array{String}(["Mick Jagger","Nina Hagen",
                        "Berthold Daum","Markus Scheller"])

fldTABLE1 := tool.findHTMLElementbyAttr ("guests", BServletToolbox.ID)
     // find table in HTML page (the table was marked with id="guests")

For valuedGuest In earlyBirds do
     // just to make sure we get SOME guests!
     fldTR1 := BHTMLTableRow () // create new table row
     fldTABLE1.#add (fldTR1) // add it to the table
     fldTD1 := BHTMLTableCell () // create new table cell
     fldTR1.#add (fldTD1)     // add it to the table row
     fldTD1.#add (BHTMLAnyText(valuedGuest)) // fill cell with content
end For

selection:=Select guestvar.Name from Guests as guestvar
     // OQL statement to select registered Guests

For valuedGuest In selection do
     fldTR1 := BHTMLTableRow ()    // create new table row
     fldTABLE1.#add (fldTR1)       // add it to the table
     fldTD1 := BHTMLTableCell ()    // create new table cell
     fldTR1.#add (fldTD1)                // add it to the table row
     fldTD1.#add (BHTMLAnyText(valuedGuest)) // fill cell with content
end For
   end implementation
end method buildTable
end class invitati
```

The resulting dynamically created web page could look like Figure 15.6.

The servlet as a client

Bolero's WebAPI allows an HTML page to be loaded from a URL dynamically. The elements of the page can then be modified. So it is possible for a program to fill in the blanks in an HTML form and finally hit the SUBMIT button. The servlet is acting as a client – possibly as a client of another servlet.

This technique can be used, for example, for business-to-business transactions. A client application can visit a partner's web site, request pages and post messages.

In the following example we do just that. We have highlighted the parts entered by the programmer.

Figure 15.6 A dynamically created web page.

```
class bigbrother.invitati
   extends javax.servlet.http.HttpServlet is public
   doc
      "This is a generated class from Bolero. It is invoked "
      "within a HTTP-Server and creates one HTML-page"
   import com.softwareag.bolero.language.standard. #transaction,
      javax.servlet.http,
      javax.servlet,
      com.softwareag.bolero.webapi.dom,
      java.net,
      com.softwareag.bolero.webapi.html,
      com.softwareag.bolero. #transaction,
      com.softwareag.bolero.webapi.util,
      java.io

....
....
instance method doGet overrides and is public
   doc
      "The doGet method calls the generateDocument method"
```

```
          "to fill in the pure HTML tag classes. After that"
          "you can put your business logic and calls"
          "to persistent objects or DCOM objects into this class"
          "or into a class that is called from this class"
      parameter req type javax.servlet.http.HttpServletRequest
      parameter res type javax.servlet.http.HttpServletResponse
      throws java.io.IOException
      implementation
  Field tool Type BServletToolbox
      Field myDoc Type BHTMLDocument
      Field body Type BHTMLBody Value Null
      Field head Type BHTMLHead Value Null
  // Fields required to hold page elements
      Field fldINPUT1 Type BHTMLInput Value Null
      Field fldINPUT2 Type BHTMLInput Value Null
      Field fldFORM1 Type BHTMLForm Value Null
  // Field servletGen Type bigbrother.invitatiServletGen
      Field mySession Type com.softwareag.bolero.#transaction.Session

      tool := BServletToolbox (req, res)

  // These two lines call the class that generates the static part of the
  HTML page
  // servletGen := bigbrother.invitatiServletGen ()
  // myDoc := servletGen.generateDocument (tool, This)

  // As an alternative you can load the HTML page dynamically with this
  statement.
  // You need to import java.net and
  // put the lines above (....generateDocument(tool....etc.) in comments.

      myDoc := tool.loadHTMLPage
              (URL("http://<your-webhostaddress>/<htmldir+file.htm>"))

  // This line passes the generated doc to the toolbox, no matter how it
  was created.
      tool.setDocument (myDoc)

      Decide On First type of x := myDoc.getBody ()
        Case BHTMLBody
          body := x
      End Decide
      Decide On First type of x := myDoc.getHead ()
        Case BHTMLHead
          head := x
      End Decide
```

```
//** If you want to make modifications to the generated HTML page, here
//** is a good place to put them. If you regenerate this class only
//** invitatiServletGen will be overwritten.
//** Modifications in this class will not be overwritten.
//
// your code......
//
// ... my code
// find input elements for form, name, number of guests.
// (The DECIDE clauses are Bolero's way of type casting.)
Decide On First type of x :=
        tool.findHTMLElementbyAttr ("F1", BServletToolbox.NAME)
    Case BHTMLForm
        fldFORM1 := x
End Decide
Decide On First type of x :=
        tool.findHTMLElementbyAttr ("T1", BServletToolbox.NAME)
    Case BHTMLInput
        fldINPUT1 := x
End Decide
Decide On First type of x :=
        tool.findHTMLElementbyAttr ("D1", BServletToolbox.NAME)
    Case BHTMLInput
        fldINPUT2 := x
End Decide

// everything located – now ready to fill form
fldINPUT1.setValue("Big Brother")
fldINPUT2.setValue("1")
// (Big Brother is attending with 1 person)
// and submit
fldFORM1.submit()
```

```
    end implementation
end method doGet
end class invitati
```

Going live

JavaScript was developed by Netscape. One should not conclude from the name
a close relationship to Java – the concepts of the two languages are quite different. JavaScript was first named LiveWire and later renamed JavaScript for
marketing purposes.

Because it originated from Netscape, the support for JavaScript in Microsoft
Internet Explorer is lagging behind, usually by one version number. Microsoft
provides a similar scripting language JScript which also supports features not

Using scripts in applets

found in JavaScript. Both Microsoft and Netscape claim to conform to ECMAScript, the web's standard scripting language.

JavaScript can invoke methods of applets contained on the same web page:

```
<APPLET CODE="BoleroApplet.class" WIDTH="200" HEIGHT="150"
        CODEBASE="classes/"
        ARCHIVE="my.jar">
          NAME="myApplet"
   ...
   </APPLET>
```

The name attribute defines a name for this applet instance. This name is then used in JavaScript to invoke applet methods:

```
document.myApplet.show("Hello world");
```

The other way round – applets calling JavaScript functions – is only possible under Netscape with LiveConnect (Howque 1999) (via the JSObject class).

Downloading object data

Now, when we create HTML pages dynamically with a servlet, and the HTML contains some scripts, it is often necessary to pass data objects from the server to the client. For example, the HTML page contains a script to display product information. We must pass the product data from the business objects on the server to the script in the HTML page.

Microsoft provides for this purpose Visual Basic Scripting Edition, a subset of the Visual Basic programming language. VBScript can be used to 'glue' together ActiveX controls, Microsoft Automation servers and Java applets. Because VBScript supports DCOM it can be used to communicate with server-side DCOM components, such as Bolero servlets.

However, this works only in a Microsoft environment. RMI is another option for an applet to communicate with a servlet, but this is not unproblematic (see Section 13.1).

A portable and pragmatic way to transfer data objects from the server to the client and make them accessible to JavaScript is to generate some code in the HTML page.

In the following we show how Bolero can generate business data objects expressed as JavaScript code and contained in a servlet-generated HTML page. The technique is based on Allaire's WDDX (Web Distributed Data Exchange) proposal (Allaire 1999).

Consider the following Bolero classes:

```
class ProductDetail
instance field Color type String
instance field ProductNo type String
instance field Price type Decimal
...
end class ProductDetail
```

```
class Product
instance field Name type String
instance field Description type String
instance field Specification type String
instance field Detail type ProductDetail
...
end class Product
```

Using the BHTMLScript class from Bolero's WebAPI it is not difficult to generate a SCRIPT element that begins like this:

```
<SCRIPT language="JavaScript"><!--
var myProduct=new Product();
   function Product() { }
myProduct.Name = "Walkman";
myProduct.Description = "Elegant Long-Play Walkman";
myProduct.Specification = "Mega Bass Dolby B, Auto Reverse";
myProduct.Detail = new ProductDetail();
   function ProductDetail() { }
myProduct.Detail.Color = "silver";
myProduct.Detail.Price = "59.90";
myProduct.Detail.OrderNo = "34 97 11-65";
```

When the web page is loaded, a JavaScript object is created and initialized with the specified data. The object can then be used in other script functions, for example in a function like the following:

```
function printProduct() {
  document.write(myProduct.Name);
  document.write("<BR>");
  document.write(myProduct.Description);
  document.write("<BR>");
  document.write(myProduct.Specification);
  document.write("<BR>");
  document.write(myProduct.Detail.Color);
  document.write("<BR>");
  document.write(myProduct.Detail.Price);
  document.write("<BR>");
  document.write(myProduct.Detail.OrderNo);
  document.write("<BR>");
}
```

A Bolero–JavaScript bridge

It is quite simple to write servlet code that generates a script like the one shown above. However, this would require writing new code for each new class that we want to transfer to a client.

A more generic solution is to write a method that can analyze any object and convert it to JavaScript. This can be done by using the Java Reflection library (see Section 14.1). Reflection allows you to find out which methods and fields an object has.

Serious programming starting here

The following is a not so trivial example of programming in Bolero. It demonstrates how to use the Java Reflection API and how to use Java class libraries in Bolero.

The program does what we described above. A given Bolero object is translated into JavaScript. When the script is run at the client side it constructs a new object containing the data of the original Bolero object.

What we want to do is to identify all public fields of a given object and retrieve the content from these fields. As these fields may contain references to other objects, we must be able to handle a whole object hierarchy.

There is one glitch: the Java Reflection classes reflect Java code, not Bolero code. This is normally not a problem, as compiled Bolero classes result in Java byte code. In this case, however, it is a problem. Bolero implements all instance fields (including public fields) as private Java fields. The consequence is that reflection does not find a single field. Fortunately, the Bolero compiler generates a get*Fieldname*() method for each public field. So, instead for scanning for fields, we scan for methods beginning with get.

Here is class b2js. The method export returns the resulting JavaScript segment as an ArrayList{String}.

```
class b2js
    extends com.softwareag.bolero.language.standard.Object is public
    import java.lang.reflect,java.util,
        com.softwareag.bolero.language.standard.collections

class field classdefs type HashMap{String,Object} is private
    value HashMap{String,Object}

class constructor is public
    implementation

    end implementation
end constructor

class method export is public
    doc
        "Parameters:"
        "n: name of target field"
        "v: object to assign to target field"
        "This method converts a whole hierarchy"
        "of nested objects into statements that"
        "construct an equivalent hierarchy in"
        "JavaScript."
```

```
      "The method tries first to call an object's"
      "jsExport() method. Only if such a method"
      "does not exist, a default translation"
      "is executed. The default translation"
      "exports all public fields."

      "The following Bolero types are handled:"
      "- Number and Subtypes"
      "- Boolean"
      "- DateTime"
      "- Amount and Subtypes"
      "- String"
      "Java primitives are handled, too."
      "Arrays and classes that possess a"
      "toArray() method are handled as well."
      "If a class implements the toJavaScript() method"
      "this method will be used for conversion instead of standard"
      "conversion. toJavaScript() must deliver a result of"
      "type String."
      " "
parameter n type String
parameter v type Object
implicit parameters unchecked
result type ArrayList{String}
      value ArrayList { String } ()

implementation
      Field   className type String
      Field   fieldValue type Object
      Field   methodName type String
      Field   fieldName type String
      Field   oneMethodFromClass type #Method
      Field   m type #Method
      // Hash sign to identify as a Name, not a keyword
      Field   jsDefSize type Integer
      Field   classWasDefinedHere type Boolean Value False

      Exit method When v Is Null
         // we do nothing when the object is null
      begin
         m := v.getClass ().getMethod ("toJavaScript",null)
         // check if we have a to JavaScript method
         // if yes we use it!
         decide on first type of js := m.invoke (v, Null)
         Case String
            Result.#add(js)
```

```
      Exit method
    end decide
    on exception e
      // not user method, continue with processimg
    end exception
  end
  Decide On First type of vv := v
    // we have to write an assignment when deciding on type
  // for different standard classes, we simply print out the
  // string representation, some quoted.
Case Number
  Result.#add (n + " = " + v + ";" )
Case Boolean
  Result.#add (n + " = " + v + ";" )
Case String
  Result.#add (n + " = \"" + v + "\";" )
Case DateTime
  Result.#add (n + " = \"" + v + "\";" )
Case Amount
  Result.#add (n + " = \"" + v + "\";" )
No Case
    // that seems to be a complex class.
      className := v.getClass ().getName ()
    // get class name
    If classdefs.#get (className) Is Null then
      // check if already defined in this script
      classdefs.put (className, className)
      classWasDefinedHere := True
      Result.#add ("function " + className + "() {}")
      // no - output a function definition to define JS class
    End If
    Result.#add (n + " = new " + className + "();")
      // create a new instance in JS
    jsDefSize := Result.size ()
    For oneMethodFromClass In v.getClass ().getMethods () do
      // loop over all public get methods in object
      methodName := oneMethodFromClass.getName ()
      If methodName.startsWith ("get")
        And methodName <> "getClass"
        And methodName.length () > 3
        And oneMethodFromClass.getModifiers().bitAnd
                           (Modifier.STATIC) = 0 then
          fieldName := methodName.substring (3)
          fieldValue := oneMethodFromClass.invoke (v, Null)
          // get field value.
```

```
                    Result.addAll (exportField(n.fieldName,fieldValue))
                      // process the field value recursively
                End If
                On  Exception e
                   // catch any exception
                End Exception
            End  For
            If Result.size () = jsDefSize then
               // Empty object. Remove already made definitions
               Result.clear ()
               If classWasDefinedHere then
                    classdefs.#remove (className)
               End If
            End  If
        End  Decide

    end implementation
end method export

class method isJavaIdentifier is private
    parameter t type String
    implicit parameters unchecked
    result type Boolean
            value true

    implementation
       Field i type Integer

       If Not java.lang.Character.isJavaIdentifierStart(t.charAt (0)) then
         Exit method With Result := False
       End  If
       For  i In 1..t.length () – 1 do
         If Not java.lang.Character.isJavaIdentifierPart(t.charAt(i)) then
           Exit method With Result := False
         End If
       End  For

    end implementation
end method isJavaIdentifier

class method exportField is private
    parameter n type String
    parameter fieldName type String
    parameter fieldValue type Object
    implicit parameters unchecked
    result type ArrayList{String}
        value ArrayList { String } ()
```

```
implementation
   Field j type Integer
   Field jsSubSection type ArrayList { String }
   Field longName type String
   Field classDescriptor type String
   Field v type Object

   Field m type #Method
   If isJavaIdentifier (fieldName) then
      longName := n + "." + fieldName
   // get field name and prefix with path
   classDescriptor := fieldValue.getClass ().toString ()
   // get class descriptor for new field
   If classDescriptor.startsWith ("class ") then
      // is it a class or a java primitive?
   begin
      m := fieldValue.getClass ().getMethod ("toArray",null)
      // check if we have a toArray method: Probably a collection
      v := m.invoke (fieldValue, Null)
      // yes - convert to array
      classDescriptor := v.getClass ().toString ()
      // reevalautae class descriptor
      on exception e
         v := fieldValue
         // not convertible to array, use original value
      end exception
   end
   If classDescriptor.startsWith ("class [") then
         // is it an array?
         Result.#add (longName + " = new Array();")
         // yes - create new Array instance in JS
         For j In 0..java.lang.reflect.Array.getLength (v)-1 do
         // process all array elements
            jsSubSection := export (longName + "[" + j + "]",
                           java.lang.reflect.Array.#get (v, j))
         // call this method recursively for array elements
            Result.addAll (jsSubSection)
         End For
      Else
         jsSubSection := export (longName, v)
         // call this method recursively for scalars
         Result.addAll (jsSubSection)
      End If
   End If
End If
```

```
      end implementation
   end method exportField

   instance constructor is public
      implementation

         end implementation

      end constructor

   end class b2js
```

The export method can be called in the following way:

```
class method main is public
   parameter argv type Array{String}
      implicit parameters unchecked
   implementation
      field o type TestObject
      field s type String
      o := TestObject()
      for s in b2js.export("myVar",o) do
         System.out.println(s)
      end for
   end implementation
end method main
```

This is of course just to test the class b2js. In the context of a web application, the results obtained with the export method would be generated as script into an HTML page, using the BHTMLScript class from Bolero's WebAPI.

15.4   Components – the building blocks of electronic business

We have already discussed component-based system architecture (Chapter 9) and had a look at which component models are supported by Java (Section 12.7).

Bolero supports all these components models: JavaBeans, Enterprise JavaBeans, CORBA and DCOM (Figure 15.7). Bolero thus takes an integrative approach to the different component technologies: in an enterprise environment single model component scenarios are hard to find – a mix of several component technologies dominates.

Figure 15.7   A Bolero component can be deployed as a DCOM component, as an EJB component, or as an RMI-based component. Each Bolero class can only be deployed under one component model.

Creating components

Bolero allows classes to be deployed in a variety of component models. No changes are required in the code of the class. Instead, a deployment option is set (such as *Enable DCOM*). If there are additional parameters required, such as for DCOM, Enterprise JavaBeans or RMI, the parameters are all generated by Bolero. They are shown in the class definition on a separate property sheet, allowing these settings to be customized.

COM/DCOM

Software AG has a strong stake in DCOM technology. Their middleware product EntireX, for example, provides a DCOM runtime environment on enterprise UNIX platforms and mainframes, while their 4GL Natural allows DCOM component-based applications to be developed (Software AG 1999-3).

Consequently, Bolero offers strong support for DCOM, too. Bolero does not rely on the DCOM support found in some Java Virtual Machines but provides its own native DCOM runtime support. A Bolero class can easily be made into a DCOM component by just declaring it as such. The required DCOM settings, including global unique identifiers (GUIDs), are automatically generated by Bolero (Figure 15.8). Bolero also maps the Bolero data types of method parameters and results onto DCOM data types.

Bolero builds all files that are required for automatic deployment of the component with the Bolero Deployment Tool, and also takes care of registration of DCOM components.

These components can then be used by any DCOM-enabled application, including, of course, applications written with Software AG's Natural (Software AG 1999-3).

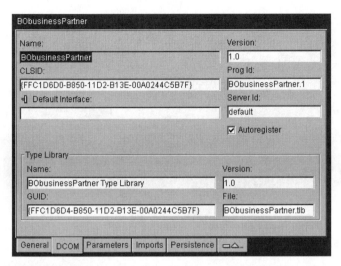

Figure 15.8 The DCOM property sheet of a Bolero class. The attributes generated by Bolero can be modified by the programmer, if required.

JavaBeans

The creation of JavaBeans in Bolero is just as simple: all that is needed is to set the property 'JavaBean' in the general setting for a class. JavaBeans is best suited for making components available to other Java- and Bolero-based applications. The JavaBeans component model should be used for non-enterprise objects. A typical application domain is beans that are used in the context of graphical user interfaces.

Enterprise JavaBeans

For enterprise objects in a Java or CORBA environment, EJBs are the component model of choice. We have already discussed EJBs in Section 12.7. Bolero allows EJBs to be created and supports persistent entity beans. All EJB aspects are defined in an extra property sheet (Figure 15.9).

Separate settings allow the transaction policies for the EJB to be specified (Figure 15.10).

- BEAN_MANAGED. This policy indicates to the EJB container not to interfere with the application's transaction control. When this policy is selected, the native Bolero transaction model consisting of persistent objects and transaction-control objects is used (see Section 15.7): transaction-control classes can be deployed as EJBs.

- With all other policies (see Sections 12.7) transaction control is handled by the EJB container (*container managed*). With these policies the native Bolero transaction model consisting of persistent objects and transaction-control objects cannot be used – database access in such a bean is possible via JDBC.

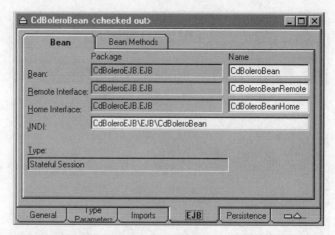

Figure 15.9   EJB property sheet (early prototype).

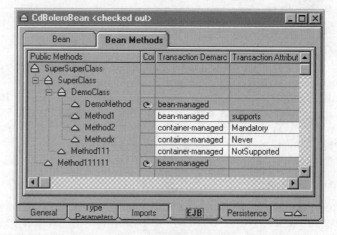

Figure 15.10   Defining transaction policies for EJB methods (early prototype).

CORBA

CORBA (Common Object Request Broker Architecture) is a vendor-independent architecture that is well suited for enterprise components. Bolero supports the creation of CORBA components with its support for Enterprise JavaBeans (see above).

Enterprise JavaBeans is the component model of choice in the context of CORBA and Java. CORBA object request brokers (ORBs), like Iona's Orbix or IBM's CICS, provide EJB containers which act as a runtime environment for EJBs. EJBs communicate with other CORBA components transparently through RMI-IIOP.

Using components

Bolero applications can use foreign components, whether DCOM components, JavaBeans, Enterprise JavaBeans, CORBA components, RMI-based components or CICS transactions (see also Section 15.12).

The Bolero Component Studio can import foreign components, but it is also possible to access external components that have not been imported. Importing a component into the Component Studio means that the component appears in the Component Studio like a Bolero class. The Bolero compiler can perform type checking for method parameters and results when such a component is used.

In the following example we show how to import a Natural DCOM component into the Bolero Component Studio.

Natural is Software AG's 4GL in the OLTP area. In cooperation with the module NaturalX, Natural can create DCOM components and can incorporate external DCOM components into Natural applications (Figure 15.11).

We can then use the imported Natural component like any other Bolero class, create a new instance, perform method calls, etc. (Figure 15.12). The Bolero compiler checks type compatibility for method parameters and results.

External DCOM components, such as Office 2000 components or user-written DCOM components, can be imported into the Bolero Component Studio and are then used like any other Bolero class. This includes the mapping of DCOM data types to Bolero data types and type checking when DCOM methods are called.

Alternatively, Bolero allows DCOM components to be used explicitly as external components. The components in this case are not imported into the Bolero Component Studio. Compile-time type checking is not, of course, performed.

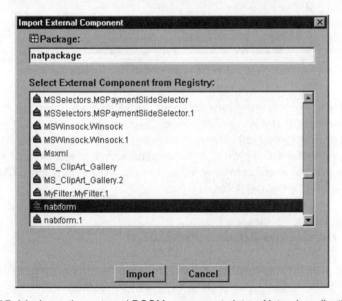

Figure 15.11 Importing external DCOM components into a Natural application.

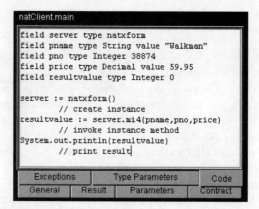

Figure 15.12   Using an imported Natural component.

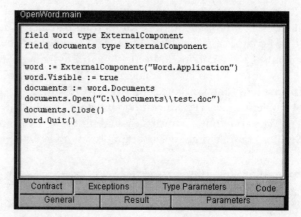

Figure 15.13   Accessing a DCOM component that has not been imported.

In Figure 15.13 we show how to access a DCOM component that has not been imported into the Bolero Component Studio. We do this using an example of Microsoft's Word application.

First, a reference to the `Word.Application` server is established, and then the features of the Word component, such as `Documents`, or `Open`, `Close` and `Quit`, are used like normal Bolero features.

15.5   The Bolero Application Model

Similar to the Java Enterprise Application Model introduced with Java 2 Enterprise Edition (J2EE) (see Section 13.6), Bolero features a four-tier architecture (Figure 15.14):

- Enterprise database systems are accessed through Java APIs, such as JTA or JDBC. On the programming level, Bolero abstracts from these APIs and supports high-level modelling of data objects through Bolero's concept of persistence-capable and transaction-control classes (see Section 15.6).

  CICS and DCOM support allow legacy applications to be leveraged, while XML is supported via Bolero's Tamino CLIP.

- The second tier contains the business logic which can include components of different models: DCOM and Enterprise JavaBeans. While EJBs must run in an EJB container, DCOM components can run directly under the Bolero Application Server.

- The third tier handles server-side presentation logic, such a navigation. Bolero servlets can work in cooperation with Java servlets and Java Server Pages. Similar to Java Server Pages, Bolero servlets generate HTML pages dynamically – but they do it differently (see Section 15.3).

- Finally, the fourth tier deals with client-side presentation. Clients can be web browsers (either pure HTML or Java enabled). Bolero can be used to create both applets and desktop clients.

Four-tier architecture

Enterprise-level applications require the Bolero Application Server, a collection of Java classes that provide the necessary support for constructs such as long transactions, persistency, transaction control, etc. Except for the DCOM support, the Application Server is completely written in Java.

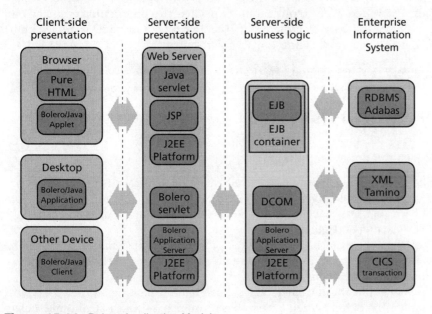

Figure 15.14   Bolero Application Model.

15.6   The Bolero persistency model

Of course, it is possible to use SQL through JDBC within a Bolero program. But this would ignore one of the major features of Bolero, an object-oriented persistency model. Bolero provides an automated but customizable way to map objects to relational tables.

- Object–relational mapping is used to create relational database schemata from object class definitions.
- Relational–object mapping can create object class definitions from existing database tables.

Establishing a database connection

Bolero provides a special language construct to connect to a database.

```
connect user "myLogin" to "url"
  using password "myPassword"
...
disconnect
```

Pooling connections

Alternatively, a session pool object can be used to connect to databases. Frequent connection and disconnection to and from a database can incur considerable overhead. A database session pool can solve this problem. Instead of disconnecting from a database the session is kept open but returned to a pool manager. When a new connection is needed the pool manager assigns an already existing session to the client. The Bolero pool manager can scale up by opening new database connections when required.

```
myPool:=BSessionPool.getPool()
mySession:=myPool.join("myLogin","url"," myPassword")
...
myPool.leave(mySession,"myLogin","url"," myPassword")
```

Object–relational mapping

Creating relational tables from class definitions

Object–relational mapping is activated when a Bolero class is marked as persistence-capable. Bolero generates a relational database table for this class. Each field is mapped to a table column – Bolero also takes care of mapping data types to SQL data types (Figure 15.15).

This mapping can be edited by the programmer, for instance, to customize database field names. Individual instance fields can be excluded from persistency by declaring them as `transient`.

Bolero automatically generates a hidden field containing a primary key that identifies the object. When a new object instance is created at runtime, Bolero generates a unique key value. In the case of aggregated objects, fields for foreign keys are generated automatically to enable SQL JOIN operations.

Distributor <locked>

△ Name		▦ Name	
Distributor		Distributor	

▭ Name	▭ Type	▭ Name	▭ Type
Name	String	Name	VARCHAR(128)
Town	String	Town	VARCHAR(128)
Street	String	Street	VARCHAR(128)

▭ Name	▭ Type	▦ Name

General	Type Parameters	Imports	Persistence	▭△…

Product <locked>

△ Name		▦ Name	
Product		Product	

▭ Name	▭ Type	▭ Name	▭ Type
Name	String	Name	VARCHAR(128)
Price	BigDecimal	Price	NUMERIC(18,7)

▭ Name	▭ Type	▦ Name
Distributor	Distributor	Distributor

General	Type Parameters	Imports	Persistence	▭△…

Figure 15.15 Mapping of object fields to database fields: fields that can be mapped directly to SQL data types are shown in the middle section of the property sheet. Fields that require an additional table like `Distributor` are shown in the lower section. The fields for primary and foreign keys used to connect the two tables are not shown.

In an aggregation, each single object must be defined as persistence-capable. This excludes some predefined Bolero data types from persistency. Most container types, such as `LinkedList`, are not defined as persistence-capable. For good reasons: their recursive definition can hardly be mapped onto relation structures.

However, a special collection class `PersistentList` exists to cater for situations where a persistent list is required.

The capability of being persistent

Persistence-capable classes can have persistent instances as well as transient instances. For example, given the persistence-capable class `Customer`, the statement

```
myCust := persistent Customer()
```

creates a persistent instance of the persistence-capable class `Customer`, while the statement

```
myCust := Customer()
```

creates a transient instance. Transient instances can be made persistent at any time:

```
add persistence to myCust
```

while persistent instances can be made transient:

```
remove persistence from myCust
```

This is also the only way to delete an object from the database.

Using persistent objects within an application is totally transparent to the programmer. Object fields and methods can be accessed in the usual way:

```
System.out.println(myCust.status)
myCust.status := "preferred customer"
myCust.address.setPostalCode(64297)
```

Internally, Bolero converts read accesses into SQL SELECT statements which are deployed via JDBC.

Write accesses to objects are collected by Bolero in a client-side cache. Once the transaction has been committed (see Section 15.7), all modifications are written internally to the database via SQL INSERT, UPDATE or DELETE statements – if necessary across multiple tables.

The advantages of this technique, compared to native JDBC, are obvious:

● Objects and object hierarchies can be accessed in an object-oriented way; access to transient and persistent objects is identical.

● Bolero takes care of the synchronization between the persistent object in the database and the transient copy in system memory.

● Type safety is maintained, because the mapping between Bolero data types and SQL data types is done by the system.

Transitive persistence

When working with aggregated objects, additional considerations are required. When we add or remove persistency to or from an object, we do this only with the object specified, but not with aggregated objects that are possibly contained in that object. The same applies when a new persistent object is created.

For example, our `Customer` class may contain a constructor that creates an `Address` instance as an aggregated object:

*Propagating
persistence through
aggregations*

```
class Customer is persistence capable
...
instance field address type Address is public
...
constructor
  address = Address()
end constructor
...
end class Customer
```

This definition always creates a *transient* `Address` object, independently of whether the `Customer` object was created persistent or not. In Bolero, the operation of making an object persistent is not *transitive*.

We can modify the constructor in order to achieve transitive persistence for object creation:

```
constructor
  if this is persistent
    address = persistent Address()
  else
    address = Address()
  end if
end constructor
```

Transitive operation is not possible with

```
add persistence to myCust
```

and

```
remove persistence from myCust
```

Here we must add a second statement:

```
add persistence to myCust
    add persistence to myCust.address
```

and

```
    remove persistence from myCust
    remove persistence from myCust.address
```

The last statement, however, should only be applied when we are sure that the `Address` object is not contained in any other persistent object!

If, however, we forget to remove persistency from the `Address` object, and the object is not contained in any other persistent object, it becomes an orphan – and the database after several such operations becomes a crowded orphanage.

Unfortunately, we are back here to a situation similar to that of a C++ programmer who is risking either null pointer exceptions or memory leaks, when he or she fails to destroy objects correctly. For transient objects we have the comfort of garbage collection, but for persistent objects in the database it is the programmer's responsibility to remove persistency from objects correctly.

Enterprise objects vs. member objects

Most OODBMSs (Object-Oriented Database Management Systems) automate this process by implementing disk garbage collection. The OODBMSs remove all persistent objects that are no longer referenced by other persistent objects. However, in an enterprise scenario we deal with RDBMSs in most cases: existing data is stored in relational databases.

The development of relational algebra and RDBMSs was motivated by the exact opposite: not to lose information that was no longer referenced. Let us consider the following relational schema:

Product					
Name	Price	...	Distributor	Town	Street

As soon as the last product of a given supplier is deleted, the information about the supplier is gone, too. This is what is called a *delete*-anomaly in relational theory. To avoid such situations, relational database design uses a series of normalization steps, from First Normal Form (1NF) to Fifth Normal Form (5NF). The main technique is to decompose complex schemata into multiple (and simpler) schemata:

Product			
Name	Price	...	Distributor

Distributor		
Distributor	Town	Street

Now it is possible to delete product records without affecting the supplier information.

In an object-oriented environment we would similarly model this scenario with `Product` objects referencing `Supplier` objects. Deleting `Product` objects must not of course cause the deletion of `Supplier` objects, even if the `Supplier` object is not referenced by anyone else. The orphan `Supplier` object could still be retrieved with an OQL or SQL query, or used by another application using the same database.

In contrast, an `Order` object usually contains several `OrderLine` objects. Deleting an `Order` object must imply the deletion of the connected

`OrderLine` objects, otherwise we would end up with a database full of use-less `OrderLine` objects.

Obviously there are two categories of persistent objects:

Enterprise object vs.
member object

- **Enterprise objects** are objects that exist in their own right – they do not require references from other objects to justify their existence.

- **Member objects** are objects whose existence depends on the existence of other persistent objects (enterprise objects or other member objects). If no other object is referencing such an object, their *raison d'être* ceases and they can be deleted.

When designing an object-oriented database-related application, we should determine for each object whether it is an enterprise object or a member object. This will allow us to define a clear deletion policy for these objects.

Relational–object mapping

While object–relational mapping provides an elegant way to create a new RDBMS-based object-oriented application, Bolero's relational–object mapping helps to build object-oriented applications from existing relational schemata (Figure 15.16).

Creating class defini-
tions from relational
tables

Because relational database schemata do not contain all structural information, the process is semi-automatic. After logging into the database, the programmer selects all the tables that are required to construct an object class. Bolero then suggests field mappings for each table, which the programmer can

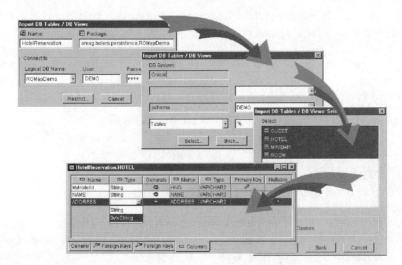

Figure 15.16   Import of relational schemata from a database into the Bolero Component Studio (Source: Software AG).

accept or modify. The programmer must also define a primary key for each table to enable Bolero to identify each object instance.

During object–relational mapping (see above) such a primary (and hidden) key was automatically created by Bolero. This is not possible here, because existing database tables should not be extended with an extra column. Therefore an existing key field must be identified by the programmer (field combinations are also possible).

If multiple tables are involved in the construction of a Bolero class, it is necessary to describe the relationship between these tables. This information is not usually stored in the database, but is defined in the application domain. The programmer must therefore describe to Bolero which are the foreign keys, and to which primary keys they should be joined.

Once the class code has been generated, the programmer may complete the class definition with transient fields and methods.

While relational–object mapping is more elaborate compared to object–relational mapping, it has the same advantages when compared to JDBC:

● Objects and object hierarchies can be accessed in an object-oriented way; access to transient and persistent objects is identical.

● Bolero takes care of synchronization between the persistent object in the database and the transient copy in system memory.

● Type safety is maintained, because the mapping between Bolero data types and SQL data types is done by the system.

Object queries and proper populations

Bolero uses the Object Query Language (OQL) to retrieve data from a database. Using standard SQL query constructs, OQL can be used to select and load data from persistent storage into a transient application address space.

Compiler checks

OQL is fully integrated into the Bolero language on a statement level. OQL phrases can therefore be checked by the compiler. Queries are precompiled for improved performance.

```
for c in (select cvar from Customer as cvar
        where cvar.Balance < 0)
....
end for
```

The OQL query enclosed in parentheses defines the result set which is processed by the for statement.

Dynamic queries?

However, when using OQL, it is not possible to construct dynamic queries by a program. In this case it is necessary to use the JDBC interface and to construct an SQL query string (see Section 12.8).

OQL is closely related to the ODMG's (Object Data Management Group) query language specification and is almost fully compatible with retrieval constructs in SQL:1999.

Like SQL, OQL is a set-oriented query language. The programmer does not specify a procedure to retrieve objects from the database, but rather an algebraic expression that defines a result set. OQL supports the usual relational operations, such as Selection, Join, Grouping, Ordering, and nested queries. *Set-oriented*

In Bolero, each persistence-capable class has an *extent* that holds all instantiated persistent instances of this class. The clause `with population` makes this extent available to the FROM clause of an OQL query. *Populations*

Normally, the extent of a class includes instances of subclasses, too (i.e. it is polymorphic). If this is not wanted, it is possible to exclude subclasses by using the clause `with proper population`.

```
class Customer persistence capable with population
  instance field Name type String
  instance field Balance type Decimal
  ...
end class Customer

class CorporateCustomer extends Customer
  ...
  method sendFriendlyReminder
  ...
  end method sendFriendlyReminder
end class CorporateCustomer
```

The extent of this class can hold both `Customer` and `CorporateCustomer` instances.

In the next example we show how the results of a query can be separated by type, and depending on the type specific steps are taken.

```
for c in (select cvar from Customer as cvar
                        where cvar.Balance < 0)
  decide on first type of cc := c
    case PrivateCustomer
      c.sendSharpReminder()
    case CorporateCustomer
      c.sendFriendlyReminder()
    case EnterpriseCustomer
      c.sendCollegialReminder()
  end decide
end for
```

Finally, OQL provides a special mechanism for queries that are intended to return a single object only. This simplifies application development and is faster than retrieving a whole set of objects, using only the first element and ignoring the rest.

```
select single c from Customer as c where c.Balance < 0
```

15.7 Database transactions

Locking strategies

In Chapter 4 we discussed the requirements for database transactions: ACID transactions must be atomic, consistent, isolated and durable.

In multi-task systems the database system must establish a policy for clients that access the same data.

- Competing clients that update the same data items at the same time could bring the data into an inconsistent state.
- A client that reads data while another client concurrently updates the same data could retrieve an inconsistent object, a *ghost*.

Locking

Database systems implement locking strategies to inhibit conflicting database accesses:

- **Pessimistic locking.** This strategy locks all data records that are accessed during a transaction at the beginning of the transaction, and unlocks them when the transaction ends. Pessimistic locking can create scaling problems: in heavy traffic the probability of hitting a locked record increases. The client has to wait until the lock is released. Bad application design can lead to the situation where clients mutually lock the records that the other client wants to access: a deadlock has occurred.

- **Optimistic locking.** This strategy locks the data records involved in a transaction only when the transaction is committed and only for the short duration of the commit operation. During the commit operation the current state of the data involved in the transaction is compared with a data image made at the beginning of the transaction (or by comparing time stamps that reflect the last update). If the two differ (because another client has modified the data during the course of the transaction) an exception is raised. Optimistic locking scales better than pessimistic locking, but is less user friendly, because a client can get an error message after committing a transaction.

- Mixed forms between pessimistic and optimistic locking.

Separating transaction control from persistency

Typical of the object-oriented model is that objects define their own access methods. If this is so, should persistent objects contain demarcations for the beginning and the end of a transaction?

Should a persistent object control transactions?

The answer is no. In Chapter 7 we discussed the difficulties with objects that participate in concurrent processes and try to synchronize these processes. The same problems exist when we try to control a transaction (which is in effect a concurrent process) from an object that takes part in the transaction.

A method of a persistent object, for example, that contains a `commit` statement would be hard to reuse: it must always be the last one in a complex transaction.

The solution to this problem is the same as the one found in Chapter 7: separation of concerns. The transaction logic must be separated from the business object.

Bolero therefore provides, besides persistence-capable classes, *transaction-control* classes. The two attributes are mutually exclusive, so it is not possible to mix persistency and transaction control.

Transaction-control classes explained

Transaction-control classes can have both transaction-control methods and non-transaction-control methods. Each transaction-control method defines exactly one database transaction. The transaction begins when the method is invoked and is committed when the method returns. A rollback is performed when the method throws an exception, or if an `Exit Transaction with Abort` statement is executed.

Within each of these transactions, methods from other objects can be called, especially methods from persistent objects. Properties of persistent objects can be modified, or persistent objects can be created or deleted by adding or removing persistence.

During the execution of a transaction-control method all changes made to persistent objects are collected. The transient copies of the persistent objects always reflect the current state of the object. When the transaction is rolled back, the transient copies are also set back to the initial value. When the transaction commits, all changes are written to the database.

Synchronization

Bolero uses here a strategy similar to optimistic locking. The database records are only locked during the short time of the write operation. An exception is thrown, however, if the persistent objects involved in the transaction were modified by another process during the course of the transaction.

Locking strategy

By default, all read operations to persistent objects can be performed outside a transaction-control method. Bolero uses a lazy read strategy, reading from the database only those data fields that are required by the application.

Performing a read operation outside a transaction-control method and afterwards performing an update operation within a transaction-control method could lead to inconsistencies if the programmer is not careful. For critical data, for example a bank account, an additional safeguard can be defined: instances of a persistence-capable class defined with the clause `requires transactions` must perform all operations (including read operations) within a transaction-control method. By this means, data consistency is ensured for all operations.

Read access and transactions

By providing transaction support on the language level, Bolero abstracts from the underlying transaction infrastructure. In a J2EE environment where a transaction manager is present, Bolero will use the Java Transaction API (JTA) for transaction control, thus allowing the use of distributed databases with two-phase commit. If no transaction manager is available, Bolero uses JDBC transaction control instead. The Bolero application code is the same in both cases.

J2EE support

15.8   Bolero and XML

The Tamino CLIP

We discussed XML in Chapter 14. While Bolero also offers low-level access to XML documents via SAX and DOM (see Section 14.4), a more comfortable way exists in connection with Software AG's Tamino Information Server (see Section 14.5). To support the Tamino XDBMS, Bolero's Tamino CLIP[1] adds the required functionality to Bolero.

Generating classes from XML schemata

Bolero's Tamino CLIP is based on the SAX parser. To process a given XML document type, the CLIP extracts the required schema definitions from Tamino's data map, and uses this definition to generate a hierarchy of Bolero classes, where each class maps one element type from the document schema. In addition, the CLIP generates SAX event handlers that link into the SAX parser (Figure 15.17).

When a document is read (a generic reader class is contained in the CLIP), the document is parsed by the SAX parser, which in turn calls the document type-specific event handlers. The event handlers use the generated class definitions to create object instances and assign the XML content to the fields of the object instances.

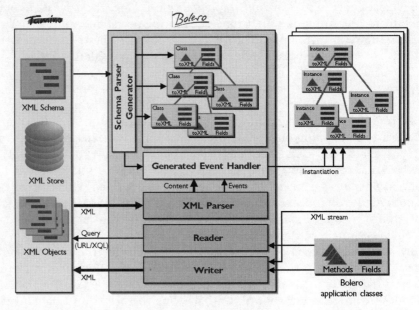

Figure 15.17 Reading and writing XML documents in Bolero. XML schemata are used to generate class definitions and the required SAX event handlers. (Source: Software AG)

[1.] Component library integration package

When retrieving documents from Tamino, Bolero can retrieve either a single document by URL, or a document set by content. Similarly to how a set of objects is retrieved from an RDBMS via OQL, documents can be retrieved with the XML Query Language (XQL) (see Section 14.4). Bolero can handle such sets and can create corresponding object instances for each of the returned documents.

When the CLIP generates class definitions from XML schemata it automatically equips each class with a toXML() method. Calling this method for the root object converts the whole object hierarchy into an XML stream. The process can be compared to Java serialization (see Section 12.8) with the difference that the output format is XML.

The generated XML is not only *well formed* (syntactically correct) but also a *valid* XML document because the toXML() methods result directly from the XML schema definition. A generic writer class then writes the XML document to Tamino.

Basic access

On a more basic level, Bolero can process XML documents by using the SAX and DOM classes provided with Bolero's libraries (see Section 14.4). The classes provided here are the same as in Sun Microsystems' Project X library.

- DOM (Document Object Model) (W3C 1998-2) allows the programmer to load an XML document, navigate its structure, retrieve and modify elements and attributes, create new elements and attributes, delete existing elements and attributes, and finally write out the modified document.

    Bolero's DOM support goes beyond the W3C DOM Level 1 Core Recommendation and includes support for XML Namespaces, document printing, element identification via the id attribute, and the exchange of nodes between documents.

    Because DOM has to keep the whole document structure in memory it needs substantial resources when large documents are involved.

- In contrast, SAX (Simple API for XML) (SAX 1998) is an event-based parser. As the parser scans through the document and detects syntactical units (nodes) it calls event handlers that must be provided by the programmer (or generated by Bolero's Tamino CLIP, see above). This allows an XML document to be processed without building up a large object tree in memory. However, SAX does not allow XML documents to be modified – it is a read-only API.

XML in user interfaces

While in an Internet solution HTML is still the markup language of choice, XML becomes an alternative in intranet scenarios. Microsoft's Internet Explorer 5, for example, supports XML and an early version of XSL (XML Stylesheet Language). InDelv Inc. provides a Java-written XML browser with more complete XSL support.

Microsoft's Data Source Object (DSO) is a technique to bind elements from an XML document to elements in an HTML page. Here, an XML document acts as a small client-side 'database' from where HTML pages can retrieve data elements. The XML document contains the data, while the HTML page defines the presentation.

While these solutions can be used in an intranet scenario where a consistent client technology (browser versions) can be ensured, XML solutions for the Internet are the exception because many browsers in the field do not support XML. However, there are two exceptions:

- Pages on a web site that are accessed not with a browser, but with an XML client. These pages can be read and processed, for example, by agents or custom web-enabled applications, typically in a business-to-business scenario (see Section 15.11).
- Pages for WAP (Wireless Application Protocol) devices, such as mobile phones. The markup language used in WAP is WML (Wireless Markup Language), which is XML and is defined through a WML DTD (see Section 14.3).

Bolero supports such XML applications in a similar way as the Tamino CLIP (see above). XML DTDs can be imported into the Bolero Component Studio, where a class hierarchy and event handlers are generated in the process.

15.9   Business processes

Database transaction vs. business process

In Section 15.7 we discussed how database (or ACID) transactions are handled in Bolero. Each database transaction is encapsulated within a method of a transaction-control object.

In traditional applications, database transactions are closely related to the work units (tasks) within a business process. A typical application function (invoked, for example, via a menu function and committed via an OK button) usually consists of a single database transaction. The end user or operator selects the appropriate application functions step by step to perform the tasks that make up the whole business process. When a mistake is made or when the business process is cancelled, it is the responsibility of the operator to apply corrective functions.

This is not possible in an electronic business environment, because the role of the operator has been replaced here by program logic. An electronic business application must therefore model a business process not only function by function, but as a whole organic process, where the actions of the end user lead from one well-defined state to another. The application is responsible for the coordination of all business functions.

We find similar requirements in enterprise application integration (EAI) (see Chapter 3). Where formerly a human operator invoked application functions step by step, a now seamless process integrates the formerly independent application functions and usually excludes human intervention.

Obviously, it is impossible to model a whole business process as a single database transaction. A business process can take any amount of time, from a few seconds to days or even weeks. And that is a fairly modest time span: when it comes to administrative tasks, processes may last over a whole human life.

Locking the data objects involved in a business process for such a long time would exclude many other users from access to the same objects. The golden rule with database transactions is that a transaction should not span across user interactions. Rolling back a business process to the very beginning possibly after weeks have elapsed when an error occurs is also not an option. So, we need a different architecture.

In the first step we identify the units of work that form atomic business functions. Each of these functions contains one database transaction. We call these items *business tasks*.

Business task defined

Examples of such functions are:

Add item to shopping cart
Write invoice

In the second step we create a framework to coordinate these business tasks. This framework defines several states for a business process, such as

```
CART_EMPTY

PAYMENT_RECEIVED

etc.
```

This framework also defines which events and conditions change the state of a business process, and which business tasks are executed (*triggered*) in such a case. Events can come from the user interface, or are system events, or events posted by the application. In Bolero such a framework is called a *long transaction*.

To summarize:

Long transaction introduced

- **Business tasks** incorporate atomic function units within an electronic business application. A business task incorporates one and only one database (ACID) transaction. Business tasks are implemented in Bolero as transaction-control objects (see Section 15.7). This means that a business task is a first-class citizen in the object-oriented environment of Bolero.

- **Long transactions** coordinate the execution of business tasks. In an electronic business application a long transaction takes over the coordination functions that in classical desktop applications are executed by a human operator. In the following sections we will discuss long transactions in detail. A long transaction implements a business process.

So far we have talked only about the process, not about the data. In an object-oriented world we model real-world business objects as object classes. In the example above we find objects like `Product`, `Shopping_cart`, `Invoice`, `Customer`, etc.

All of these objects have one thing in common: they are persistent and continue to exist outside the boundaries of a session. Consequently, the electronic models of such real-world objects are implemented as persistent objects in Bolero (see Section 15.6). They are modelled by persistence-capable classes. We call these objects *business objects*.

Business objects defined

● **Business objects** constitute the data of an electronic business application. Business objects are persistent, they are stored in a database. Within the context of a business process, business tasks can process several business objects, and business objects can be processed by several business tasks (*n:m* relationship).

Three building blocks for business applications

Business model

The triad of business objects, business tasks and business processes constitutes the basic building blocks of the business model. With business processes, business tasks and business objects, we possess a solid but simple concept for the design of electronic business applications.

Bolero matches these building blocks with persistence-capable classes, transaction-control classes and long transactions, which form a similar triad on the implementation side (Table 15.2).

Long transactions in detail

A long transaction models a whole business process from start to finish. Each long transaction consists of several business tasks. Long transactions coordinate and orchestrate the business tasks within the context of a business process. In principle, a long transaction can span several server sessions and can involve several end users in collaborative roles. It can also communicate with other long transactions.

Bolero provides long transactions as a separate meta-object within the development context. Within the Bolero Component Studio, long transactions appear as separate items and are edited with a specialized long transaction editor.

Business events introduced

Electronic business applications – like other client-server or GUI-driven applications – are event driven. The client sends business events to the server. These business events trigger business tasks which in turn manipulate business objects.

Table 15.2 Mapping the business model to Bolero.

Business model	Bolero
Business process	Long transaction
Business task	Transaction-control object
Business object	Persistent object

What sounds simple in theory is actually quite difficult. The random sequence of business events (they may arrive in any sequence) mismatches with the linear behaviour of computers – a computer executes one instruction after another in a predefined sequence. Most programming languages are also organized in this linear (procedural) fashion: statements are executed one after another.

Writing an event-driven program is therefore a difficult task – especially for programmers used to the data-driven paradigm of traditional business programming. The situation becomes even more difficult if the system involves – as in the case of business objects – persistent data. Faced with an unpredictable sequence of business events, it is not easy to keep persistent business data in a consistent state.

With traditional desktop systems (Figure 15.18) the job of orchestrating various business tasks depending on the incoming business events is left to a human operator. In an electronic business scenario the long transaction takes the place of the operator (Figure 15.19). The state of the long transaction represents the overall state of the business process. Depending on incoming business events and the current state of the long transaction, the long transaction initiates the execution of the appropriate business tasks and assumes a new state.

Long transaction takes role of human operator

In the theory of computing an operator or agent can be modelled as a *finite automaton*. The semantics of a finite automaton are described with a simple state transition table: each row in the table describes a tuple of old state, event, new state, and task (Table 15.3).

State transition table introduced

While the theory looks simple, practical solutions require some refinement. The following elements constitute a long transaction:

- Identifying object. An object that identifies the long transaction. This should be the central business object in the business process.

Long transaction ingredients

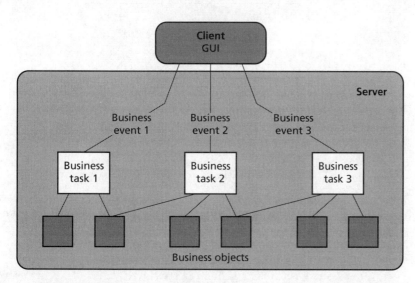

Figure 15.18 Traditional implementation of a business application. The client invokes business tasks separately.

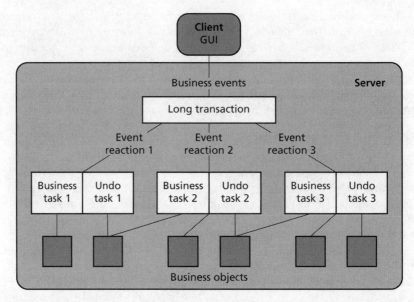

Figure 15.19 A long transaction organizes event-driven program logic. Because the human operator has been excluded from coordination, the application has to know how to undo a business task.

Table 15.3 Finite automaton state transition table.

Old state	Event	New state	Task
START	e1	S2	t1
START	e2	S3	t2
S2	e3	S4	t3
...		...	...

In order processing, for example, an Order object would be the identifying object for the long transaction that models the process.

- States. At any time a long transaction is in a defined state. There are two predefined states: START and STOP. All other states are defined by the application. Examples of states are ORDER_RECEIVED, SHIPPED, PAID.

- Events. Events trigger a state transition. When an event occurs the long transaction goes from one well-defined state to another well-defined state. Events can come from a client, from another long transaction, or they can be internal events, which are triggered by a post processing condition (see below) from the same long transaction. There are also some predefined system events, such as CANCEL, DELETE, STOP, UNDO, etc. All other events are defined by the application programmer.

An event is represented by an event object. Event objects can carry additional data:

- Business event data. Additional information supplied by the sender of the event.

    For example, if the event is adding an item to a shopping cart, the business event data is the object that represents this item.

- Long transaction event data. Additional status information about the long transaction and the sender of the event.

- Event reaction condition. An event reaction condition can inspect the business event and check the status of business objects. It can influence which business tasks will process the event. If the event cannot be processed, the event reaction condition can throw an exception.

- Business tasks. This is a transaction-control object (see above). The methods of a business task used in a long transaction must accept the following parameters:

  - Event object. The business event or system event that triggered the execution of the business task is passed to the business task. The business task can access and modify the event data.

  - Result object. Result objects carry the result information of business tasks. This information can be used in post processing conditions (see below).

    Result objects are kept by the long transaction in a history file and are passed to compensating (UNDO) tasks (see below), when business tasks must be undone.

  - Identifying object. The object that identifies the long transaction (see above). The business task can access and modify this object.

  The long transaction runtime system guarantees that each business task is executed exactly once for a given event, even in the case of a restart.

  Bolero's long transactions know two special types of business tasks:

  - Init business task. This task is called when a new long transaction is initialized. This business task has to accept only the event object parameter and must return the identifying object as a result. It is not required to perform a database transaction, but may do so.

  - Exit business task. This task is called when a long transaction exits. It is called with two parameters, event object and identifying object. It must control a database transaction.

- Event receiving task. Event receiving tasks are an alternative to business tasks. They differ from business tasks by not controlling their own database transaction. Instead, event receiving tasks run in the transactional context of the long transaction.

  Event receiving tasks cannot be used to implement business-critical tasks, because the long transaction runtime system guarantees only that the event receiving task is executed. In the case of a crash and subsequent restart an event receiving task could be executed *a second time* for the same event.

Event receiving tasks are used to perform an action not related to business objects, for example send an email notification, or invoke a function of a legacy application.

- Compensating (UNDO) tasks. Each business task can be paired with a compensating action that provides a semantic Undo for the business task. Compensating actions are called when an UNDO event has been received or when a long transaction is cancelled.

    For example: a cancellation of an order is received. If the long transaction is already in state SHIPPED, the cancellation is rejected. If the long transaction is still in an early state, the cancellation is accepted.

    Goods that have already been removed from the warehouse must now be returned to the warehouse. An ACID transaction would do this by resetting the stock counts in the warehouse database to their previous values (the before image). This is not possible here because other processes may have changed the stock counts in the meantime. To reset physically to their previous values would cause inconsistencies in stock-keeping.

    The UNDO action must therefore understand some of the semantics of warehouse management. A long transaction cannot itself know about these semantics, so a compensating task must be provided by the application programmer.

    When a compensating task is called by a long transaction, the result object (see above) that was prepared by the corresponding business task and stored in the history file by the long transaction is passed to the compensating task. This is to provide the compensating task with the required information to perform the compensation.

- Post processing. A post processing condition can inspect each business event (including the event data) and analyze the result object returned by the business task. Depending on the results, the post processing condition can:
    - influence the state transition;
    - trigger another business event which is sent either to the same long transaction, to an event receiver task, or to another long transaction. The event data of the original event is passed to the new event.

- Query events allow a client to obtain information about the current state of a long transaction and about the state of event processing.

Long transaction data flow

The data flow within a long transaction is organized as follows:

- Event objects carry information between
    - a long transaction client and business tasks;
    - a long transaction client and event receiving tasks;
    - a long transaction client and the long transaction instance;
    - the long transaction instance and business tasks;
    - the long transaction instance and event receiving tasks.

- Result objects carry information
  - between the long transaction instance and business tasks;
  - from a business task to the corresponding Undo business task, probably activated much later.

So, a state transition within a Bolero long transaction is influenced not only by an event, but by other criteria, too, in the following order:

1. Business event
2. Event reaction condition
3. Post processing condition.

In a long transaction, data integrity is achieved not by locking business objects but by using event reaction conditions and post processing conditions. Business objects are only locked within the business task's database transactions, but not across the whole business process. Integrity and consistency in a business process are achieved on a semantic level.

For example: a customer has selected only items that are in stock. But by the time the customer checks out, items might have gone out of stock. An event reaction condition could detect this situation and throw an exception.

In the Bolero long transaction editor, state transitions are shown not as a state transition table but as a tree structure. We show here how a state transition table (Table 15.4) transforms to a tree (Figures 15.20 and 15.21).

Long transaction representation

Let us consider, for example, an order processing example in an electronic business application (Table 15.5 and Figure 15.22). Customers enter an order via the World Wide Web, by adding items to the order line by line, finally confirming the order. Once the consumer has completed the order it must be picked, i.e. the ordered items must be collected from the warehouse. When all parts of the order are available, the order can be packed and eventually shipped. An invoice for the order must be sent to the customer and payment of the invoice must be tracked.

Long transaction example

Table 15.4 A long transaction state transition table.

Old state	Event	Event reaction condition	Task	Post processing condition	New state	Trigger
START	e1	r1	t1	p1	S2	
START	e1	r1	t1	p2	S3	
START	e1	r2	t2	p3	S4	e4
START	e2	r3	t3	p4	S5	
START	e2	r4	t4	p5	exception	
...	...	...	...	...	...	...

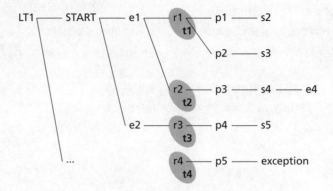

Figure 15.20   The resulting long transaction tree structure.

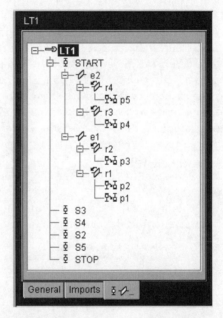

Figure 15.21   A long transaction tree in the Bolero long transaction editor. New states, triggered events, business tasks and Undo tasks do not appear in the tree but appear in dialogue forms when tree items are edited.

Long transaction persistency

LT recovery

Bolero's long transactions are persistent. Event delivery and long transaction states are stored in a *history file* in the database. The stored information is used by the long transaction runtime system to recover the long transaction after a crash and to continue with event execution (*forward recovery*).

Table 15.5 An order-processing long transaction. For simplicity we have omitted exception handling, post processing and the handling of the CANCEL event.

Old state	Event	Condition	Task	New state
START	eADD_ITEM	Item available?	Add_Item_to_Order	RECEIVING_ORDER
RECEIVING_ORDER	eADD_ITEM	Item available?	Add_Item_to_Order	RECEIVING_ORDER
	UNDO		**Remove_Item_from_Order**	RECEIVING_ORDER
	eCONFIRM	Customer data valid?	Add_customer_data	SCHEDULED
SCHEDULED	eITEM_PICKED		Update_warehouse	SCHEDULED
	eALL_ITEMS_PICKED		Notify_packer	PICKED
PICKED	eORDER_IS_PACKED		Prepare shipping_docs	PACKED
PACKED	eSHIPPED		Send invoice	SHIPPED
SHIPPED	ePAYMENT		Update_balance	PAID
PAID	eSTOP			STOP

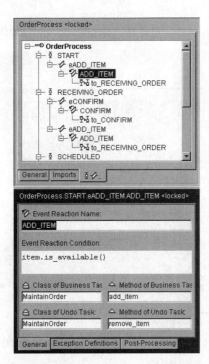

Figure 15.22 The example from Table 15.5 in the Bolero long transaction editor. The window pane below shows the event reaction, consisting of the business task and the compensating task. We use the same business task class for both, but with different methods.

The history file is not only used for recovery. It is also used for UNDO events, to find out and roll back previous events and business tasks by calling the corresponding compensating tasks. If necessary (for instance in the case of a CANCEL event), the whole long transaction can be undone step by step, provided the required compensating tasks are defined.

Special *query events* allow the client to interrogate the long transaction history file. This feature can be used to inform the client about current and previous states of a long transaction and whether a certain event was successfully executed.

Local and remote long transactions

Because long transactions are persistent they need to set up a connection to a database. Clients can use Bolero's *long transaction runtime system* in different modes:

- Local mode (same JVM as the client), using its own database connection (Figure 15.23).
- Local mode, using the same database connection as the client (Figure 15.24).
- Remote mode. Long transaction runtime systems are set up on both client and server (Figure 15.25). The remote communication between both runtime systems is established via DCOM. (Software AG's EntireX is required for DCOM support on UNIX and mainframe.)

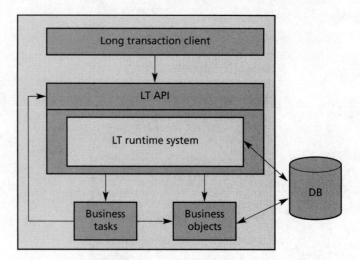

Figure 15.23 Long transactions runtime system – local mode, using its own database connection.

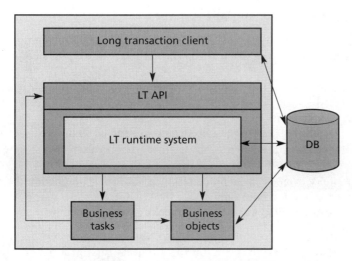

Figure 15.24 Long transactions runtime system – local mode, using the same database connection as the client.

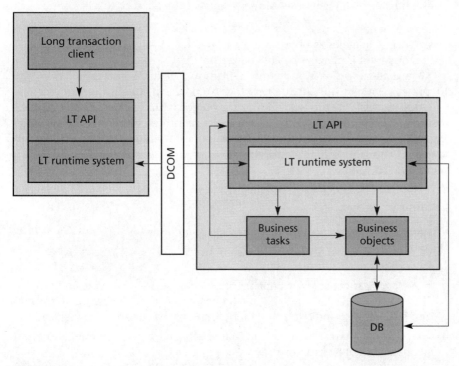

Figure 15.25 Long transactions runtime systems on both client and server – remote mode.

Using the long transaction API

After initialization, the client can send business events and event data to the long transaction. This is done through method call `sendLTEvent`. Control is returned to the client as soon as the long transaction has processed an event and all cascading events that were triggered by post processing actions. Status information and event data, possibly modified by the business tasks invoked, are returned to the client.

During this interval a long transaction is considered to be *busy*. A long transaction is locked for other clients during this time. Another client trying to send a business event to a busy long transaction will receive an `LTBusyException`. However, query events can be processed by a busy long transaction. This allows long transaction to be monitored at any time.

Multi-threading and LT   Multi-threaded operation for long transactions is possible in the following way:

- Remote mode. The remote long transaction runtime system with business tasks, event receiver tasks and business objects runs in a remote thread on the server. Clients may run in separate local threads.

- Local mode. The long transaction runtime system with business tasks, event receiver tasks and business objects may (but is not required to) run in a separate thread. Each client may run in a separate thread, too.

Note, that while business tasks, business objects and business events are first-class citizens in Bolero's object-oriented universe, a long transaction is not. A long transaction is a meta-object (a pattern).

LT instances   Nevertheless, a long transaction definition can have instances. When the LT runtime system initializes a new long transaction, the Init business task is called. This task creates an identifying object which is tied to the new LT instance. The particular LT instance can be identified either via the identifying object or via an `LTHandle`. `LTHandle` is an address-space-independent identification (unlike the identifying object), and can therefore be used by a remote client, too.

Summary

We conclude this section by summing up the characteristic features of long transactions.

Long transactions:

- provide a clear concept for implementing complex event-driven applications. They act as a filter for valid and invalid business events depending on the current state of the transaction, and orchestrate the execution of business tasks;

- solve the mismatch between long-lasting business transactions and short database (ACID) transactions;

- provide forward recovery in case of a system crash;

- can handle the Undo of previous events, if necessary rolling back the whole business process.

- enhance reusability of business task classes, because coordination issues are removed from the business tasks.

15.10 Long transaction scenarios

In the previous section we discussed the basic relationship between business process, business task and business object, and discussed long transactions (which implement business processes) in detail.

In this section we discuss scenarios with single and multiple cooperating long transactions. When we speak of a long transaction, we implicitly include the associated business tasks and business objects.

Single long transactions

In the simplest long transaction scenario, there is one long transaction and a client. The client, usually a graphical user interface, initializes the long transaction and then sends business events to it. The long transaction manages the whole business process.

Embedding subsystems

We have already discussed the implementation of basic business tasks, which are implemented by Bolero's transaction-control classes. In an enterprise, however, there may be business tasks that cannot be implemented as transaction-control classes because they are already implemented. These are existing subsystems, third-party components, legacy systems or ERP-systems.

These subsystems are embedded into a Bolero long transaction via an event receiving task (see Section 15.9). Such a task is implemented as a non-transaction-control Bolero class and accesses the subsystem to embed.

Usually these subsystems do not run in the same transaction context as the long transaction. This makes it difficult to ensure consistency over the whole long transaction. We have already mentioned that the long transaction runtime system cannot guarantee to an event receiving task that it is not executed twice in the case of a restart. It can only guarantee that the event receiving task is executed at least once per event.

Dealing with event receiving task

The subsystems that are embedded via an event receiving task must therefore adhere to *one* of the following conditions:

- The subsystem's event processing must be idempotent. This means that if the same event (identified perhaps by a time-stamp or a reference number) is sent twice, the subsystem guarantees that it is processed only once.

- The subsystem must be testable – it can provide information on whether a certain event was processed or not. In this case the event receiving task must test the subsystem before sending an event to it.

Nesting other long transactions

For large applications it may be sensible not to model the whole business logic in one huge long transaction. Instead, it is better to decompose the long transaction into several smaller long transaction, which then cooperate. This allows application parts to be exchanged separately. One technique for decomposition is to nest long transactions.[2]

> *In our order processing application, for example, we could set up the shopping process (adding order-lines to the order) as a separate long transaction. This embedded long transaction receives all events until the eCONFIRM event happens. The main long transaction takes over and processes the completed order. Similarly, the picking process could be implemented as a separate subaltern long transaction. These different long transactions can share one identifying object, in this example the business object* Order.

Asynchronous events

Bolero's long transactions work synchronously. A client that sends an event to a long transaction via the sendLTEvent method has to wait until the long transaction has executed all business tasks that are involved in the processing of this event. This includes cascading events (events triggered by post processing actions). Only after all processing steps are executed does the sendLTEvent return.

Requirements for asynchronous processing

However, especially in distributed applications, it is often necessary to handle events asynchronously. This means that when a client sends an event to a server (here: a long transaction runtime system) control is immediately returned to the client. The client can now process other tasks, for example accept additional data from the user, while the server is busy processing the event (*latency hiding*).

When an event is sent asynchronously, the client has no knowledge of whether the event was processed successfully or not, because the sending method returns before the event has been processed.

Several techniques exist to solve this problem:

- The client periodically checks if and how the event was processed (polling). This technique has the advantage that the client not only checks for the status of the processed event, but also detects if the server is still alive. The technique, however, incurs a high overhead, especially in a distributed situation when messages are sent across a wire. If polling intervals are long, the overhead is lower, but the responsiveness of the system suffers. If polling times are short, the system responds better, but the overhead is high and the system may not scale so well.

[2.] The nesting of long transactions is not implemented in the current Bolero version (2.1) but is planned for future versions.

● The client asks the server to notify it when the event has been processed. This technique is very responsive (compares to a polling interval of zero) and overhead is low. However, when the server dies, the client is not notified. It is therefore necessary that the client specifies a time-out interval with each request for notification.

In the following we show on a basic level how a client can interact asynchronously with a long transaction. The technique we use is based on C.A.R. Hoare's CSP (communicating sequential processes) which we discussed in Chapter 7. Both client and long transaction are implemented as independent processes which communicate with each other through *channels*.

CSP

How the channels are actually implemented depends on the requirements of the application. One option is to use Message-oriented Middleware (MoM) to set up a communication channel between processes. Software AG's EntireX is such a system. Bolero supports EntireX by providing a library with the EntireX API. Also, Java 2 Enterprise Edition provides the Java Message Service (JMS) API which acts as an interface to MoM products from different vendors (see Section 12.6).

In an object-oriented environment each message is a first-class citizen. The message object carries the message information, but may also have methods of its own, for example a method for acknowledging receipt of the message. Each message object holds additional meta-information. The list of meta-information attributes shown in Table 15.6 is closely related to the message header attributes used in JMS.

Message objects

Table 15.6 Meta-information attributes.

Attribute	Description
Destination	Receiver's identification, for example a URL. This ID is used to route the message to the receiver.
DeliveryMode	This attribute indicates whether the message is to be treated as a persistent message by the messaging system or not. Persistent messages require additional overhead.
MessageID	A unique identification string. The message ID must be unique within the universe of the messaging system.
Timestamp	Date and time when the message was passed to the messaging system.
CorrelationID	The ID of another message to which this message relates. A receipt message, for example, relates to the original message
ReplyTo	The address where the reply is to be sent. In our case this is identical with the sender's address.
Status	The message status reflects the current processing status of a message, such as MESSAGE_CREATED, MESSAGE_SENT, MESSAGE_RECEIVED, MESSAGE_ACKNOWLEDGED. This status information can be used for restart purposes after a crash.
Type	A message type. For example, the message could be a business event, a receipt or an administrative message.
Redelivered	This attribute indicates that this message is a repetition of an earlier message, for which no reply has been received.

When exchanging messages asynchronously, sender and receiver run in separate processes, for example separate threads or on separate Java Virtual Machines. In our long transaction scenario, long transaction client and long transaction runtime system run in different threads (or on different JVMs). We call the thread where the long transaction runtime system runs the 'server thread'.

Using channels   According to CSP we connect clients and servers using channels. Instead of sending an LTEvent directly to the long transaction runtime system, the client wraps the long transaction event into a message object and sends it to the server thread's input channel. When the event has been processed, the server thread sends a return message to the client's input channel. The client eventually checks its own input channel for return messages.

This channel-based approach has the advantage that the channels handle all synchronization issues. This simplifies the implementation of clients and servers considerably (see Chapter 7).

In the following we will develop the concept of asynchronous long transactions from the simplest case (one client, one server, one long transaction) (Figure 15.26) to more complex cases.

To receive messages – business events sent by the client and return events sent by the server – we define an interface InputChannel. We leave it open as to how such a channel is implemented: simple channels can be easily implemented in Java or Bolero, more elaborate ones may use the services of EntireX or of another MoM product through the JMS API.

```
interface InputChannel is public

    // dispatch a message to the channel
    method send
        parameter message type Message
    end method send

    // take a message from the channel
    method receive
        result type Message
    end method receive

    // take a specified message from the channel
    method receive
        parameter ID type MessageID
        result type Message
    end method receive

    // browse messages in channel
    method browse
        result type List{Message}
    end method browse


end interface
```

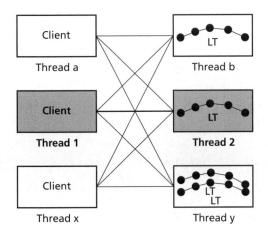

Figure 15.26   While in principle we allow multiple clients to access multiple servers, we concentrate first on the one-to-one relationship.

To send messages we define an OutputChannel interface. The output channel is responsible for locating the receiver, establishing a connection with it and passing messages to the receiver's input channel.

```
interface OutputChannel is public

    method setSenderAddress
        parameter sAddress type String
    end method setSenderAddress

    method send
        parameter message type Message
    end method send

end interface
```

With these two channel interfaces in place, we are now able to establish an asynchronous communication between client and server:

A long transaction client creates a new message object containing the LTEventObject it wants to send to the long transaction server. It then calls the send() method of its own output channel, passing the message object as a parameter.

When the channel method send() accepts a message it immediately returns – before or after the message is delivered to the receiver, depending on the implementation. This allows the client to continue processing.

The server thread has a separate life. The run() method of the thread object reads messages arriving from the input channel by invoking the channel's receive() method. It extracts the LTEventObject from the message and passes it to the long transaction. When the event has been processed by the

Building a server

long transaction runtime system, control is returned to the `run()` method. The
`run()` method can then read the next message from the input channel.

When there are no more events in the channel, the channel causes the
thread's `run()` method to wait.

```
class LTserverThread
        extends java.lang.Thread
        and implements ILTServerAdmin
        and is public

    instance Field inChannel // channel instance
            Type InputChannel is public

    instance constructor
        is public
    implementation
        // create new channel instance
        inChannel := SomeInputChannelImplementation()
    end implementation
    end constructor

    instance method run
        is public and overrides
    implementation
        Field message type Message
        Field bEvent type LTEventObject
        Field ltEvent type LTEventObject
        Field ltSysEvent type LTSysEvent
        Field ltQueryEvent type LTQueryEvent
        Field ltHandle type LTHandle
        Field ltInit type Boolean value false
        Field outChannel type OutputChannel

        // the following loop dispatches events
        // to the Long Transaction runtime system
        loop
            // read message from channel
            message := inChannel.receive()

            // check for administrative message (shutdown)
            exit loop when message.Type = SHUTDOWN

            // extract the business event from the message
            decide on first type be := message.Data
                case ltEventObject
                    bEvent := be
            end decide

            // intialize
            if not ltInit then
```

```
                    // connect to database
                    connect user "<UserID>" to "<DB>"
                              using password "<Password>
                    // Note: it is the application's
                    //    responsibility to construct a
                    //    suitable database UserID.
                    //    In our One-client-One-server example
                    //    message.replyID would be a choice.
                    //    In more complex cases the use
                    //    of the JNDI naming & directory
                    //    interface could be an option.

                    // initialize LT runtime system
                    //    the parameter specifies the maximum
                    //    time to wait on a busy LT (msec).
                    LTSys.initLocal(90000)

                    //    Send START system event to obtain
                    //       LT handle
                    ltsysevent :=
                       LTSys.sendLTSysEvent(START, ltName, null)
                    ltHandle := ltsysevent.getLTHandle()

                    ltinit := true
                end if

                // we use the Long Transaction handle
                // to send the event to the LT
                LTSys.sendLTEvent(bEvent.getEventType(),
                                            ltHandle,message)

                // we send here the full message as event data
                // to enable us later to identify the event.
            end loop
            on exception e
                System.out.println("Uncaught exception"+e)
            end exception
            finally
                LTSys.release()
                disconnect
            end finally
        end implementation
    end method run
  end class LTServerThread
```

At a later time the client may arrive at a situation where it needs to know if the event sent to the long transaction has already been executed and whether it was successfully executed. This can be done by querying the long transaction directly (the required information is stored in the long transaction history file and can be retrieved with a Query Event). If the event has not yet been processed, the client has to wait a short while and try again. This polling technique, however, introduces a high overhead, especially in a remote situation (see above).

A better solution is to use a notification mechanism (Figure 15.27).

Message objects are equipped with a `ReplyTo` method which allows an answer to be returned to the sender's *return channel*. When the client requires a receipt it uses the return channel's `receive()` method. If the receipt has not yet arrived, the return channel makes the client wait for it.

The dispatcher loop of class **LTServerThread** is modified to send the receipt:

```
Field outChannel type OutputChannel
        value OutputChannel()

    if not ltInit then

        ....
        // setup output channel
        outChannel.setSenderAddress
                        ("www.serverdomain.com/.../")

        ltinit := true
    end if

    ...
    // send to Long Transaction instance
    ltevent := LTSys.sendLTEvent(bEvent.getEventType(),
            ltHandle,message)

    // send the result to client
    outChannel.send(message.ReplyTo,ltevent)
end loop
```

This is all that we need to process a business event asynchronously and return the result back to the client. However, the logic presented here is not crash proof.

For a crash-proof solution we would need a robust channel, definitely a case for a middleware product. However, when a crash happens at the wrong moment, the channel can redeliver a message that has already been processed. When this happens we have to look at the long transaction history file (by using an LTQuery event). If the business event has already been processed, we just return the result, instead of processing the event again.

We must also force the messaging system to remember a message until it has been processed by the long transaction runtime system. To do so, we run the messaging system in CLIENT_ACKNOWLEGE mode instead of AUTO_ACKNOWLEDGE mode, and use the `acknowledge()` method of the `message` object to acknowledge the message explicitly.

```
...
do_message := true
if message.Redelivered then
  // search event in LT history file
  ltQueryEvent :=
    LTSys.sendLTQuery(QUERY_EVENT_HISTORY,ltHandle)
  for ltevent in ltQueryEvent.getEventHistory() do
    if ltevent.getAddData().MessageID
              = message.MessageID then
      do_message := false
      exit loop
    end if
  end for
end if
if do_message
  // send to Long Transaction instance
  ltevent :=
  LTSys.sendLTEvent(bEvent.evType,ltHandle,message)
end if
  // send the result to client
  inChannel.sendResult(ltevent)
  // acknowledge to messaging system
  message.acknowledge()
end loop
```

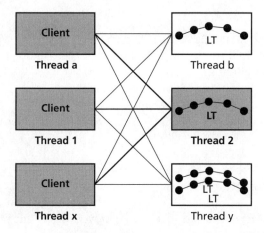

Figure 15.27   This concept allows multiple clients per server. Receipts are sent back to the right client because the message object keeps the client identification.

Concurrent long transactions

So far, we have only looked at the server. We have developed a concept that allows the client to send a message with a business event asynchronously to the server. While the server processes the event, the client is free to do other things. At a later time, the client can ask for a result message which was delivered to its own input channel. The client uses the return channel's `receive()` method to retrieve (and possibly wait on) an incoming result message.

Here is the code for a client starting a long transaction and posting an event to it. Note that this code is simplified; exception handling, detecting server death and restart logic are not shown here.

```
field message_1 type Message
field ltEvent_1 type LTEvent
field eResult_1 type LTEventObject

// create return channel instance
field retChannel type InputChannel
          value InputChannel()

// create output channel instance
field outChannel type OutputChannel
...       value InputChannel()
// setup output channel
outChannel.setSenderAddress("www.clientdomain.com/.../")
...

// create and send Business Event
ltEvent_1 := LTEventObject().setEventType(eADD_ITEM)
ltEvent_1.setLTName("OrderProcessing)")
ltEvent_1.addAddData("Some event data")
outChannel.send("www.serverdomain.com/.../",
                               Message(ltEvent_1))
...
// wait on result to arrive
eResult_1 := returnChannel.receive()
System.out.println("Event processed")
```

After sending an asynchronous event to a server, the client may send other asynchronous events to other servers (Figure 15.28). These servers, however, must run in different processes (different Java Virtual Machine), as a busy long transaction runtime system blocks its own process (Figure 15.29).

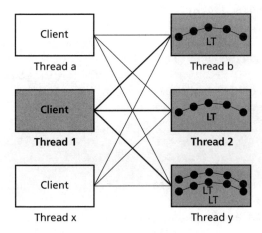

Figure 15.28   A single client (or multiple clients) can access multiple servers to run several long transactions concurrently.

This new situation requires some additional mechanisms for receipt handling. To continue with its work the client may want to check on the arrival of a single receipt, or on the arrival of a combination of receipts. The input channel interface provides additional methods to receive a message with a specified identification, and to browse all waiting messages.

```
field message_1 type Message
field ltEvent_1 type LTEvent

field message_2 type Message
field ltEvent_2 type LTEvent

field eResults type List{LTEventObject}

// create return channel instance
field retChannel type InputChannel
         value InputChannel()

// create output channel instance
field outChannel type OutputChannel
...
// setup output channel
outChannel.setSenderAddress("www.clientdomain.com/.../")
...

// create and send Business Event 1
ltEvent_1 := LTEventObject().setEventType(eADD_ITEM)
ltEvent_1.setLTName("OrderProcessing)")
```

```
ltEvent_1.addAddData("Some event data 1")
outChannel.send("www.serverdomain_1.com/.../",
                                    Message(ltEvent_1))
// create and send Business Event 2
ltEvent_2 := LTEventObject().setEventType(eASK_RATE)
ltEvent_2.setLTName("ApplyForCredit)")
ltEvent_2.addAddData("Some event data 2")
outChannel.send("www.serverdomain_2.com/.../",
                                    Message(ltEvent_2))


...
// wait on results to arrive
loop
    eResults.add(returnChannel.receive())
    System.out.println("Return value arrived")
    exit loop if eResults.size() = 2
end loop
System.out.println("All events processed")
```

Summary

We summarize what we have achieved so far. We have defined:

- Messages that can carry, among various meta-data, business events, system events or return data.

- Input channels that accept incoming messages and dispatch them to a process as they are required. Channels can queue messages and can be implemented in various ways. By using appropriate middleware products, channels can be made persistent.

- Output channels are responsible for setting up a connection to the receiver and delivering messages to the receiver's input channel.

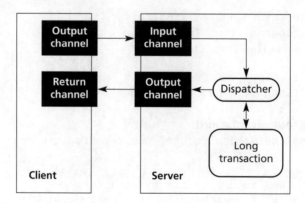

Figure 15.29 Driving a long transaction asynchronously. The channels (black) are the only objects that need thread synchronization.

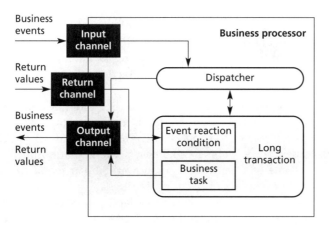

Figure 15.30   A business processor, which can be used as a building block for a network of asynchronously communicating long transactions. Only the channels (black) need synchronization.

With these relatively few new elements we can;

- dispatch a business event asynchronously;
- send the result of a long transaction invocation asynchronously to the client;
- allow several clients to participate in one long transaction;
- allow a single client to drive multiple long transactions that run concurrently on separate JVMs.

Finally, we can combine a client and a server into a business processor (we will spare you the code). The LT server can now act as a client to other LT servers (Figure 15.30).

Business processor defined

Within the course of a long transaction, business tasks can so invoke other remote long transactions, by sending a business event through the output channel to the remote server.

In such a case it might be necessary in later steps of a long transaction to check on incoming return values. This can be done in event reaction conditions which can read return messages from the return channel (they might have to wait until a return value arrives).

Accessing an output channel from a business task (and similarly the return channel from an event reaction condition) is a bit tricky because these tasks don't know these channels. Here is how it is done:

```
// use Java static method to get current thread
decide on first type t := Thread.currentThread()
// cast on LTserverThread
case LTserverThread
// and retrieve channel object
    c := t.outChannel
end decide
```

and similarly for the return channel.

Application layers and long transactions

The application model discussed in Section 15.9 works quite well for simple applications: a graphical user interface acting as client generates business events. The events are received by a long transaction which controls the execution of business tasks.

For complex applications and sophisticated user interfaces, however, this is not sufficient. A user-centric design approach means designing an application's navigation logic for ease of use and intuitive behaviour. In consumer-oriented applications issues like 'shopping experience', 'friendly atmosphere', 'impulse buying', etc. become more and more important. Similar requirements exist of course in the other categories of electronic business.

OOHDM revisited

In Section 10.4 we discussed how user interfaces can be designed in a systematic way. We discussed the design method OOHDM (Object-Oriented Hypermedia Design Method) which separates business logic from navigation logic from presentation. We feel that this three-layered approach fits well with the requirements of electronic business.

In this three-layer architecture the end user does not navigate between business objects. What the end user sees are views of the business objects, which we call *view objects*. The end user navigates between these view objects.

The end user also does not generate business events, but navigational events which in turn may result in business events.

Consequently, we can use long transactions on both the navigation layer and the business layer. We have already discussed how a long transaction can control a business process (see Section 15.9). Similarly, a long transaction is well suited to controlling a navigation process comprising navigation tasks and view objects.

- **Navigation events** are events generated by the graphical user interface as the user navigates through a site (follows links).

- **View objects** are the *nodes* in the navigational network and are derived from business objects. The relationship between view objects and business objects is not necessarily a 1:1 relationship. A business object may require several view objects for representation, or one view object can display a combination of several business objects. The composition techniques used here are well known from conceptual modelling: specialization, generalization, aggregation, or classification. It is clear, that under such circumstances navigation events are different from business events.

- **Navigation tasks** incorporate processing steps on the navigational level. They also provide transaction control for persistent view objects. Alternatively, navigation tasks can be implemented as event receiving tasks, if persistency is not required on the navigational level.

- **Links** reflect relationships intended to be explored by the user. Typically, links describe the relationships between objects of the conceptual model. Links are implemented as first-class citizens. Link classes define specific link attributes and behaviour, source and target objects, and cardinality. For one-to-many links the link object itself behaves as a node, acting as an intermediate object between the link source and the destination.

- **Access structures** support the end user in finding the desired information. Menus, indices and guided tours are examples of access structures.

- **Context classes** complement the definition of a node (view object), of a link or of an access structure. They determine which information is shown and which anchors are available when accessing the object in a particular context.

- **Navigational contexts** are induced by navigational classes such as nodes, links and access structures. A navigational context consists of a set of navigational classes (nodes, links, access structures), context classes and other (nested) navigational contexts. Different types of user may possess different navigational contexts, but also a single user may possess different navigational contexts, if the application supports different navigation modes. For example, in a product catalogue we might support different modes to list products: if we list all products of a certain manufacturer, it is not necessary to include information about the manufacturer in every product description. However, if we list products by product class, information about the manufacturer (and maybe a link to the manufacturer) should be included in all product descriptions.

- The **navigation process** is implemented by a long transaction. It receives navigation events and brings navigation tasks to execution. Depending on the navigation event, the current state of the navigation process, the outcome of event reaction conditions, and the results of the navigation tasks, appropriate business events are sent to the business layer.

In a synchronous set-up, both long transactions can run in the same thread. The navigation process sends a business event to the business process and gets control back when the event has been processed. However, if business tasks are complex, this can cause delays in the navigation process.

In an asynchronous set-up, the navigational and business layers run in separate JVMs, possibly on different machines (Figure 15.31). Business events sent by the navigation process are sent as messages to the remote business process. They are accepted by an input channel and are processed as discussed earlier. Return values are sent as messages to the return channel in the navigation layer. Later, the navigation process can check on the presence of return values. This is done in the event reaction condition of the navigation events.

Asynchronous communication between layers

An alternative design would be to regard the responses (return values) from the business layer also as navigation events that change the state of the navigation process. This would relieve us from the effort of checking these responses in the event reaction conditions of the navigation events. However, we feel that this design would lead to an explosion in the number of possible states in the navigation process.

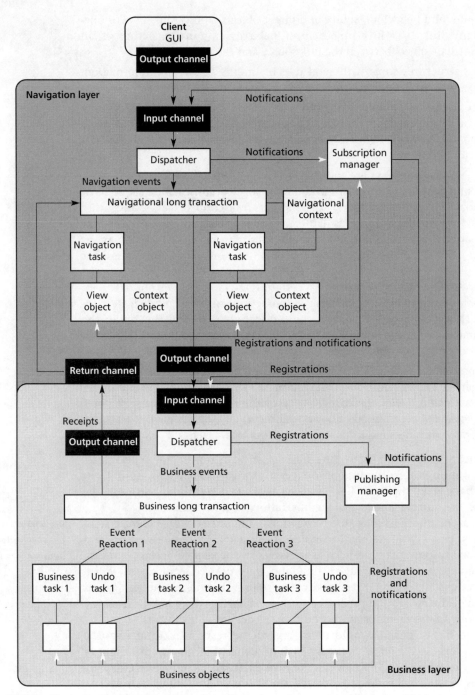

Figure 15.31   Navigation layer and business layer in an asynchronous architecture. All black units are synchronized, other units do not need synchronization. Black arrows represent events and receipts, white arrows registrations and notifications.

Compared to classical multimedia applications (such as CD-ROM titles) for which OOHDM was designed, there is a significant difference from electronic business applications. In electronic business applications the business objects do change. This requires that all view objects derived from a changed business object must be updated.

Business objects change!

This mechanism is a well-known technique in object-oriented programming, and is known as the *Publish-Subscribe Pattern*. In our case we have a *n:m* Publish-Subscribe relationship. One or many view objects (subscriber) register with one or many business objects (publisher). The subscribers want to be notified when a business object changes. When a business object does change it notifies all the view objects that have registered with it. The business views can then take the appropriate action.

Publish-Subscribe Pattern

However, this direct mechanism introduces a tight coupling between the two layers and does not work well in an asynchronous environment.

Instead, we suggest the following mechanisms:

Using managers

A subscription manager in the navigation layer takes all registrations (subscriptions) from the view objects. It stores these registrations in a local table and forwards registrations to the business layer's input channel as an asynchronous event. A dispatcher routes this special event to a publishing manager in the business layer. The publishing manager in turn registers with the business objects.

When a business object changes, it notifies the publishing manager (possibly adding application data to the notification). The publishing manager sends the notification to the input channel in the navigation layer. A dispatcher routes this special event to the subscription manager. The subscription manager now notifies all view objects that had registered for the notifying business object.

This construct separates the navigation layer and business layer well. The channels are the only synchronized objects. All other objects do not need synchronization. This architecture also reduces data traffic between navigation layer and business layer, because a business object with several business views has to send a notification only once. With an *n:m* relationship between view objects and business objects, only *n* registrations and *m* notifications must be transmitted between the two layers, instead of $n*m$ registrations and $n*m$ notifications.

Not every application will need the three-layer architecture discussed here. Simple applications can start with a one-and-a-half layer architecture, consisting of a business layer made up of servlets and a plain HTML user interface. Large sites and scenario servers, however, are well advised to invest in an architecture that separates the concerns of presentation, navigation and business logic.

Collaborative applications

In Chapter 11 we discussed several concepts and techniques for the implementation of collaborative applications, i.e. applications where multiple (and possibly distributed) users collaborate to achieve a common goal.

Collaborative applications revisited

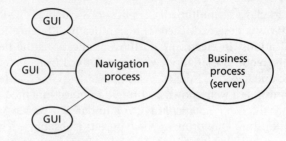

Figure 15.32 Common navigation process.

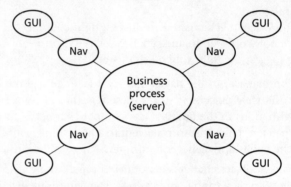

Figure 15.33 Common business process.

The business processor described above can be used to implement long transaction-based collaborative systems.

In the following we describe some possible scenarios.

In Figure 15.32 several users with replicated or specialized graphical user interfaces send navigation events to a common navigation process. The navigation process informs all users about state changes and sends business events to the business process.

In Figure 15.33 several users with replicated or specialized navigation processes and graphical user interfaces send business events to a common business process. The business process informs all users about state changes.

In Figure 15.34 each user runs its own business process, but the business processes communicate with each other. Each business layer must inform its user when another business process causes a state change.

In Figure 15.35, a main business process controls slave business processes. Concurrent operation is a possibility, but also sequential execution of the slave processes, as in a workflow system.

In Figure 15.36 we show our order processing example as a simple workflow model.

Process parts, like ordering, picking of items, packing and shipping, and finally the tracking of payment, can be identified as separable steps and are implemented

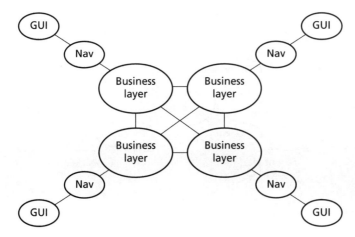

Figure 15.34   Communicating business processes.

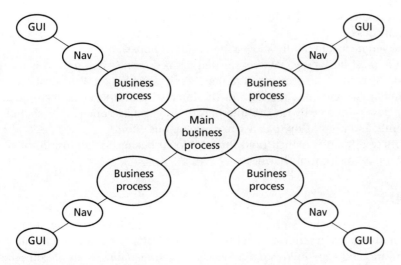

Figure 15.35   A business process controlling slave business processes.

as individual business processes. Each of the user roles (customer, picker, packer, accountant) uses specialized navigation layers and graphical user interfaces. The central business process orchestrates the workflow between these components.

In all of these scenarios it is usually necessary to implement some kind of locking mechanism for business objects. Business events must carry information about the owner of the event (the end user or the navigation process). A locking manager on the business process level can safeguard access rights to business objects. Business tasks can inform the locking manager which business objects they plan to access and how (read/write). The locking manager can then acknowledge the request or raise an exception in the case of a locking conflict.

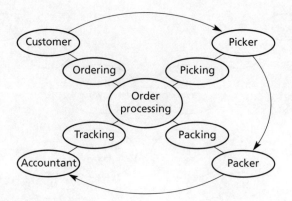

Figure 15.36   A simple workflow model.

15.11 Crossing the enterprise boundary

'Well, mate, just go to the backyard and see what you can find.' Not many enterprises operate like this – although some might, like the car breaker quoted. But even he would hardly allow a look into his books.

No, most businesses have set up well-defined facades and protocols for their business contacts, customers, suppliers, services, for financial institutions, government agencies, etc. It is also in the interest of business partners not to get too closely involved with the internals of an organization. Things change frequently and keeping up to date can cause serious effort.

These principles, which hold for traditional business relations, do of course also apply to electronic business.

B2B

For this reason electronic business-to-business (B2B) communication differs from internal communication within an organization. Within a corporation the software landscape increasingly consists of a fine-grained web of components and processes, using middleware through mechanisms such as remote procedure call (RPC), remote method invocation (RMI), DCOM or CORBA to communicate with each other.

These fine-grained imperative interface contracts are usually not suitable for the communication of software instances between businesses. In some cases they might be useful, for example if partners work on the same project, or work together in a common virtual enterprise. We discussed this topic in Chapter 11 and Section 15.10.

Loose coupling   However, in the usual client–supplier relationships these mechanisms provide a much too tight coupling – giving rise to security concerns, and forcing the partner to update his or her software frequently. Particularly when moving from a one-to-one business relation to a web of business relations, the resulting software enterprise model would gain a complexity that would be hard or impossible to manage.

Instead, it is necessary to shield the partners from the internal processes and complexities of each other's enterprise software system. This is done by setting up facades (interfaces for external partners) with which the partner systems can interact and protocols to which external partners adhere.

Open worlds and closed worlds

The design of an electronic business scenario differs considerably for open and closed business worlds.

In an open system:

- the number of potential partners is high;
- the relationship between partners is brief;
- mutual trust has no time to develop;
- the number of transactions is low;
- business is often done with the help of a third party (agent, distributor);
- the level of coordination between partners is low.

In a closed system:

- the number of partners is small;
- the working relationship extends over a long time;
- the relations are based on mutual trust;
- the number of transactions is high;
- a middleman is not usually required;
- the coordination between partners is high.

This means that an open system has to rely much more strongly on public standards than a closed system. A closed system can be based on mutual agreements.

EDI

We have already given a short review of EDI in Section 14.2. Electronic data interchange (EDI/EDIFACT) began as a typical closed-world system. Initiated by the car industry (General Motors), it has a long track record. Started in 1970, it has greatly enhanced the turnaround time for business transactions compared to paper-based transactions. However, today EDI serves only 2 per cent of US companies.

There are reasons for this:

The economic advantages of Electronic Data Interchange (EDI) are widely recognized. However, the cost of setting up an EDI relationship is still very high due to the need for a detailed bilateral business and technical agreement between the involved business partners. The initial high cost of establishing such an agreement does not justify short term partnerships. It has also been found that implementations involving the management of a large number of partners and their associated agreements are not productive. Consequently, most EDI implementations have been successful only:

– in long term partnerships;

– between a limited number of partners. (ISO/IEC 1997)

One problem is that there are different national EDI standards. A global standard EDI/EDIFACT was created by the UN and the target year of 1997 was set to migrate national standards to EDIFACT. However, the US X12 standard is still in use by many companies and will continue to be used over the next few years. Even the OBI (Open Buying on the Internet) Technical Specification V2.0 (OBI 1999) released in 1999 is based on EDI X12, and mentions EDIFACT and XML/EDI only as future options.

To establish a client–supplier relationship via EDI can be a long and difficult process:

At one conference on EDI law, James Pitts, a purchasing manager at R.J. Reynolds, said he spent 18 months negotiating a single trading partner agreement. That left him with only 349 other trading partners to go. (Euridis)

But now, the advent of the Internet has given a new lease of life to the EDI business.

OBI

One example is Open Buying on the Internet (OBI 1999). OBI concentrates on high-volume, low-dollar transactions, such as purchasing office supplies or maintenance materials. These transactions follow the 80/20 rule: they account for 80 per cent of all transactions but for only 20 per cent of transaction value. Often the purchasing cost is higher than the product cost. OBI has defined standardized scenarios (when to send a particular message and what to reply) by integrating electronic product catalogues with EDI messages.

Efforts were made by traditional EDI companies, too, to bring EDI to the web. Companies like FORESIGHT Corporation, Harbinger Corporation, IBM and OAO provide web-EDI solutions, either as client-side implementations in the form of a Java applet, or as a server-side solution. Small business partners simply use a web browser to fill out forms that have been generated from the EDI definitions. While this is certainly an option for the occasional user, it is not a solution for automated B2B transactions because data must still be entered manually into the web browser.

Some EDI companies have developed systems that use the Internet as the communication medium by transmitting encrypted EDI data over TCP/IP connections. This reduces communication costs, but the 'closed world' approach of EDI, with the drawbacks of inflexibility and high maintenance costs, acts as an inhibitor for integrated electronic business solutions. Standardized APIs for these proprietary systems are also lacking, so that integration with back-end applications remains a problem area.

In 1997 the International Organization for Standardization (ISO) and the   *Open-edi*
International Electrotechnical Commission (IEC) released a joint international
standard for the Open-edi reference model (ISO/IEC 1997). This model separates business rules (Business Operational View) from interoperability rules
(Functional Service View). It also stipulates the definition and registration of
business scenarios by business communities. This allows new users simply to
adopt a scenario instead of renegotiating all details.

Each scenario consists of:

- Several **roles**. A role defines a partner involved in a business scenario.

- **Information bundles**. These describe formally the semantics of the information which is exchanged between Open-edi parties in an Open-edi scenario.
  Information bundles are constructed using semantic components.

- **Semantic components**. A semantic component is a unit of information unambiguously defined in the context of the business goal of the business transaction.

- **Scenario attributes** (information that is independent of roles or information bundles).

Additionally, the dynamic aspects of scenarios are defined using existing formal
methods such as state transition diagrams or documentary Petri nets (Bons
et al 1995).

The Open-edi reference model is generic; it does not define an operational
standard but serves as the basis for the coordination of work between the different agencies involved in EDI standardization.

At the time of writing, there are several activities relating to Open-edi.
At the Erasmus University Research Institute for Decision and Information
Systems in Rotterdam, Netherlands, for example, a design tool is being
developed for the interactive definition of Open-edi scenarios (Lee 1999).
Business rules are not hardcoded into applications (as in classic EDI) but
are kept in declarative form and are stored in libraries, allowing applications to be adapted more easily to new situations or to different international practices.

XML

XML (see also Section 14.2) has set new ground rules on how to represent infor-   *XML/EDI*
mation. The independent XML/EDI group is working on an XML/EDI standard
(XML/EDI 1998). Two European pilot projects are currently evaluating the
XML/EDI proposal. Once finalized, XML/EDI is an option for the exchange of
Open-edi information bundles. Also, the OBI Consortium intends to integrate
XML/EDI into the OBI specification.

In the context of B2B communication, XML is not a solution but a base technology. When partners use different tag systems to mark up content, they
might be able to parse each other's XML documents, but they still cannot
understand each other. It is therefore necessary for partners to agree on

common tag systems.[3] This is done by defining common Document Type Definitions (DTDs) or XML Schemata (XML Schema). In an EDI context these definitions correlate to the semantic components which are part of Open-edi information bundles.

Because XML provides a flexible way to package complex information, XML-based B2B communication can adapt very well even to changes in the communication protocol itself. For example, a company might change their data exchange protocol by adding a new element to a defined document class, in order to cater for the requirements of a specific partner. Other partners using the same protocol are not required to act on that change. Their systems can still process the new document class but simply ignore the new tag – XML processors must be able to process any syntactically correct (well-formed) XML document.

XML support

XML has attracted a lot of industry support. Parsers and editors are freely available, and the first commercial native XML databases (XDBMSs) are appearing on the market. XML–Java bindings are available (DOM and SAX) so that XML documents can be parsed, created and modified by a Java or Bolero application.

Bolero, in particular, in combination with Software AG's Tamino XML database, offers a high-level approach for integrating XML data into an object-oriented electronic business environment (see Section 15.8).

Agents

Agents (see also Section 13.7) are another option to achieve the loose coupling required for B2B communication. When an XML document is the electronic equivalent of a business letter, agents are the liaison officers.

Agent as liaison officer

Using an agent requires the agreement and cooperation of the partner. Because the agent is deployed into the partner's computer network, the partner has to set up an agent server. The agent server provides the infrastructure so that the agent can run, communicate with the home base, and survive system crashes.

From there we can follow two different paths:

● The agent server grants the agent certain access rights to the system. The agent, for instance, might browse the partner's product catalogue and report new entries back home.

● The agent server does not grant any access rights to the agent. Instead, its own agents are deployed, which service the foreign agent. This has the advantage that the agent server is not subject to frequent version changes, and that a given scenario can be more easily reconfigured by just exchanging agents.

In both cases the agents do not necessary have to be mobile. They can be deployed at the partner's site as stationary agents.

---

3. The recently launched XML.ORG serves as a central repository and portal for XML Document Type Definitions. XML.ORG is run by the Organization for the Advancement of Structured Information Standards (OASIS) and is backed by major industrial players in the XML field.

Coordinating multi-party business processes

In the following we represent a simplified example of an international trade contract which involves several partners (Figure 15.37).

Because enforcing payment or delivery in an international environment can turn out to be difficult, banking institutions are used as middlemen. One bank, called the issuing bank, issues a letter of credit. Trusting this letter, the corresponding bank pays the seller who in turn dispatches the goods. The shipping documents are issued by the carrier and go from there via the seller and the corresponding bank to the issuing bank, which then pays the corresponding bank. On payment by the buyer, the issuing bank will hand over the shipping documents to the buyer who can then collect the goods from the carrier.

B2B example

Tables 15.7–15.11 show how the diagram is segmented into different roles. Each role (Seller, Buyer, Issuing Bank, Corresponding Bank, Carrier) can act according to the state tables defined below. An alternative approach could be to represent the state transitions as Petri nets (see Chapter 4), but we find state transition tables easier to read. They are also easy to implement as collaborating long transactions (see Section 15.10).

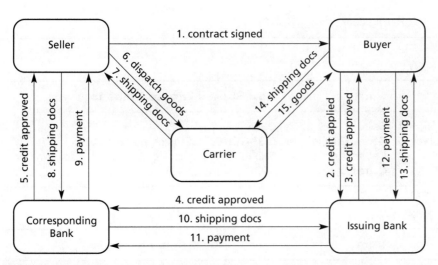

Figure 15.37 Flow of documents and goods between the partners in international trade.

Table 15.7 Role 1 – Buyer.

State	Event	from	New State	Trigger Event	to
START	contract_signed	Seller	CREDIT	credit_applied	Issuing Bank
CREDIT	credit_approved	Issuing Bank	PAYED	payment	Issuing Bank
PAYED	shipping_docs	Issuing Bank	NOTIFIED	shipping_docs	Carrier
NOTIFIED	goods	Carrier	STOP		

Table 15.8 Role 2 – Issuing Bank.

State	Event	from	New State	Trigger Event	to
START	credit_applied	Buyer	CREDIT	credit_approved	Corresponding Bank
				credit_approved	Buyer
CREDIT	shipping_docs	Corresponding Bank	PENDING	payment	Corresponding Bank
	payment	Buyer	PAYED		
PENDING	payment	Buyer	STOP	shipping_docs	Buyer
PAYED	shipping_docs	Corresponding Bank	STOP	shipping_docs	Buyer
				payment	Corresponding Bank

Table 15.9 Role 3 – Corresponding Bank.

State	Event	from	New State	Trigger Event	to
START	credit_approved	Buyer	CREDIT	credit_approved	Seller
CREDIT	shipping_docs	Seller	SHIPPED	shipping_docs	Issuing Bank
				payment	Seller
SHIPPED	payment	Issuing Bank	STOP		

Table 15.10 Role 4 – Seller.

State	Event	from	New State	Trigger Event	to
START	contract_signed	Seller	OPEN		
OPEN	credit_approved	Corresponding Bank	DISPATCHED	dispatch_goods	Carrier
DISPATCHED	shipping_docs	Carrier	SHIPPED	shipping_docs	Corresponding Bank
SHIPPED	payment	Corresponding Bank	STOP		

Table 15.11 Role 5 – Carrier.

State	Event	from	New State	Trigger Event	to
START	dispatch_goods	Seller	SHIPPING	shipping_docs	Seller
SHIPPING	shipping_docs	Buyer	STOP	goods	Buyer

Communication methods

In the most general case these five roles represent five separate partners. Their business applications are separate operational entities. How they communicate with each other depends on mutual agreement (or agreement on industry community standards).

As we stated above, using tight imperative methods for interoperation, like Java RMI, DCOM or CORBA is not appropriate. Instead these applications

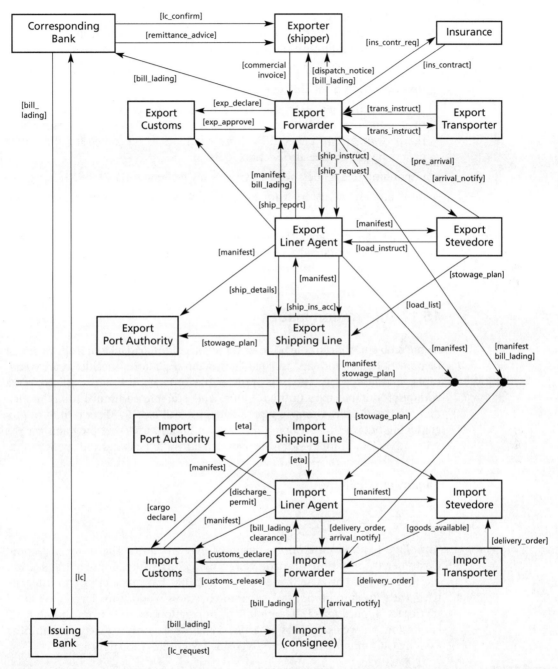

Figure 15.38   A more complete picture of the flow of documents and goods in international trade. (Source: Euridis project (Euridis))

would use company facades providing the necessary services for secure and stable interoperation with external partners. There are several technical options to implement communication between facades:

- sending messages via TCP/IP (depending on firewall set-up) or e-mail, for instance sending an XML document (slow).

- visiting each other's web sites and posting replies on web pages. Such web sites contain both HTML and XML pages. While XML is easier to interpret by the partner, HTML pages allow form elements to be embedded that allow data to be posted (see also Section 15.3).

- responding to a request with a dynamically generated HTML or XML page.

- providing an agent server for the partner's agents and deploying one's own agents.

Exercise for the daring   As we have already stated, the example above has been simplified. A more complete picture is contained in Figure 15.38. We leave the definition of the state tables as an exercise for the reader.

15.12 Integration issues

A core problem in electronic business is the integration of data islands. A variety of incompatible data formats, isolated IT structures, platform-specific security concepts, highly specific and non-transferable software solutions, all these are counterproductive to a unified, global and scalable communication model. According to Gartner Group, a typical enterprise will use 35–40 per cent of its programming budget in developing data extraction and updating programs for the sole purpose of information transfer between different databases and applications.

Legacy applications

CICS

'CICS/390 is IBM's enterprise e-business server' (Lamb). The now 30-year-old Customer Information Control System (CICS) is still a popular transaction monitor installed at 20,000 sites worldwide. IBM has made efforts to integrate CICS with the important new electronic business world, thus leveraging existing legacy applications. The amount of integration extends from simple 3270 emulation on web browsers to arbitrary complex *n*-tier systems combining existing CICS transactions with server-side Java beans and applications.

Interfacing CICS   • The *CICS Transaction Gateway* (Shanesy and Compton 1999) provides a comprehensive library of Java classes to access CICS applications from a web browser or from a web server application (Figure 15.39). The CICS Transaction Gateway provides different ways to integrate CICS into a web environment:

- CICS/390 provides a plug-in for the OS/390 web server. This allows Java and Bolero **servlets** running on the server to access CICS services via the plug-in's API. Typically, an incoming HTTP request from a client is processed by the servlet which in turn requests services from CICS. The Gateway provides all the necessary data conversion and manipulation functions that are necessary to invoke CICS transactions with a 3270 or COMMAREA interface (access to the 3270 interface is only available for non-S/390 servers). On return from CICS the servlet processes the data received and generates an HTML page which is sent back to the client. *CICS and servlets*

- Similar Gateway facilities are available for **applets**. The difference is that the processing is done at the client site and that typically the applet does not generate an HTML page for display but uses Java AWT classes to present the information within the applet's graphical user interface. *CICS and applets*

- The CICS Transaction Gateway supplies a turnkey 'terminal servlet' which translates the classical black and green 3270 CICS screens (you asked for it, you got it) into HTML on a one-to-one basis. This allows CICS applications to be run in the same way from a browser as from a 3270-compatible screen. This functionality is not available on S/390 servers. *Black and green screens*

  The Gateway allows outgoing screens to be customized (for example to extract data) or several CICS transactions to be combined into one HTML page.

- *CICS native IIOP Interface.* **CORBA IIOP** (Internet Inter-ORB Protocol) support is provided for inbound access to CICS applications. In connection with Java's CORBA support and the CICS language support for Java, CORBA clients can communicate with Enterprise JavaBeans running within CICS. CICS acts here as an object request broker (ORB) and an EJB container. The CICS JavaBean objects can be either pure Java or can implement Java wrappers for existing applications. *CICS, CORBA and EJBs*

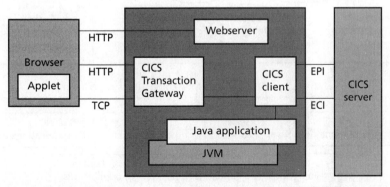

Figure 15.39 The CICS Transaction Gateway supports Java-based client- and server-side application logic.

CICS and Bolero   For Bolero, support for CICS is based on the CICS support for Java:

- Enterprise JavaBeans created with Bolero can run under CICS.

- By utilizing IBM's CICS CORBA interface, Bolero can access CICS transactions as CORBA components.

- CICS transactions can be imported into the Bolero Component Studio with the same transparency as DCOM is supported: CICS transactions show up in the Bolero Component Studio and are treated transparently as Bolero classes.

- On a low level, Bolero can utilize the CICS Transaction Gateway for OS/390: the Bolero program uses the classes in `ctgclient.jar` to access the CICS Transaction Gateway for OS/390 which in turn accesses the CICS application programs. When accessing CICS in this way, it is the Bolero program that is responsible for presenting parameter data in a format that is understood by the CICS application.

Third- and fourth-generation language applications

EntireX and DCOM   Third- and fourth-generation language-based applications, such as applications created with COBOL or Software AG's Natural development system, can be leveraged for electronic business by using Software AG's middleware product EntireX (Figure 15.40). Working as a message broker, EntireX organizes the flow of information between components of different component models. Non-componentized business functions can be wrapped by EntireX as DCOM/ActiveX components. EntireX, which is available for a variety of platforms – from Windows NT over Linux and UNIX to mainframe – acts as a container application for DCOM components.

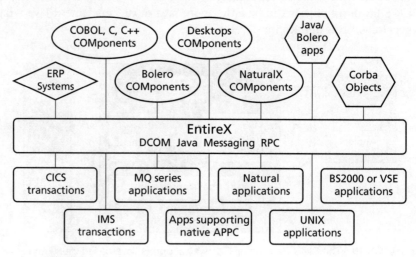

Figure 15.40   Enterprise application integration with EntireX. (Source: Software AG)

This alone allows a legacy application to be integrated with a Bolero application (see Section 15.4). In addition, EntireX can offer the functionality of existing components and business functions in the form of Java class libraries (EntireX), thus providing support not only for Bolero but also for 'pure' Java.

EntireX and Java

Software AG's Natural 4GL OLTP development system has been supplemented with the NaturalX component development system. NaturalX allows DCOM components to be implemented by means of the Natural 4GL, and to access existing DCOM components from the Natural language. This means that components created with Natural and NaturalX can be imported into the Bolero Component Studio and can be used transparently like Bolero classes. Vice versa, Bolero classes can be deployed as DCOM components and can be accessed by Natural. For an example see Section 15.4.

Natural

Legacy data

RDBMS

Java accesses relational database systems (RDBMSs) through the JDBC interface. Some RDBMSs provide their own JDBC drivers, while others can be accessed via a JDBC–ODBC bridge.

We discussed how relational data can be processed with native JDBC (see Section 12.8), or in a more object-oriented manner through Bolero's relational–object mapping (see Section 15.6).

Adabas

Software AG's Adabas database management system has been around for three decades. Invented before terms like relational and normalization were coined, it is a table-based database management system allowing multiple dimensions in table elements.

Now, Adabas supports the full SQL-2 standard, but the original Adabas direct calls are still in widespread use, mainly because they offer unparalleled performance.

Bolero's Adabas CLIP (Component Library Integration Package) allows data to be stored and retrieved from Adabas. Instead of using the JDBC interface internally, it directly translates Bolero's operations into Adabas direct calls. In addition the CLIP can import Adabas DDMs (Data Description Modules – Adabas' schema definitions) and can generate Bolero class definitions from the DDMs.

Adabas and Bolero

Third-party applications

SAP R/3

Beginning with version 4.0 of their R/3 system, SAP has started to componentize the system. R/3 4.0 now includes 14 business components (BCs), 45

Internet application components (IACs), 200 finer-grained business objects (BOs), and more than 400 BAPIs to access business functionality (Mauth 1998).

- **Business components** provide business functionality on a larger scale, such as human resources, availability-to-promise, product data management, consolidation, and pricing.

- **Business objects** represent smaller business functions (for example, an order). They are accessed through BAPIs (Business Application Programming Interfaces).

SAP and Java

In the long term, SAP plans to encapsulate all R/3 functionality in BAPIs. Because not all R/3 functionality is covered by BAPIs at present, DCOM and Java programmers might have to resort in some cases to remote function calls (RFCs) to access R/3 functionality. Both BAPIs and RFCs offer Java and DCOM support (contained in the SAP Automation package and the SAP DCOM Component Connector package, respectively) and can work synchronously or asynchronously.

SAP and Bolero

Bolero supports R/3 with a special SAP R/3 CLIP (Component Library Integration Package) (Figure 15.40). Based on the JRFC class library and assisted by the R/3 repository, RFC and BAPI types can be imported as components into the Bolero Component Studio. They can then be used transparently like other Bolero classes.

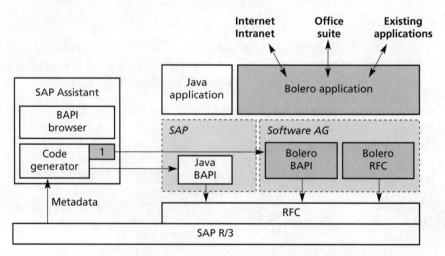

Figure 15.41 The Bolero SAP R/3 CLIP supports the generation of Bolero RFC-type and BAPI-type classes assisted by SAP Assistant and SAP Metadata. (Source: Software AG)

Baan

Most other manufacturers of enterprise resource planning (ERP) software provide access to their systems in the form of Java APIs, DCOM or CORBA.

Like SAP, Baan have started to componentize their applications:

- **Functional components** (FCs) define larger business functions, such as finance or warehousing.
- **Business object component sets** (BOCS) model finer-grained business objects. In contrast to SAP's BOs, BOCS can maintain persistent data.

Business object interfaces (BOIs) control the information flow and transactional context between business objects. In our terminology they can be compared to business tasks. BOIs are designed to be used with an ORB (object request broker) such as CORBA or DCOM. BOIs currently work synchronously, requiring online connections (LAN, WAN) between applications.

From Bolero, BOIs can be accessed via either DCOM or CORBA.

Methodology

Method is the soul of business.

The Business Man, *Edgar Allan Poe*

Part 4 discusses aspects of software reusability and software engineering methodology. Readers will benefit from basic knowledge of project management and object-oriented principles.

● Chapter 16 argues that reusability is not a business goal in itself. Instead reusability must be seen in the context of software engineering and quality assurance, in order to achieve business goals such as flexibility, time-to-market and cost effectiveness. Several developments in software technology, especially in programming languages, are discussed in this context.

● Chapter 17 discusses a reuse methodology based on a component-based architecture. Guidelines are developed to maximize the benefit from the reuse of components.

● Chapter 18 introduces Software AG's SELC, an incremental and iterative life-cycle model developed in particular for object-oriented electronic business applications.

Software reuse? 16

Since programmers started to write applications for computers they have fundamentally agreed with the rulers of the Roman empire: *Divide et Impera*. In fact, D&I had long before become the motto of all engineering art: if a problem is too complex to be solved in a brute force attempt, divide it into several smaller sub-problems, and tackle each of them separately.

When we use this strategy repeatedly we will soon find out that some sub-problems appear again and again, and that we start to reinvent the wheel. For example, if we have successfully partitioned the task of cleaning our lounge into the sub-tasks of vacuuming the carpet and cleaning the windows, we will soon find out that the task of cleaning the lounge windows is very similar to the task of cleaning the kitchen windows, and so we might use the same procedures.

This is what software reuse is about. It is about reusing existing designs, programs and procedures, to make the computer execute similar tasks in a *different* context. It also means that an existing design or implementation must be generic enough to adapt to a new context. To stay with the example, the windows cleaning procedure should be able to adapt to different window sizes and shapes.

Software reuse, however, is *not* a business goal in itself. Software reuse is one strategy among others to achieve a given business goal. *Reuse a business goal?*

Business goals may be:

- Re-engineer business processes for a more effective enterprise.
- Minimize the cost for software development and maintenance.
- Solve the software crisis within an enterprise.
- Shorten the time-to-market for a product.
- Increase customer satisfaction.

These goals are often contradictory. The fourth point especially can create much havoc. Time pressure has often led to quick-and-dirty implementations that cause heavy maintenance costs in the future. Usually written to solve an urgent problem, these 'solutions' tend to live on, and on, and on, ... the Y2K problem is in part the result of this type of 'engineering'.

The rapid development of the Internet and of electronic business has led to similar problems. To get businesses quickly on the net, many shortcuts were taken; properly engineered sites are the exception, not the rule.

In June 1998 IEEE Software (Pressman 1998) held a roundtable with experts from the software engineering field under the title 'Can Internet-based Applications Be Engineered?'. *Can Internet-based applications be engineered?*

The very fact that this question was raised suggests that many sites have become chaotic jungles of web pages, CGI scripts, Java applets and ActiveX elements, Active Server Pages, Dynamic HTML pages, plug-ins, etc. The results show in huge unmanageable sites, with maintenance scheduled for a few hours sometimes lengthening into weeks.

At a growth rate of 70 per cent per annum electronic business will dominate IT in a few years' time. It is vital to discuss engineering strategies for electronic business now if the industry does not want to be faced with problems that will make the Y2K problem appear miniscule.

Tool support for software engineering

So, we are arguing strongly for taking an engineering approach to electronic business applications. What we then have to ask of the tools and programming systems is:

- That they provide a way to *create* new applications quickly. This does not necessarily mean that a new application must be *written* quickly. The creation of a new application includes several phases. The writing of code takes only 10–20 per cent of the whole effort. Work invested during the early design and implementation phases usually pays off during alpha- and beta-test and during maintenance.

  Programs should be well designed and documented. Bugs should be detected as early as possible, preferably during compilation. The programming system chosen should implement standard tasks as language features, because language features (other than library features) are subject to compiler checks.

- That the applications created must be robust. Constructs that are difficult to debug in a test environment should be avoided. Typical candidates are low-level memory management, low-level process and thread synchronization, and low-level database transaction control.

  For electronic business applications it is essential that not only functional tests are executed but also high volume 'crash' tests.

- That the applications created must be flexible. It must be possible to adapt applications to changing requirements quickly and without surprises.

  The program code must be easy to read and to understand, and the programming constructs used intuitive. Separate concerns in an application should appear as separate code units. Changes to components should not have remote effects on other components.

- That they allow existing designs or components to be reused, including third-party components and legacy systems. Programming systems must provide ways to 'glue' external components into an application, and to customize components for the purposes of the application.

If it seems that we are drifting away from the theme of the chapter (software reuse) that impression is correct. We see software reuse as one point in the wider context of software engineering. We find that some of the techniques formerly advertised under the banner of software reuse, such as object orientation and inheritance, are in fact techniques that are more relevant to solid software engineering, correctness, robustness and flexibility.

In recent years, component-based software development systems have become a reality. Here we see chances for significant software reuse: not just a few lines of inherited code from an abstract class are reused, but whole customizable plug-and-play software components.

16.1   Simple things first

Sorry to mention this, but the readability of a language is directly related to the quality of the software that is implemented with it. A program that can be read and understood easily is also easier to debug, to change, and to reuse. Information hiding, David Parnas' (Parnas 1972) famous principle for modular programming, does not mean code obfuscation.

In fact, the most effective technique for achieving code correctness is peer code revision – to have the code checked by somebody other than the author. Some of the most successful software products rely on open, published code. The more people can read and understand the code, the better.

Here are a few hints.

Avoid terseness

The first commercial programming language was COBOL, a language anything but terse. Statements such as

COBOL vs. APL

```
ADD a TO b GIVING c
```

today make us smile at such verbosity, but at the time when COBOL was introduced it made a lot of sense. Programmers used to write their code on paper (with a pencil!). The code was then transferred to punched cards by trained typists, and the cards were then printed out and proof-read by the programmer before the program was submitted for compilation. With turnaround times of hours or days between compilations, typographic errors were fatal. A programming language that spelt everything out in full words was easy to type and easy to proof-read, and was reasonably safe against typos.

Then came APL. APL was launched when timesharing systems became available. Each user was connected to his or her own APL session – the terminal at that time was an IBM ball-point typewriter, a mechanical miracle. APL was an interpretative language; it was possible to type in a program, run it, and get the result immediately. What progress!

However, there was a problem. Programmers and scientists could not type! So the extreme terseness of APL (mostly a single character for one instruction) made it popular (not so much to type). And because it used Greek characters (you needed a special ball-point), a trained typist would have to hunt for them, too, so you did not look too silly when typing with two fingers.

Consequently, APL programs were difficult to read – even for the author – and APL soon gained the reputation of being a WOL (write-only language). The language never made big inroads into commercial programming, despite IBM's effort to market it as a business programming language in the early 1970s. APL is still in use today, but its significance for the development of mission-critical enterprise applications is nil. In the meantime, programmers have learnt how to use a keyboard, so extreme terseness is no longer cool.

Intuitive syntax

Equality vs. assignment

A computer language should use operators and commands in the way they are expected to be used. A good example is the assignment operation: we all know from school that the equality operator is '='. We know that $a = b$ means a equals b. We also know that if $a = b$ holds, then also $b = a$.

Then FORTRAN appeared. The equality sign was used for a different operation: in FORTRAN a = b means: assign value b to variable a, destroying the former content of a. Obviously, if a = b is correct, b = a is dead wrong. Not so good. However, FORTRAN had started a tradition. C, C++ and Java all use = for the destructive assignment.

COBOL does not run any risk of being misunderstood by spelling out what is meant – loud and clear: MOVE b TO a. ALGOL expressed the different semantics of assignment and equality by using a := b for assignment, and so do Pascal and Delphi, Modula, Eiffel, Natural and Bolero. The asymmetric form of the operator makes clear that the operation is not symmetric.

Operator overloading

Operator overloading was and is the subject of a heated debate in the object-oriented world. It is also an often misunderstood term. The term *operator overloading* does *not* refer only to infix operators but to *methods* in general (the term operator overloading has historical reasons). Operator overloading means that the very same method name can be used for different method implementations, depending on the type and number of its arguments.

Both method calls

```
a.add(b)    // b Integer
a.add(c)    // c BigDecimal
```

address different implementations, and can mean very different things. They are, in fact, different methods with different method signatures (a method signature consists of the method name and the types of the parameters).

In addition, the actual method executed depends on the content of the left argument a. This field may contain a subtype of the specified (static) type, and the subtype may have overridden the method implementation.

For the argument on the right (b and c), however, it is the static type that determines which method is executed. The actual content of these variables does not matter.

By now, it should be clear why operator overloading is controversially discussed in OO circles. Operator overloading requires discipline from the programmer, to use the same method names consistently for the same meaning. Operator overloading is not suitable for languages implementing multiple inheritance. In these languages method implementations are possibly inherited from a large number of parent classes and things become rather unpredictable.

In single inheritance languages, like Java or Bolero, however, we think that operator overloading has more benefits than disadvantages – using the same name for the same operation makes much sense.

User-definable *infix operators* are a useful feature to improve readability, too, especially for object-oriented languages. Why should we be forced to express the same meaning with different notations?

Infix operators

```
a + b    // a is Integer
a.add(b) // a is BigDecimal
```

In contrast

```
a + b    // a is String
```

Instead, we would like to write a + b in all cases. For that reason, Bolero allows infix operators to be used in library classes and user-defined classes.

C was designed as a language to implement an operating system: UNIX. It was designed close to the hardware (special operators like << or ++ refer directly to common hardware operations like *shift* and *increment*). C helped to replace assembler in many applications and paved the way for platform-independent programming. C, however, was not defined as a commercial programming language.

C syntax

Java adopted the somewhat cryptic syntax of C with good reason: there was a huge audience of frustrated C++ programmers who were to become Java programmers. The Java for statement, for example, looks just like a C for statement:

```
for (int i=0; i<8; i++) ...
```

Bolero's syntax, in contrast, is more spelt out and is closer to the business world.

```
for i type Integer in 0..7 do
     ...
end for
```

We also notice a difference in the semantics of the control structure: while C and Java use an algorithm to describe the possible values of the variable (initialize with 0, continue while smaller than 8, increment by 1 after each pass), Bolero uses an active object (in this case a range type) that iterates through all possible values. The argument could be any object that implements an Iterator, such as range objects, arrays, collections, and results of database queries.

Clear demarcation of control structures

Languages like C, C++ and Java do not feature explicit control structures. Instead they have control statements, like if or for, which are used in conjunction with another statement or statement block. Statement blocks are neutral and are demarcated with neutral delimiters { } .

In more complex routines this often leads to sequences of demarcation characters, for example

```
        }
      }
    }
```

This has the disadvantage that it is not easy to see where the scope of each control statement ends, and programmers often help themselves by appending comments:

```
      }   //  if
    }   //  for
  }   //  method
```

A programming language that features real control structures (here, Bolero) improves the readability of source code. It can also apply more advanced syntax checks to ensure valid control structures.

```
method m1
    ....
    if a < b then
        for i type Integer in 1..10 do
            ....
        end for
    end if
end method m1
```

16.2   Divide and conquer

As much as engineers agree on this concept, they disagree on how to put it into practice. In the history of computing many strategies for the implementation of *Divide et Impera* have evolved. We name only the most important of these strategies:

- In *procedural programming* a computational process is segmented into several steps, called procedures. Often these procedures share data structures with other procedures, so procedures usually depend on each other. This makes it not only difficult to reuse procedures in another context, but also to apply changes to one procedure without affecting others. In the history of procedural programming, several principles, such as data encapsulation and information hiding (Parnas 1972), have evolved. These principles finally led to the development of object-oriented languages.

- *Functional programming* sees a whole computer program as a single mathematical function. The function is broken down into smaller functions, until a level of primitive functions is reached. Functions are stateless; they do not have data structures, so they can't overwrite each other's data structures. Instead all data is passed as parameter or as result. Functions can easily be reused in other contexts, and the resulting programs are very robust. However, functional programming has never made big inroads into commercial programming, probably because the concept of stateless functions is too alien for the data-driven environment of commercial programming.

16.3 The object-oriented approach

Object-oriented programming evolved from procedural programming, by combining a shared set of data with the procedures (methods) that access this data into one software object. The data set defines the object's state, while the methods implement the object's behaviour. Because objects have the characteristic stimulus/response behaviour known from real-world 'animals', they are usually quite intuitive. In business programming, we can model real-world objects, such as customers, products, orders, into software objects which we call business objects. Objects lend themselves well to reuse, because they have a clearly defined interface and don't depend on their context.

A common metaphor for an object in object-oriented programming is that of the machine (Meyer 1997). The state of the machine is changed by 'command' methods, while 'query' methods interrogate the machine's state. Query methods should *not* modify the object's state, i.e. they should not have any side effects. The rationale for separating methods into command-style methods and query-style methods is to increase the reusability of object classes, and to make class specification easier to understand and to reason about. Database management systems use the same approach: the functions to access a database are strictly separated into commands and queries – commands modify data, and queries retrieve but do not modify the data.

Command and query

In a large application, we will find that many object classes have features in common. Object-oriented programming languages therefore allow a hierarchy of classes to be defined. The classes at the top contain the most common features. Subclasses inherit these features and can extend the class definition with new features (or override inherited features).

Older object-oriented languages, such as Simula or Smalltalk, support single inheritance – each class can have only one parent class. This was often found not to be sufficient: classes are often multifaceted, they can be seen as combinations of different types. For example, a class might implement the types Printable, Observable and Serializable.

Newer languages, such as C++ or Eiffel, implement multiple inheritance – a class can inherit features from several parents. Especially in C++, this has caused problems when inheriting implementations of methods. There is always the problem of name clashes when inheriting from multiple ancestors, and the programmer has to decide on a method by method basis how these conflicts

Multiple inheritance?

Class and interface

should be resolved: prefer the method of one ancestor, rename methods, concatenate methods (in which sequence?). This introduces additional coupling between ancestor and child class. Applications become more complex and more difficult to change (Sakkinen 1988).

Java, and with it Bolero, has learned from this experience. Here, the concepts of class (the implementation) and type (the interface) are separated. Inheritance between classes is only allowed from a single ancestor, but inheritance between interfaces allows multiple ancestors.

This means that a class can inherit only a single implementation, but it can be used as a subtype of many ancestor types, providing the required flexibility for polymorphism. This solution maintains most of the benefits of multiple inheritance while avoiding the tight coupling between child and ancestors.

In the past, inheritance has been praised as a major concept for software reuse. In the meantime it has become clear that over-exploitation of inheritance works counterproductively – vast inheritance structures are directly opposed to the principle *Divide et Impera*. Program readability suffers; the term 'yo-yo effect' (wandering up and down the class hierarchy to understand what is going on) has its origins here (Taenzer et al. 1989). So, the advice is – despite the contradictory advice in many OO-related publications – to keep inheritance paths short.

> *The inheritance principles used in object-oriented programming were inherited (excuse the pun) from the taxonomy system developed by the Swedish biologist Carl Linné (1701–78). However, Linné developed his system to classify existing material, not as a method for construction. Bertrand Meyer (Meyer 1997) gives a good three-page overview of the history of taxonomy, and about all other issues of object-oriented programming in the rest of the 1,254 pages.*

16.4   Software safety

Type safety

Almost any programming language has some mechanism to check for the compatibility of data types within an operation, or to admit only certain data types as parameters in a function call. Especially in object-oriented languages, where each class and interface introduces a new data type, type safety is in high demand:

Dynamic vs. static typing

- Languages like Smalltalk execute source code statements directly with an interpreter. It is not required to compile a program before it can be executed. The consequence is that type compatibility can only be checked during execution. These languages therefore do not require a type to be specified when a variable is defined: the type of a variable is the type of its content; this is called *dynamic typing*. Type safety in such languages is low: incompatibilities are found only when testing a program.

● Languages like Eiffel, C++, Java, or Bolero compile programs before they can be executed. This allows data types to be checked by the compiler throughout the program; the result is better type safety. All these languages require the specification of a type when a variable is declared (static typing), this enables the compiler to perform the necessary checks.

It is not always possible to follow the strict type algebra of static typing. When acquiring data from external sources, such as a file or database, when talking to external modules such as a DCOM component, or when using generic constructs such as collection classes (see Section 15.2) , it is often necessary to assign data content to variables of a formally incompatible type. This is called *type casting*. Type casting disables type checking by the compiler and is therefore a source of type compatibility errors at runtime.

Type casting

The design of a type-safe language should reduce the necessity for type casts to a minimum. One strategy is to use generic types (see Section 15.2). While generic types allow the required flexibility for collection classes and similar constructs, they still allow type checking by the compiler – no type casts are required.

Generic types

Another strategy to reduce type errors is to include access methods to external data and components into the language. This has been exercised by fourth-generation languages (4GLs) where access to databases is fully integrated into the language. Bolero follows the same path: using object–relational mapping and relational–object mapping, structures and data types in the database are automatically mapped onto Bolero classes and Bolero data types (see Section 15.6). No type casting is required. In contrast, access to a database through JDBC does require type casting.

Automatic type mapping

The same is true when importing DCOM, CORBA components or CICS transactions into the Bolero Component Studio. Data types from these component models are automatically mapped onto Bolero data types, and no type casting is required (see Sections 15.4 and 15.12).

Semantic safety

Software constructs often rely on certain assumptions about the context in which they are deployed. This can make the reuse of software constructs dangerous. Bertrand Meyer (Meyer 1997), who had pioneered contracts in the Eiffel programming language, tells the story of the Ariadne5 rocket that had burst into pieces shortly after being launched because of a software problem. A numeric routine (written in ADA) caused an unhandled exception. The assumptions made by the authors of the routine were correct, but only for Ariadne4. The routine was originally written for Ariadne4 and was then reused for Ariadne5 where the assumptions did not hold.

Programming by contract (see Section 15.2) is not a construct to make a software unit more generic or more reusable. Instead, its task is to make reusable software components safer. When a software component is reused in

Contracts

another context, it may encounter parameter values that were not foreseen or planned when the component was implemented. The contract makes sure that an exception is raised as soon as possible before an unforeseen value combination causes havoc.

16.5 Separation of concerns

We discussed separation of concerns (Hürsch and Lopes 1994) and aspect-oriented programming (AOP) in Chapter 8.

Systems have to deal with a multitude of concerns, such as persistency, transaction control, error recovery, concurrency, location control (which object is remote and which is not), performance issues, robustness, logging, auditing, internationalization, GUI-fication, etc. More often than not the amount of this 'overhead' code far exceeds the amount of code necessary for the business logic.

In the example from Section 15.2:

```
class Product
  is public and is persistence capable with population

instance field Name type String is public

instance field Price type BigDecimal is public
  contract
    precondition newValue >= 0
    postcondition result >= 0
  end contract
  value 0

instance method getVAT is public
  parameter Rate type Decimal
  result type BigDecimal
  throws VatError, VatRateError, PriceError
  contract
    precondition Rate >= 0 else throw VatRateError()
    precondition Price >= 0 else throw PriceError()
    postcondition result >= 0 else throw VatError()
  end contract

  implementation
      result := Price*Rate/100
  end implementation

end method getVAT
end class Product
```

the business logic is contained in just one line:

```
result := Price*Rate/100
```

Often, the 'overhead' code intermingles with the program's business logic, making business classes difficult to read, reuse, change and maintain (Lopez 1997).

'Separation of concerns' postulates that those individual aspects should not clutter business logic but should be handled separately. On the design level 'separation of concerns' is well known and well practised. At implementation level, however, most programming languages do not allow the separate formulation of aspects. Several new language developments, for example Xerox' AspectJ, have been designed and implemented to explore the new paradigm of aspect-oriented programming (Kiczales et al 1997-2). The different aspects of a software construct are formulated in different sections of a program, in some systems by using different languages. The aspect code is later *woven* into the main program logic, either by a program generator, by a preprocessor, or by the compiler.

That doesn't sound like object-oriented programming, does it? The object-oriented paradigm postulates that all functions applied to an object should be part of the object definition. But there are objects and objects, just as there are people and people. There is the average person who has to do everything himself – make his appointments himself, fix the car himself, and mow the lawn at weekends. And there is the business person, who has a secretary managing his time, a chauffeur to look after the car, and a gardener to keep the lawn in optimal shape. All this is done smoothly, efficiently and professionally, allowing our friend to attend to business without distraction. With objects it is just the same. The average object has to look after everything itself: exception handling, transaction management, coordination with other objects. And then there is the business object which is looked after and which can concentrate on doing business. A class society? Sure, that is where objects live … .

Business class service

Bolero supports 'separation of concerns' on two levels:

- First, it suggests a methodology for implementing business applications: the triad of business object, business task and business process (implemented through persistent objects, transaction-control objects and long transactions) separates different concerns (Figure 16.1). (See also Section 15.9.)
- Second, the Bolero Component Studio separates the different aspects of program logic by presenting them on different sheets of a tabbed notebook (Figures 16.2 and 16.3). On the class level, things like object persistence, object–relational mapping, the component model used, DCOM and EJB properties, and transaction control are kept away from the code.

  On the method and field level, a similar separation exists. Contracts and exceptions are kept away from the code, and also other meta-information.

Business Object (persistence-capable class)	Business logic Persistency Object–Relational mapping
Business Task (transaction-control class)	Database transaction control Business Object relations
Business Process (long transaction)	Coordination Semantic Undo Recovery Logging

Figure 16.1   Separating different concerns.

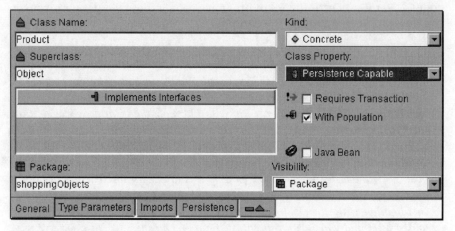

Figure 16.2   General properties sheet for class `Product`.

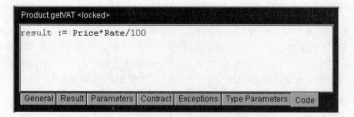

Figure 16.3   Code sheet for the `getVAT` method of class `Product`. The business logic clearly stands out.

This makes the business logic of classes easier to understand and to maintain. Programs that are easily understood can also be easily adapted for other purposes. It also becomes possible to modify certain aspects, such as transaction control or the component model, without touching the business logic.

16.6 Exception handling

If business logic is the rule, what is the exception?

Exceptions are situations that cannot be handled with the normal programming structures of business logic, such as:

- Hardware exceptions: no disk space, broken communication line.
- Network errors: wrong URL, no response from server.
- Operating system exceptions: too many windows open, not enough resources, file I/O errors.
- Unintentional application exceptions, such as: bugs, missing modules, version errors, type errors.
- Intentional application exceptions such as:
  - exceptions caused by the execution of a `throw` statement;
  - exceptions caused by the violation of a contract;
  - exceptions caused by long transactions, for example, if an event reaction condition detects an invalid situation.

Wrong input of data by the *end user* is *not* an exception but the rule. Validation of user input is part of the business logic.

Exception handling in most modern programming languages is based on the onion skin model introduced with the ADA programming language: an exception raised in an inner program block tries to get out, but exception handlers on each block level may catch it on the way (Figure 16.4). Exceptions that do get out bring the application down. *The onion skin model*

In most object-oriented languages exceptions are first-class citizens, usually subtypes of class `Exception`. Exception objects may carry additional data with detailed information about the cause and context of the exception, allowing a detailed diagnosis of what went wrong where. This is a significant improvement compared to many non-object-oriented languages where only a mere error code is returned. *Exceptions are first-class citizens*

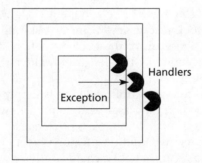

Figure 16.4 The onion skin model of exception handling.

In Java and Bolero, proper exception handling is enforced by the compiler: a program block that raises an exception or calls a method that may raise an exception must either have an exception handler for this exception type or must declare that it may raise this exception type itself.

In Bolero exception handlers are always located at the end of a block:

```
begin
        connect("DataBase", "User", "Password")
...
        something.dangerous()
...

        on exception e
        case IOException
            System.out.println("IO error")

        case OverflowException
            System.out.println("Overflow")

        default
            System.out.println("Exception" + e)
        end exception

        finally
            disconnect
        end finally
end
```

In this example the on exception clause checks on the dynamic type of exception e. The default clause is executed when none of the case clauses match. The finally clause is always executed to clean up things at the end of a block.

16.7 Design patterns

Innovations are rarely conceived in isolation, especially when writing software. Programmers usually look first at how a similar task was solved before, before they formulate the design goals or the implementation strategy. 'Make it look like a Macintosh' was reportedly the design imperative that finally resulted in the Windows operating system.

That does not mean that an existing solution is simply copied. It only serves as the blueprint of a vision, and as a road map on how to get there. In the course of design and implementation, parts of an already existing solution are accepted, modified or rejected, and new features are added. On the way, new innovative solutions appear, but they could not have appeared if there had been no discourse with the state of the art.

Graphical designers, for example, use the same method. For a new project one of the first actions is to browse catalogues of already existing (and successful) designs. On the basis of these existing designs new designs are created.

The same applies to architects. There is a strong market for architectural magazines and books that inform architects about the works of the masters, new trends, and problem solutions.

It is appropriate that it was an architect who put this process of innovation into a formal method: the concept of design patterns was first formulated by the architect Christopher Alexander (he also had a background in mathematics). Alexander published on urban planning and building architecture in the late 1970s.

Origin of design patterns

Design patterns in their original meaning describe the *relationship* between a *problem*, the *context* of the problem and the *solution* of the problem. They describe this relationship in such a way that it becomes possible to transfer the means of solving the problem into a different context. Design patterns are not invented: they are discovered when similar solutions are found to solve similar problems in various contexts.

Unlike object-oriented inheritance, where knowledge transfer is vertical (from an ancestor to a descendant), knowledge transfer through design patterns happens horizontally: the new solution (B) found with the help of an existing solution (A) is a solution in its own right and is independent of solution (A).

In software design, work on design patterns began in the late 1980s and reached its culmination in the work of the 'gang of four', Erich Gamma, Richard Helm, Ralph Johnson and John Vlissides (Gamma et al 1995). Since then, patterns have become popular in software design.

For example, let us consider the relationship `customer:order`. This relationship between the two classes `Customer` and `Order` could be implemented with a field in class `Order` that refers to the order's owner (`Customer`).

Design patterns explained

With more experience we find out that there are similar problems that require similar solutions, for instance the relationship `supplier:invoice`, or `department:employee`. We find that these problems have something in common (modelling a `OneMany` relationship).

Formulating a design pattern requires us to abstract from the concrete scenario. Instead of speaking of the relationship `customer:order` we speak of the relationship `roleB:roleA`, and we formulate the problem in an abstract way based on `roleB` and `roleA` (Figure 16.5).

Transferring this new `OneMany` pattern to a new context requires only the assignment of concrete classes, such as `supplier` and `invoice`, to the abstract roles `roleA` and `roleB`, and lo!, the pattern should deliver a solution for this problem.

In Bolero, we find support for design patterns in the Bolero Component Studio (Figure 16.6). A pattern scenario consists of:

Design patterns in Bolero

- the *pattern class*, for example the `OneMany` pattern class. The abstract roles (in our case `roleA` and `roleB`) are properties of this class;
- a *source*, consisting of all the classes constituting the source context, such as the role classes `Customer` and `Order`, and all additional classes, fields and

methods that belong to the solution of the specific problem, in our case of the `Customer:Order` problem;

- a *source pattern instance*, in our example an instance of the `OneMany` pattern class, describing the relationship between source context and abstract pattern. The properties implementing the abstract roles are instantiated with the concrete roles of the source context. The concrete roles of the source context are mapped onto the abstract roles of the pattern class, for example `Order` ⇔ `roleA`, `Customer` ⇔ `roleB`;

- a *target*, consisting of the classes constituting the target context, such as `Supplier` and `Invoice`. Only empty class definitions are required here, because fields, methods and auxiliary classes will be generated automatically in the process.

Cloning a solution

Given these ingredients, the patterns can transfer the solution from the source context to the target context in three steps:

1. In the first step a target pattern instance is created, in our example another instance of the `OneMany` pattern class, now instantiated with `Invoice` ⇔ `roleA`, `Supplier` ⇔ `roleB`.

2. Under the control of both source and target pattern instances, the solution formulated in the source scenario is then *cloned* onto the target context. In this cloning process the pattern acts as the transport mechanism, copying all class definitions, fields and methods from the source to the target and adapting them to the target context.

3. The resulting target classes can be compiled and tested immediately. If the result does not match expectations, the target can be *uncloned*, i.e. reset to its initial definition.

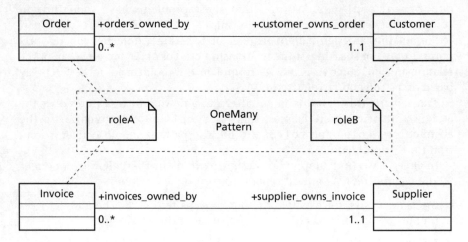

Figure 16.5 Formulating a design pattern.

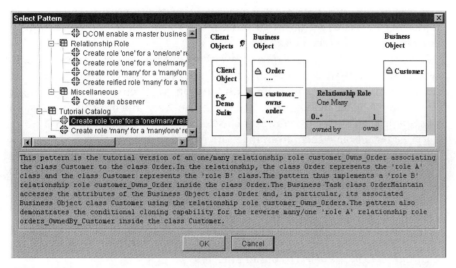

Figure 16.6 Design patterns in Bolero: predefined patterns transfer an existing solution to another problem domain.

The transfer of an existing solution to another context is, of course, only the first step in the engineering process. Changes can be made to the target solution generated. Changes in the source solution will have no influence on the target solution after cloning.

It is important to realize that a pattern does not provide a solution to a problem but a method to transfer a solution from one context or scenario to another. Documentation is a must: like any design decision, the use of a design pattern should be clearly documented in an application.

Patterns can be used in different granularity. It is possible to use patterns for very small problems, like the example above, but also for very large problems, like an application framework. It is possible to use small patterns within large patterns, which can result in very powerful constructs.

A set of predefined patterns is available in Bolero. These include: *Standard patterns*

- relationship patterns, such as one-one, one-many, many-one;
- business task patterns, such as single-platform-elementary-object, single-platform-aggregate-object, distributed-platform-elementary-object;
- publisher-subscriber pattern.

16.8 Components

'Objects lend themselves well to reuse, because they have a clearly defined interface and don't depend on their context.' That is what we wrote when we discussed object-oriented programming, and that is also how object-oriented programming was advertised.

It is certainly true that objects have clearly defined interfaces and that they do not suffer the main problem of procedural programming: the overwriting of variables in common data areas.

In recent years, however, experience with a large number of commercial software projects has shown that this claim does not hold. Objects in fact are independent of their context, but only in a physical sense. On the semantic level, or in their behaviour, most objects depend very much on their peers, on other objects in the same context. Most objects only make sense in a given object pattern. Isolate them from that pattern and they are useless.

Of course, there are certainly objects of general interest. Most of these objects are already contained in developer kits and libraries. In terms of reusability, OO techniques have in part reached a 'saturation' point.

So, the time has come for a new concept in software reuse. The new concept is called components (see Chapter 9). Components are by definition reusable:

A component is a type, class or any other workproduct that has been specifically engineered to be reusable. (Jacobson et al 1997)

Opportunities to share and reuse components are manifold. There are many business functions that are common from business to business and are replicated in the electronic business applications that support them. For example, customers requesting an enterprise's services are usually asked a set of common questions: What is your name? What is your address? What is your phone number? What is your date of birth? etc. Across the enterprise, these same functions are performed over and over in many different applications. Identifying common, reusable components provides significant benefits for maintaining application code.

These benefits include:

- *Productivity gain for the developer*. Pre-built and pre-tested reusable components that are ready for plug-in by the developer reduce the effort and time required to develop new or maintain existing applications.
- *Consistency and accuracy of processing*. Consistency and accuracy are achieved by having only one component responsible for a particular function.
- *Simplified testing*. Once a component has been thoroughly tested, it usually does not require extensive testing when it is integrated with other components to form an application.

To achieve the benefits of sharing and reusing components, a successful reuse strategy must include:

- a reuse methodology that is consistently applied by application developers;
- a component review board whose function enables the reuse program by reviewing projects and assisting with component reuse;
- documentation for each component which includes a well-defined set of input and output parameters for each interface option provided;

- a library, or repository, of information about reusable components;
- integrated error and exception handling capabilities which enable each component to operate independently of other components and applications.

We would be negligent if we ignored the issue of legacy applications in the context of componentware. Often these applications represent a value of 10 or 20 years of ongoing investment. Seriously reusing software therefore means developing a strategy to utilize existing applications in the context of electronic business.

The technique for identifying reusable components in existing applications is known as 'harvesting' or 'application mining'. Application mining involves two steps:

Application mining

- An **exploration** phase where the legacy applications are examined with the goal of isolating business functions and business objects into components.
- An **exploitation** phase where the selected business functions and business objects are made into objects. The techniques used here include a technology called 'wrapping' or 'encapsulation'. Code is implemented (manually or automatically) that wraps an API around a legacy service.

17 A reuse methodology

A successful implementation of an *n*-tier, reusable component-oriented architecture is not solely dependent on the ability to develop reusable components. Success also depends on the ability to provide the tools and management of the components for reuse.

Enterprise data model

In this context, enterprises benefit by having an enterprise-wide data model. Enterprise-wide data is data that is available for use within a single business unit, between multiple organizations or affiliates, and across the whole enterprise. Application code that maintains enterprise-wide data should be reused and shared. If more than one program updates a piece of data, then there is the risk of one program performing the update slightly differently from another. If multiple programs or applications update the same data, there is a risk of violating the integrity of that data.

Reuse strategy

The key to success in the reuse business is to put in place a solid strategy. If a componentware architecture is not explicitly designed and actively managed, the result will be a more difficult development environment than the one currently in place.

The key elements of a reuse programme are:

- Inventory
- Catalogue
- Reuse administrator and facilitator
- Methodology
- Design standards and principles
- Measurement
- Quality assurance
- Performance incentives.

A reuse programme should establish the reuse methodology enterprise-wide. A reuse methodology should be integrated with the system development life cycle.

The componentware architecture recommends the forming of a component review board that reviews projects and assists with the harvesting and implementation of components. The component review board should comprise key business users from across the enterprise. The focus of the review board is to enable the reuse programme. In order to ensure a successful reuse programme, the right people have to be involved with the knowledge and the authority to negotiate the definitions of reusable components (Jacobson et al 1997).

17.1   Techniques for reusing components

The notion of reuse is not new. Application developers have been reusing code since applications were written. Componentware architecture builds upon familiar paradigms.

Examples of code reuse are:

- **Copy code**. There are two variations for including code: (1) copying the source code from one program directly into the source code of another (cut-and-paste); or (2) using include files or copybooks.

  However, these methods produce code that is expensive to maintain and adapt to changes. If a piece of copied code implements the logic necessary to carry out a particular business rule, every time a business rule changes, the change has to be replicated in every copy instance of that code. After the change is made, each program must then be retested. Even if the rule is implemented using an include file or copybook, all programs that contain that include file or copybook must be recompiled and retested.

- **Link libraries**. Linking programs with precompiled library modules is accomplished either at compile time by using the link facility provided with the operating system, or at runtime using Dynamic Link Libraries (DLLs). This method of reuse is better than copying the code from one program to another because here the business logic exists only once. However, if a module that implements the business rule changes then any program linked with that module needs to be identified, relinked and retested.

- **Service request**. The required service is not linked into the application, but the service is requested by sending a message to a distant server. Operating system services, for example, employ this method. The application is completely independent of the service, which can even run in a different address space or on a different machine.

Service request is the preferred method of code reuse today and is the recommended technique for using components in the componentware architecture. This method also supports the *n*-tiered design recommended by the application architecture (see Section 15.5).

17.2   Types of services provided by components

Reusable components can be classified into different types:

- **Application services**. These components include business objects, business tasks and business processes.

- **User interface services**. These services include navigational functions, data views, functions for the representation of data and functions for interaction with the user. User interface services should be independent of business services. For example, it should be possible to make a legacy application

web-ready by replacing the original 3270 terminal interface with a web interface. The objective is to design the system in such a manner that it won't
matter what user interface is being used to access an application: the flow of
information will still be the same.

Typical user interfaces include:

- Graphical user interfaces (GUIs)
- Green-on-black terminals (e.g. UNIX terminals or 3270 terminals)
- Web browsers
- Point of sale devices (e.g. cash registers)
- Mobile computing devices (WAP)
- Voice interfaces, such as the plain old phone.

- **Support services**. These are services that typically provide operating system
  type functions, such as printing, faxing and imaging. These types of services
  are typically provided by purchased packages. If purchased, they should
  easily integrate into an *n*-tier environment.

- **Core services**. These components provide basic application infrastructure
  services such as security, naming and directory services. These services are
  usually provided by purchased middleware.

17.3   Guidelines for componentware

Here are a few guidelines for the design or purchase of components that support distributed, *n*-tiered, client–server, and adaptive computing across an
enterprise with high potential for reuse:

- The focus of componentware architecture is to improve business performance. A component-based development strategy enables adaptive systems
  to meet the changing business needs and technical environments. A component-based development strategy aligns information technology with the
  commonly used functions of the business.

*Share components
across the enterprise*

- Componentware architecture facilitates the reuse of components *across* the
  enterprise. Reusable components increase the productivity of the application
  development departments within the enterprise. Sharing components across
  the enterprise greatly increases the ability of the system to meet the changing needs of the business. The use of proven components enhances the
  accuracy of information processing.

  Think in application families instead of single applications (Parnas 1972).
  Application families have many components in common.

  Shareable components must be callable by any application. Reusing existing shared components eliminates duplication of development, testing and
  maintenance effort. Reusing existing shared components eliminates process-

ing inconsistencies because business rules are maintained in one piece of code. Use of components reduces the time and effort required for developing and updating applications.

- Components must be designed and developed with the understanding that the process that invokes them may or may not be developed in the same language or in the same environment. A component should be callable from any supported language on any supported platform.

  New components must be platform independent. Components must be developed so they can be deployed on any supported platform. If the business needs change or a new platform is required, the component should easily migrate to the new platform. *Language neutral and platform independent*

- Buy rather than build components whenever possible. Purchased components must be capable of being implemented in a service-oriented environment (i.e. can be integrated into an *n*-tier environment with a published application programming interface (API)). Components should be purchased whenever possible, such as class libraries, allowing developers to focus on the development of specialized business rule components. *Buy or build?*

  Rent rather than buy components. Ask your Internet Service Provider! Standard components like office products or databases will become part of the Internet infrastructure (McNealy 1999).

- Establish a repository for maintaining the information about available reusable components. The repository should be made available to all application developers as a tool for performing their jobs. The repository provides a place to store documentation about the component APIs. *Repository*

- Design components to be fully self-contained. All necessary validation, error detection and reporting capabilities, logging/debugging/tracing functionality, monitoring and alert functionality, and system management capabilities must be incorporated in the component. This facilitates operation, administration and maintenance functions. *Design for quality*

- A component should implement a single business rule or function, or a small set of related business rules or functions, such as a business task. To maximize component reusability each should contain a single function.

- Establish guidelines to optimize performance. Guidelines for request and reply message lengths should be established to avoid undue network traffic and performance problems.

- Every component must have a published API. A published API defines the (import/export) interface for a component or service. Documentation should include input and output parameters, which parameters are required, which parameters are optional, and the lengths and types of the parameters. The API should be entered into the component repository which is available to all application developers.

- Develop reusable testing suites for every component. A component testing suite contains special programs needed for calling a component as well as sample input and example output data for verifying results. Testing suites should be developed that can be reused any time a particular component is modified. The testing suites will be maintained and managed the same way as any other component.

Reuse methodology

- Establish a reuse methodology for the identification and implementation of components. Adopt effective component management methodologies, including the tools to support component reuse. In a distributed development environment, there must be a methodology in place for managing the available components. It must include the steps necessary for identifying, defining and developing reusable components. If this methodology is not in place then reuse will be very difficult to implement.

A methodology that supports reuse contains the following steps:

1. Classify the business requirements by service type (e.g. application, interface, support, or core).
2. Search the repository for reusable components that support the business or functional requirements.
3. Analyze candidate components to ensure they fully meet the requirements.
4. Incorporate the selected components into the new or re-engineered application using standard APIs.
5. Harvest components from existing applications to build the component repository initially. Legacy applications are a good resource for building a component repository. Remember that legacy software can be a source of mature, robust and efficient software. There is no need to reinvent a process or piece of functionality if software already exists that performs the desired function. If feasible, develop a wrapper that defines the API for the service and allows the legacy application to become a reusable component without major changes and effort.

Incorporate the reuse methodology into the system development life cycle (see Chapter 18).

Assign owners

- Components should have ownership and maintenance responsibilities assigned. The responsibility for the development and maintenance of the component remains with the application development team or a team specializing in components. The responsibility for the definition of a component should be assigned to the business organization within the enterprise that is responsible for the function.

Review board

- Establish a component review board to identify common components. Components used by multiple business units must be commonly understood and consistently referenced by all business users. Component development can be achieved through the context of projects. The review board should start with small, achievable and extremely strategic projects. In order to create reusable components, cooperation is needed among the business process owners. A framework needs to be put in place that allows for:

- centralized management of reusable, shareable components;
- design reviews of new and existing projects for reusable components;
- enterprise access to information about reusable components.

Establish component design reviews of all ongoing projects. Determine whether the business requirements are met by any existing components. If the business requirements are not met by existing components, determine whether there are any components that could be expanded to satisfy the business requirement (without compromising the reusability of a component).

18 The Software Engineering Lifecycle Model

Information technology is changing at an exponential rate. Product development life cycles have decreased from 10 years, to five years, to one year, to six months, and now we measure them in 'web time' – three months to six weeks. As a result, today's best practices may become tomorrow's worst nightmares.

Business architecture vs. technical architecture

Organizations that bind their business functionality to a specific technical implementation, therefore, face the prospect of having to continually re-engineer those basic business rules. A typical example is EDI/EDIFACT (see Section 15.11). A more secure approach is to make the specification of the business functionality independent of the underlying technology as far as possible – to separate the business architecture from the technical architecture.

However, we do not argue that business functionality should be defined in ignorance of the technological context. After all, the scope of an application is in its basics defined by the technology that exists at the time: no electronic business application without the Internet!

But, what comes first when planning a new application is a clear understanding of the business requirements and the architecture of the business model. This is achieved in the first phases of a project's life cycle (Yourdon et al 1995).

18.1 Phases of an object-oriented lifecycle model

SELC

Software AG's Software Engineering Lifecycle Model (SELC), which we are going to present here, supports such an approach. The steps defined in this lifecycle model are:

1. **Conceptualization phase**. The SELC covers a preliminary conceptualization phase where business process modelling (BPM) is used to understand the application domain, visualize a project and determine the scope of the project.

What

2. **Requirements analysis**. Requirements analysis modelling is the fundamental activity for the entire life cycle. The assets and artefacts developed in this phase will provide the basis of all later development activities, and enable the traceability necessary for an effective life cycle.

- An *artefact* is a tangible deliverable, necessary to define or expand upon the functionality of a system, such as diagrams, project plans, schemata.
- An *asset* is an artefact that serves a purpose outside the scope of a particular project. Examples of assets include those artefacts defining reusable components, schedules and plans used to communicate to senior management, and functional descriptions necessary for sales and marketing.

Requirements analysis presents an external view of the system from the business client's perspective. This phase captures and develops the inherent business functionality and business rules. As such, all of the activities and deliverables of this phase are expressed in the semantics of the business domain; that is, they are described in the language and terms of the business client. All deliverables obtained in this step are immediately understandable to any business user.

Some of the concepts explored in requirements analysis modelling may not be translated into a production system. Some of the business interactions, necessary to evaluate and assess business rules, may be outside the scope of any particular production system. As a result, many of the constructs identified are treated as candidates (candidate use cases, candidate business concepts). Identifying which candidates are translated into a production system is the purpose of later development phases.

3. **Analysis modelling**. The systems analysis phase involves high-level decisions concerning the problem domain of the system as a whole.

Analysis modelling translates the results of the requirements analysis into an object-oriented format. Any object-oriented notation is appropriate, as long as that notation supports integrated static and dynamic perspectives. In the context of this discussion, UML (Unified Modeling Language) is used as the modelling language (Rumbaugh et al 1998).

The business requirements are translated into *use cases*: each way an end user uses the system defines a distinct use case. Each use case defines a set of interactions with the system (Jacobson et al 1993).

Using a formal method such as UML, analysis modelling transfers the knowledge acquired during requirements analysis from the business domain to the developers' domain. The analysis model marks a 'crew' change: it contains the formal specifications that are handed over from the business analysts to the developers. The business analysts must ensure that the analysis model reflects the requirement analysis model.

The formality of the method provides the required traceability of the development process. Traceability means that later artefacts in the development can be traced back to their roots, the business requirements, and vice versa.

The analysis model is also the phase where *analysis patterns* are identified. Unlike design patterns (Gamma et al 1995) (see Chapter 16) which address common implementation constructs, analysis patterns address business constructs. Analysis patterns do not introduce new functionality into the model, rather they refer to existing solutions.

How

4. Design modelling. Now is the time to introduce technology and to define a technical architecture. Design modelling is the application of the technical architecture to the analysis model. In requirements analysis modelling and analysis modelling, we addressed 'what' to do; now we express the 'how'.

The technical architecture comprises the complete sets of technical constructs that are needed to implement the analysis model – constructs and techniques as discussed in the previous chapters. This also includes application partitioning and subsystem layering.

Where

5. Implementation modelling. This is the phase in which we address the deployment details implicit in our technical architecture. If requirements analysis modelling and analysis modelling addressed the 'what' of the system, and design modelling addressed the 'how', implementation modelling addresses the 'where'.

Implementation modelling is a crucial activity for component-based and distributed systems (see also Chapter 9). In contrast, for monolithic applications implementation modelling is trivial: the question of 'where' is easy to answer.

In this phase we also tackle the question of the integration of legacy and third-party systems.

6. Coding and assembly. Here we reach the production of executable code. This usually involves several activities: writing code, assembling application parts from already existing components, applying wrapping techniques to legacy software, and so on.

7. Quality assurance and testing. This serves the same function in this methodology as in all others: the verification and validation of technical and business functionality along the whole development life cycle.

With object-oriented design and implementation methods a test strategy for an application includes:

– **Class testing**. Classes are the smallest unit in an object-oriented test strategy. The developer ensures that the methods of the class perform correctly, and that the internal state of a class and the published properties are properly maintained. Remember that the internal state of an object changes during its life cycle, and that methods may change their behaviour depending on the object's state.

– **Scenario testing**. Here, the interaction between classes is tested by the developers, based on the scenarios and patterns developed in the modelling phases. The details of the code are visible and assessed in this process.

– **Use case testing**. By validating the use cases, the emphasis is on the verification of business functionality. Responsible for this is the quality assurance team which does not have access to the code.

– **Package testing**. Packages group together related classes that satisfy coherent subsets of functionality. The emphasis in this testing phase is on validating the interactions between those packages.

– **System testing**. This is the final activity of the quality assurance process. The emphasis is on the system as a whole, and its interactions with other systems with which the system will interact. Here, not only functional issues are important, but also issues of performance and scalability.

Additional quality assurance methods complement testing. An often repeated statement is that testing can only prove the presence of bugs but not their absence. We repeat it once more.

It is therefore necessary to apply other methods of quality assurance, too, *Peer review* of which *peer review* is one of the most effective. Peer review is applied during all project phases, starting with a review of business requirements, culminating in code review, and ending with the review of test strategies.

8. Deployment. The final step in project development. This step not only includes the distribution of the software across servers but also correlated activities: distribution of system documentation, training of users, setting up support channels, etc. In electronic business scenarios training of the end user is often not possible – effective support channels become more important.

9. Maintenance. In the SELC approach maintenance becomes simply a reapplication of the lifecycle phases defined above – a new cycle in an iterative process. One of the primary concerns of maintenance is to identify when modification and enhancement requests justify another complete development effort. The best course here is to map change requests to use cases, and assess how much effort is implied.

For each phase of the life cycle we need to identify three components:

● **Roles and resources**: The people involved in that phase.

● **Activities**: What those roles and resources will do during that phase.

● **Assets and Artefacts**: What will be produced as a result of the phase.

No life cycle can be viewed as a static entity. Any effective life cycle will have to adapt and grow, to incorporate new advances in technology, satisfy new business requirements and environments, and reflect the growing experience and sophistication of the development team through experience from project development.

18.2   The iterative incremental life cycle

The concept of incremental or evolutionary development evolved in the mid- *Evolutionary approach* 1980s. Incremental development recognizes that it is almost impossible to deliver a perfect system in a single step and without user feedback. Often it is better to implement only core aspects of the business model in a first version, instead of trying to deliver a comprehensive and perfect solution in one step. The practical experience gathered with an early version of the system is a valuable asset that helps to model and implement the new functionality added in future increments. The implementation of new functionality can be based on this growing set of experiences, and can reflect the business requirements better than a system that was completely conceived at the drawing board.

The SELC supports such an incremental developing process, while allowing several iterations within each increment.

What is an increment?

In an incremental approach, the project is broken into a number of mini-projects, each of which delivers completed implementations of selected business functionality. Each increment will contain some subset of the use cases of the system, and, when that increment is completed, those use cases will be completely developed.

What is an iteration?

Breaking the project into discrete increments has the advantage of focusing the scope of the development activity and allowing for earlier delivery of system functionality. This still leaves open the question of how to organize the activities of a particular increment.

Using an iterative development approach we break each increment into a number of iterations, usually three. These iterations cover all the phases of the life cycle, but, unlike increments, a particular iteration will not necessarily develop all of the functionality of a use case.

These iterations are:

1. **Exploration**. The initial pass of discovery.

2. **Evolution**. The expansion of constructs and processes discovered in the exploration iteration.

3. **Refinement**. The final enhancements to complete delivery.

The convergence principle

A key management strategy enabled by this three-iteration approach is the application of the *convergence principle*. This principle tells us that, given a consistent application of object-oriented technology, the solution set will converge to within 10 per cent of the final required solution within three iterations. If properly applied, this principle gives clear and early warning signs of specification errors, lack of understanding of requirements, inappropriate architectures, or an unstable environment.

Iteration loading strategies

How much effort must be devoted to each iteration?

There are three primary strategies:

- **Back-end loading**. In this approach, the majority of the work is performed on the last iteration:

    Exploration   < 20%
    Evolution   33%
    Refinement   > 50%

Paradoxically, the back-end loading strategy is used when a problem is not well understood, or if the developers are inexperienced. When confronted with an unfamiliar domain or problem space, it is best to take a quick pass through the development process in order to gain a rapid, broad understanding of the issues.

- **Front-end loading**. In this approach, the majority of the work is performed on the first iteration.

  Exploration > 50%
  Evolution   33%
  Refinement   < 20%

The front-end loading approach is best suited to problems that are trivial and well understood. In such a case it is possible to lay out the bulk of the work in one pass, without concern that later discovery will invalidate that work.

- **Linear loading**. In this approach, the level of effort is spread equally across the three iterations.

  Exploration   33%
  Evolution   33%
  Refinement   33%

Not surprisingly, the linear loading approach is the method of choice when there is no clear indication of how well the problem is understood.

Integration

While increments should be loosely coupled, there are clear dependencies between them. There will always be coordination issues that need to be resolved between increments. This process is called *integration*.

Integration is a project activity that needs to be specifically allocated and addressed. Two specific integration strategies are:

- **Increment-dependent integration**. In this approach, it is the responsibility of each development sub-team to coordinate their deliverables with those of the previous increments.

- **Separate integration**. Here, a separate sub-team is responsible for integration activities. The integration sub-team takes the deliverables of the development sub-teams, coordinates them and resolves any discrepancies.

Regardless of strategy, the project manager needs to ensure that appropriate time for these activities is allowed.

Tool support

Several tools are on the market that support the software lifecycle process or parts thereof, for example Rose and Together.

In addition, these tools can automate quality assurance tasks:

- *Automated metrics* monitor the complexity of model and implementation.
- *Audits* make sure enterprise standards and conventions are being followed.
- *Requirements traceability* allows the tracing of how requirements are matched in the different stages of the modelling and implementation process.

Round-trip engineering with Bolero

Software AG's Bolero stores development objects like classes, interfaces, methods and fields in a repository using XML internally as the storage format. This concept offers modelling tools an open interface to access Bolero's repository. In particular, Bolero teams with Together from TogetherSoft. The integration of both products allows round-trip engineering: while UML diagrams can be translated into code, changes in the code can be reflected back into the diagrams.

Appendix

Case Study 1:   Safe & Secure extranet

The following case study is based on the Limonet project done for the Safe & Secure chauffeur service company based in the city of London, UK.

The study should illustrate the following points:

- architecture of a real-world electronic business application;
- componentization of business tasks;
- integration of legacy systems.

Figure A.1 shows the logon screen for the Safe & Secure extranet.

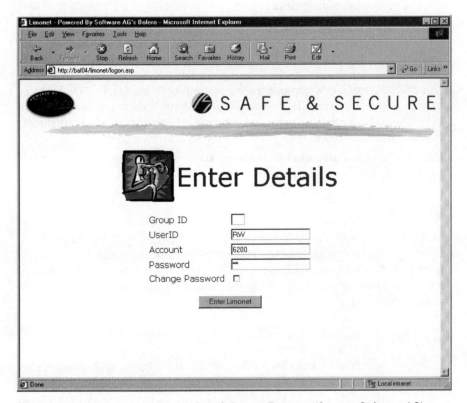

Figure A.1   Logon screen for the Safe & Secure Extranet. (Source: Software AG)

Problem domain

Safe & Secure are a chauffeur services company based in the city of London. They provide a limousine reservation facility for their customers. Currently, the company's customer base perform transactions via telephone and e-mail. The e-mails are rekeyed after reception.

Safe & Secure currently have a system called Relayer that handles these transactions. The system is implemented on a DOS version of FoxPro.

The aim is to extend this service over an extranet to Safe & Secure's current customer base. The extranet should be constructed to scale with the business.

Scope

The first release of the system deals primarily with reservations. In addition, a logon facility is provided to identify customers over the Internet. Most of the functionality is delegated to the existing Relayer system. Only the functionality that cannot be provided by the Relayer system is implemented in the new system.

Assumptions and constraints

The following have been made:

- Purchase of a new web server with Microsoft IIS and ASP and primary domain controller.
- A suitable set of COM component wrapper objects, preferably COM objects, are provided by Intersoft, the developers of the existing Relayer system. These objects expose the necessary functionality to satisfy the requirements of the extranet system.
- The main technology used is Software AG's Bolero, which will be complemented by Microsoft technologies.

Use cases

The users of the system are referred to as actors. Use case diagrams are produced to identify what business processes they wish the system to reflect (Figure A.2). Inputs to this activity are the initial requirement statements and the results of detailed requirements elicited during user interviews and workshops (business process engineering).

Packages

The overall system is broken down into individual packages, each package covering a self-contained area of required functionality.

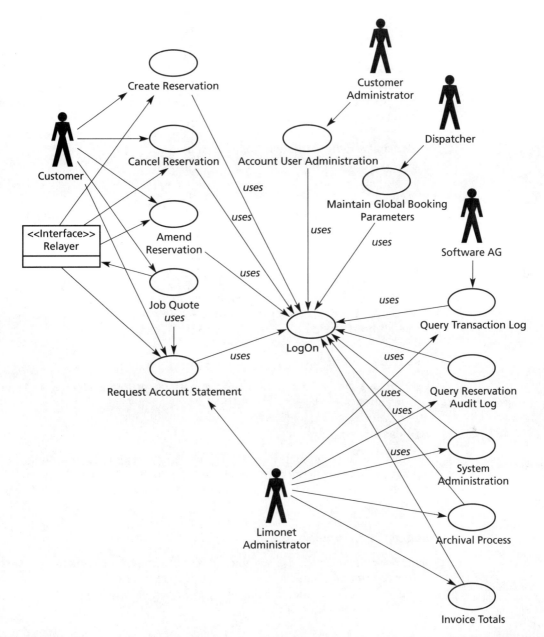

Figure A.2 The business requirements are translated into use cases: each way an actor uses the system defines a distinct use case. Each use case defines a set of interactions with the system (see also Chapter 18). (Source: Software AG)

The following packages have been identified:

- Administration.

    Use cases: System Administration, Account User Administration; LogOn; Maintain Global Booking Parameters; Archival.

    Provide system administration facilities for Limonet personnel to define and maintain users of the extranet, and for those users to define and maintain further users for their own accounts.

    Provide a secure access mechanism to the extranet with password protection and activity restrictions for defined users.

- Reservations.

    Use cases: Create Reservation; Cancel Reservation; Amend Reservation; Request Account Statement; Job Quotes; Price Breakdown.

    Provide the facilities for empowered users to add reservations to the Relayer system via the extranet; retrieve and amend or cancel those reservations; and view a list of completed jobs.

- Logging

    Use cases: Query Reservation Audit Log; Query Transaction Log.

    Log activity records to an audit log for possible transaction queries, and to a transaction log for system usage statistics. Provide access to details on these log files.

Use case descriptions

Use case descriptions define in detail the business processes pictured in Figure A.2 (not shown here).

Use case scenarios

Use case scenarios present a specific sequence of actions that illustrate behaviour. Each use case may have several scenarios defined in order to portray all possible variations on use case behaviour. A list of scenarios is provided below in the section about testing.

Sequence diagrams

Sequence diagrams present a graphical representation of the sequence of events within a scenario, defining the interactions and messaging between the elements that make up the system. They are of benefit when depicting busy or complex functions (not shown here).

Class diagrams

The business process modelling defines a number of classes that support the requirements. Each class is a self-contained collection of data items and related processes, for example a class to deal with reservations; another class to deal with user administration.

Figure A.3 details those classes and the relationships between them.

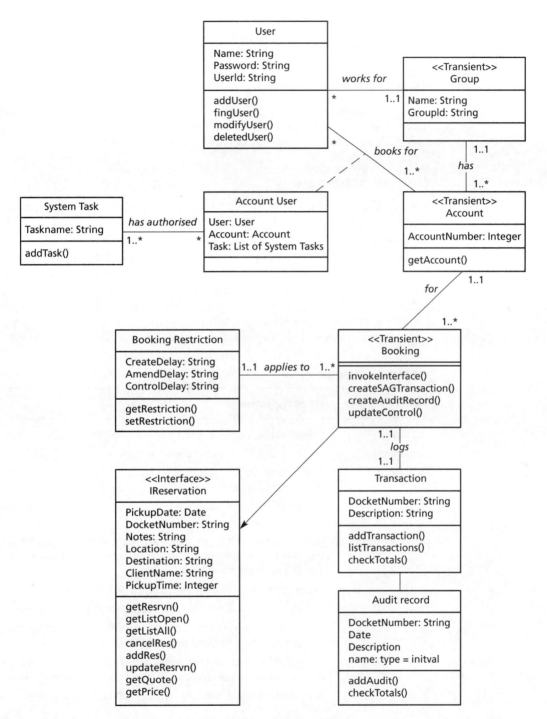

Figure A.3   Classes and their relationships. (Source: Software AG)

Class descriptions

Class descriptions are shown in Table A.1.

Relayer API requirements

These are detailed descriptions of the APIs to be provided by Intersoft in order for the Software AG Bolero components to be able to interface with the Relayer system. Table A.2 shows only a summary of those specifications.

Technical architecture

The existing LAN consists of an NT Server machine that acts as the primary domain controller (PDC). This machine also acts as the application server for the Relayer system. The PDC does not have any failover recovery.

The proposed system introduces a new NT Server machine that acts as the web server (Figure A.4). The current NT Server configuration is not altered for the extranet. Also, no additional components are introduced (with the exception of the COM wrapper for the Relayer system) on the PDC to reduce the impact on the current business processes.

Access to the Internet will be through a suitable Internet Service Provider (ISP).

Table A.1 Class descriptions.

Class	Descriptions
Account	Defines an account that exists within the Relayer system
Account User	Allows a user to access a specific account
Audit Record	A record created to record the changing state of a reservation: after creation, after each amendment, and after cancellation
Booking	Temporary record to hold reservation details passed to/from the Relayer system
Booking Restriction	Defines a period of time delay for accepting reservations onto the system, and a period of time delay against amending/cancelling reservations
Group	Not recorded within this system as held on Relayer system
IReservation	Interface class to allow communications with the Relayer system
System Task	A task that may be carried out within the extranet system, e.g. Add a reservation; Request Account Statement
Transaction	A transaction is created to reflect activity through the extranet – one per create, modify or cancel activity, for each reservation
User	A person who will use the system, either a customer or the Limonet staff

Table A.2   API specifications.

API	Description
AddReservation	Validates data provided and stores a new reservation with the specified details. Returns either the docket number or an error message.
FindReservation	Retrieves reservation/job with the docket number provided. Returns details of the reservation formatted into a String.
ModifyReservation	Validates data provided, locates the record with the specified docket number and updates the reservation details with the input details provided. Returns an error message if an error occurred, else an empty string.
CancelReservation	Locates the record with the specified docket number and cancels the reservation. Returns an error message if an error occurred, else an empty string.
GetOpenResrvns	Retrieves all reservations for the specified account id which have not yet been completed and are not cancelled. Returns a list of reservations.
GetCompleteResrvns	Retrieves all reservations for the specified account id which have been completed and have a pickup date and time greater than or equal to the startDate/Time but less than or equal to the endDate/Time input. The reservations should be ordered in ascending pickupDate/Time.
FindReference	Determines whether the input Reference value string is present on the Group reference file.
FindLocation	Determines whether the input String location code is present on the Location file.
FindAccount	Retrieves data for an Account. Returned data is separated by "~" with trailing spaces removed.
GroupAPI	Retrieves a list of all accounts for a specific Group Id. Formatting as specified in parameter format example.
QuoteAPI	For the specified journey details, calculates and returns the journey total cost.
PriceAPI	For a specific docket number, returns the journey cost breakdown.

Parallel to the extranet development Safe & Secure are upgrading their IT infrastructure. The main aim is to eliminate the single point of failure at the PDC. In order to achieve this improved resilience, the current PDC is replaced with a more up-to-date machine that has failover recovery. The current PDC is used as backup domain controller (BDC).

Figure A.5 shows the overall technical architecture of the system. The user interface is a web browser, using HTML over HTTP. HTML ensures maximum browser independence and reduced download times. The web server is a Microsoft IIS web server running under Windows NT Server. Microsoft Active

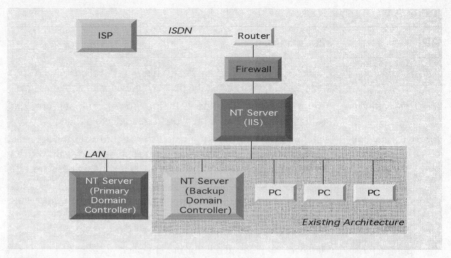

Figure A.4 Technical infrastructure of Limonet. (Source: Software AG)

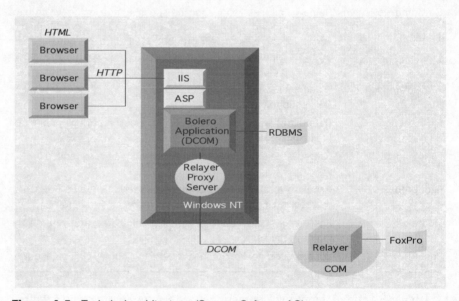

Figure A.5 Technical architecture. (Source: Software AG)

Server Pages (ASP) are used to generate HTML and interact with server compo-nents. The server hosts business objects developed using Bolero. These components use DCOM as the component model.

In order to access and delegate functionality to the Relayer system the Relayer Proxy Server is employed, using DCOM as the communication protocol.

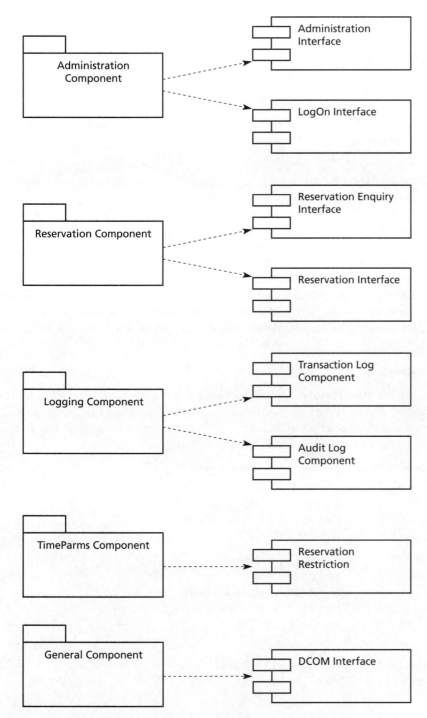

Figure A.6   The Limonet component diagram. (Source: Software AG)

Component design

The component interfaces of the system are mapped to the identified packages as defined in Figure A.6.

Object to relational mapping

The object to relational mapping for the Limonet system is handled automatically by Bolero.

Development Environment

- Platform. PC with Windows NT Workstation with Option Pack 4. Each machine has the capability to act as a host for the entire application and will facilitate development of components in isolation. Also, when necessary, the machines can be networked to test the distributed aspects of the system. The development platform has the flexibility to adapt to different configurations.
- Software tools. Bolero Component Studio will be used to develop all the business objects that will reside in the middle tier (web server). Visual InterDev will be used for developing the ASP pages.

Testing

Scenarios are developed from use cases to enhance understanding of the system. Several scenarios may be produced from each use case, each scenario being a textual description of a different path through the use case. The following scenarios are used as a basis for system testing.

Use Case	Maintain Administrators
Scenario 1	add administrator for new Group/Account
Scenario 2	find existing administrator's details
Scenario 3	modify existing administrator's password
Scenario 4	remove a definition
Use Case	Account Administration
Scenario 1	add new person
Scenario 2	find existing person's details
Scenario 3	modify existing person's privileges/password
Scenario 4	remove a definition
Use Case	Log On
Scenario 1	unsuccessful Customer logon – incorrect details
Scenario 2	successful logon by customer

Scenario 3	successful logon by Limonet person	
Scenario 4	password change	

Use Case	Maintain Global Booking Parameters
Scenario 1	set period limit for Group
Scenario 2	set period limit for Account
Scenario 3	set default period limit
Scenario 4	set specific time

Use Case	Create Reservation
Scenario 1	complete successfully
Scenario 2	incorrect data
Scenario 3	refused on booking period

Use Case	Amend Reservation
Scenario 1	amend successfully
Scenario 2	incorrect data
Scenario 3	refused on booking period

Use Case	Cancel Reservation
Scenario 1	cancel reservation

Use Case	Account Statement
Scenario 1	browse Account Statement

Use Case	Query Audit Log
Scenario 1	query by docket number
Scenario 2	query by account/date

Use Case	Query Transaction Log
Scenario 1	query transaction log

Use Case	Price Breakdown
Scenario 1	query price breakdown

Use Case	Job Quote
Scenario 1	query job quote

Use Case	Archival Process
Scenario 1	query archival process

Deployment diagram

The deployment diagram is shown in Figure A.7.

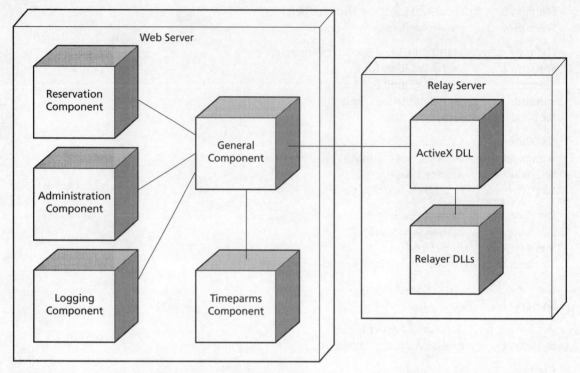

Figure A.7 Deployment diagram. (Source: Software AG)

Case Study 2: Integrating existing applications at FinRenault, Italy

The objective of the project is to handle car registrations automatically through dealers connected through the Renault intranet.

To link an existing mainframe application to the Renault intranet (Renault.Net), FinRenault used EntireX to wrap CICS transactions as DCOM components. The mainframe applications are written in Software AG's 4GL Natural and access an Adabas database. The mainframe is linked to the Windows NT application server via a Windows NT SNA server.

Bolero acts here as a middle-tier engine. Mainframe applications business functions, wrapped as DCOM components, are combined with MS Office DCOM components (WinWord) and with Bolero objects.

The Bolero application plus the Bolero application server are deployed on a Netscape Web Server running under Windows NT. JRUN as a Java servlet container provides the necessary runtime environment for Bolero.

The architecture is shown in Figure A.8.

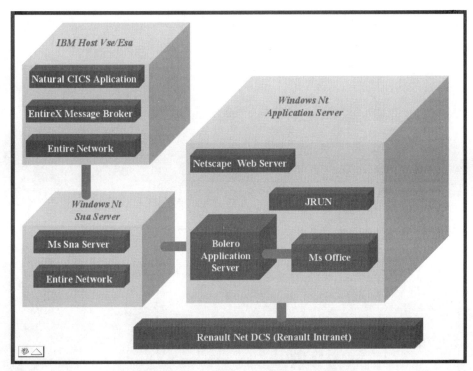

Figure A.8   FinRenault DCS-SCIC application. (Source: Software AG)

Glossary

4GL The term *fourth-generation language* was coined by James Martin to refer to non-procedural high-level languages built around database systems. 4GLs provide special language constructs for database support, report generation and user interaction.

Abstract class Abstract classes serve as a basis for further extension. While an abstract class cannot create instances, subclasses of an abstract class may.

ACID transaction ACID is an acronym for the four primary attributes ensured for any database transaction:

- **Atomicity**. A transaction cannot be divided into smaller parts. Either all or no data elements involved in a transaction are committed to a transaction.
- **Consistency**. A transaction leads to a new and valid state. In the case of a failure the transaction is reset to the previous valid state.
- **Isolation**. A pending transaction must remain isolated from any other transaction.
- **Durability**. Once data has been committed it must stay – regardless of system failures or restart – in its committed state.

The ACID concept is described in ISO/IEC 10026-1:1992 Section 4.

A COMMIT is the last step in a successful database transaction. In distributed database systems a two-phase commit is necessary.

The *two-phase commit* is a way of handling a transaction in a distributed environment, ensuring that the transaction is performed either on all participating units or on none.

ActiveX ActiveX is Microsoft's component technology based on COM and DCOM. ActiveX 'controls' can be created with many different languages, such as. C++, VisualBasic, VBScript, NaturalX, Bolero, and provide similar functionality to Java Applets. ActiveX controls can be run within the context of a container application (for example, a web browser).

Agent An entity that acts on behalf of a client.

Aggregation Aggregation is used to model whole–part structures. The whole is called a *composite object* or *aggregate* and the parts are called *component objects*. Both the aggregate and its components are modelled as object classes.

API Application Programming Interface.

Applet Small application. In the context of the World Wide Web and Java, applets are small Java programs that are embedded into a web page and are distributed over the net. Applets are used for relatively simple tasks. For security reasons access to system resources can be limited.

Application server Provides the infrastructure required to execute a component-based application. Services include transaction and state management, Internet access, security, load-balancing, etc.

Browser A program that can present HTML or XML pages on a computer screen and that supports navigation over the World Wide Web. Most browsers support the execution of Java applets (Java-enabled browser).

Business object A business object represents a 'real world' entity from the business problem domain.

Business process A business process is a collection of activities that takes one or more kinds of input and creates an output that is of value to the client.

Byte code A platform-independent and compact representation of a compiled computer program. The byte code needs an interpreter (or runtime system) to execute on a concrete target machine.

CGI Common Gateway Interface. CGI scripts are executed on web servers and are used to access legacy applications and to create dynamic HTML pages.

CICS The Customer Information Control System is IBM's prime transaction monitor.

Class In object-oriented programming a class defines the prototype of an object. Concrete objects are created by instantiating a class. The features of a class include data fields and methods (procedures). Most object-oriented languages support inheritance to create a hierarchy of superclasses and subclasses.

Client–Server The term client–server describes the relation between two computer programs. One program – the client – sends a request to the second program – the server – which in turn answers to the client. In distributed computer networks the client–server model is the usual model for distributed applications, potentially including several distributed servers accessed by one or many distributed clients.

   In the Internet the TCP/IP protocol follows the client–server model. The typical client is a web browser, an FTP client, an e-mail client, etc.

Cohesion Cohesion describes the strength of the relationships between the elements of a system. Within a system component high cohesion is desirable.

Collection class In object-oriented programming collection classes implement data structures consisting of type-neutral elements, such as lists, arrays, trees. Collection classes implement methods to manage the structure of the collection, while enforcing only minimal constraints on the type of an element (for example, tree elements must be comparable).

COM The Component Object Model is Microsoft's architecture for the development and deployment of software components. As an extension of OLE, COM is also responsible for services such as interface negotiation, version management, licensing and event services.

COMMIT See ACID.

Component A component is an independent software module designed for 'plug-and-play' reuse. Components contain an interface description and most components can be configured according to the requirements of the container application. Examples of components models are JavaBeans, Enterprise JavaBeans, CORBA, ActiveX/COM/DCOM.

Component broker A component broker acts as the container application for components. Component brokers provide the following services:

- protocol negotiation depending on a component's interface description;
- publishing of component features to other components;
- event management;
- persistence, i.e. keeping the internal state of components across requests or sessions;
- support of component-based application development environments;
- wrapping of components consisting of several resource files.

Container application An application that can bring independent software components to execution. Typical examples are a CORBA ORB, an EJB server, a web browser, or an office application that can embed ActiveX components. From creation to destruction, a component lives in a container, which is transparent to the client.

 Container applications provide services such as security, concurrency, lifecycle management, transactions, and other services.

Contracts Contracts are a software construct that guarantees to a software unit that a calling instance adheres to certain conditions, and the software unit itself guarantees certain conditions when the result is returned to the calling instance.

Cookie A cookie is an information packet sent by an HTTP server to a web browser which is sent back each time the browser accesses that server. Cookies can be made persistent (stored on the client's hard disk) and contain information such as session state or user profile.

CORBA The Common Object Request Broker Architecture is the Object Management Group (OMG) component model. CORBA defines the creation, deployment and management of distributed components in networks. CORBA requires object request brokers (ORBs) as container applications.

 An object request broker enables objects to make and receive requests and responses transparently in a distributed heterogeneous environment.

DCOM The Distributed Component Object Model extends Microsoft's COM architecture to distributed applications. Distributed components can communicate via remote procedure call (RPC). DCOM was developed for Windows platforms, but has been ported to UNIX and mainframe (Software AG).

Deployment The process whereby software is installed into an operational environment.

Design pattern An object-oriented design technique which names, abstracts and identifies aspects of a useful design structure. The design pattern identifies classes and instances, their roles, collaborations and responsibilities, while focusing on a particular object-oriented design problem.

DOM The Document Object Model provides an API to describe, access, create and modify SGML-based documents, such as XML or HTML documents.

DTD A Document Type Definition defines the valid content of an XML document.

EDI The Electronic Data Interchange standard describes the exchange of electronic documents between trading partners. EDI standards are ANSI X12 (USA) and EDIFACT (United Nations).

Encapsulation Encapsulation is any mechanism that hides the implementation of an object, so that other components of the system do not need to be aware of the internal structure and details of the object.

Enterprise application integration (EAI) The integration of enterprise resource planning (ERP) systems, existing (legacy) applications, database and data warehouse systems, front and back office into an automated business process.

Enterprise JavaBeans (EJB) A Java-based component model. EJBs abstract from the underlying infrastructure of resource and transaction managers. Services such as session and transaction control are instead contained in EJB container applications. EJBs use RMI/IIOP as communication method and can interoperate with CORBA objects. Popular CORBA ORBs provide EJB containers (see also Container Application).

Enterprise resource planning (ERP) ERP systems help businesses to manage important parts of their activities, such as product planning, parts purchasing, maintaining inventories, interacting with suppliers, providing customer service, tracking orders, finance and human resource management. Examples of ERP are SAP R/2 and R/3, PeopleSoft, Baan, J.D. Edwards.

Exception An error condition that interrupts the normal control flow in a program. An exception can be raised by the hardware, system software, or the application itself.

Extranet An extranet is a virtual private network (VPN) that uses Internet protocols and the public telecommunication system to share information between registered business partners. Extranets require security measures, such as firewalls, digital certificates and encryption.

Facade A component or component group within a larger component system. The facade acts as an interface to the system. All other components within the component system are accessed by the client through the facade.

Final class A class in Java or Bolero that cannot be extended (subclassed).

Final method A method that cannot be overridden in subclasses.

Floating point A number representation consisting of a mantissa and an exponent. Most floating point implementations are based on IEEE 754.

Garbage collection Garbage collection is the process of dynamically reclaiming allocated storage during the execution of a program. Garbage collectors must be able to detect which memory blocks are no longer in use, free them, and combine several free memory blocks into contiguous larger blocks to avoid memory fragmentation.

GUI Graphical User Interface, the use of graphical elements (pictures, icons, buttons, dialogue boxes) for interaction between computer programs and humans instead of text. GUIs usually include the use of a pointing device, such as a mouse. The GUI concept originated in the early 1970s at the Xerox PARC laboratory.

HTML Hypertext Markup Language. A hypertext document format used on the World Wide Web. HTML is an application of SGML. Tags embedded into the text describe certain properties of the text elements and can include other elements such as links to HTML pages or to other resources such as images. HTML is a recommendation of the W3C (World Wide Web consortium).

HTTP Hypertext Transfer Protocol. The Internet protocol used for communication between clients and servers. HTTP messages consist of requests from client to server and responses from server to client.

HTTPS HTTP layered over the SSL protocol.

IDL (Interface Definition Language) IDL is a CORBA-specific definition language for component interfaces. IDL gives a precise description of types and exceptions. The interfaces are independent of operating systems and programming languages.
    DCOM uses its own, DCOM-specific, IDL.

IIOP Internet Inter-ORB Protocol. A protocol used for communication between CORBA object request brokers.

Inheritance In object-oriented programming, inheritance is the ability to derive (extend) new classes from existing classes. The inheriting class (subclass) inherits the features (fields and methods), but can also add new features or override existing ones. Single inheritance supports the inheritance of features from only one superclass, while multiple inheritance supports the inheritance of features from multiple superclasses.

Instance An instance is a concrete manifestation of a class. A class can have many instances.

Interface The interface defines the features of a system as seen from another system. A graphical user interface, for example, defines the elements that are visible to a human user. A component interface defines the features (methods) that can be used by the component's client.

Internationalization Internationalization is the process of planning and implementing products and services so that they can easily be adapted to specific local languages and cultures.

Internet The largest network in the world. The Internet features a three-level hierarchy, consisting of backbone networks, mid-level networks and stub networks. It spans many different physical networks around the world with various protocols, including the Internet Protocol TCP/IP.

Intranet An intranet is a network within an enterprise that uses Internet protocols, usually implemented on a local area network (LAN).

JAR file A JAR (Java Archive) file contains byte code and other resources such as images and sound for a set of Java classes or JavaBeans. The JAR file format is a compressed format based on the ZIP file format.

Java Java is an object-oriented programming language designed for use in the distributed environment of the Internet. The language syntax of Java is similar to C++. The Java compiler produces Java byte code that can be run on any platform that supports a Java Virtual Machine (JVM): 'Write once – run everywhere'.

JavaBeans The Java component model. JavaBeans allows developers to create reusable software components that can then be assembled together using visual application builder tools. JavaBeans supports introspection, customization and an event model.

JavaScript JavaScript (formerly LiveScript, properly ECMAScript) is a script language from Netscape, also supported by Microsoft. JavaScript can be used within web pages to react dynamically to user actions. Server-side JavaScript can be used to create HTML pages dynamically.

JDBC Java Database Connectivity is an API to connect Java applications to a wide range of data sources such as relational databases. JDBC can pass SQL queries to a database and can return the results back to the application. JDBC is similar to Microsoft's ODBC, and bridge programs between JDBC and ODBC exist.

JDK Java Development Kit. A product required for programming in Java, consisting of a JVM, Java class libraries, Java compilers, Java runtime environment, and other tools.

JIT Just-in-time compiler. A compiler that is invoked directly before a Java program is executed. The JIT compiler compiles the Java byte code into native machine code, resulting in faster execution of the program. This concept does not impair portability because compilation is performed after a program has been deployed to a target platform.

JVM The Java Virtual Machine. A program that executes Java byte code on a target platform. Different JVM implementations are necessary for different target platforms. For Java programs, the JVM provides a consistent runtime environment, enabling Java programs to run anywhere a JVM exists.

LAN A local area network is a computer network restricted to a building or a small geographic area. The main LAN technologies are: Ethernet, token ring, ARCNET, FDDI (Fibre Distributed Data Interface).

Layer A layer is a set of components with the same degree of application specificity. Typically a higher layer is the client of a lower layer which serves the higher layer's requests, e.g. navigation layer, presentation layer.

Legacy system A legacy system is a pre-existing system that was created using other design methods and technologies.

Locale A locale defines a cultural region (country, language). Locales are standardized by ISO 3166.

Locking Mechanism within database management systems (DBMSs) to give a user exclusive access to a data object or a group of objects within an ACID transaction. Locking is an important concept to guarantee consistent data in multi-user databases.

Long transaction A transaction that spans a whole business transaction. A long transaction usually spans several ACID database transactions and includes mechanisms for semantic undo.

Method A method is a specific implementation of an operation for an object class.

Middleware Software systems that provide interoperability services for applications, such as distributed object computing, and conceal some aspects of hardware and operating system differences in a heterogeneous, distributed environment. Examples are CORBA ORBs, or EntireX.

Minitel The French version of Videotex. Minitel was deployed as a separate unit, consisting of telephone, keyboard and a CRT screen. Later, software emulation for PCs became available, too. Because the Minitel was provided free of charge the service became very popular in France.

Multi-tasking A concept in modern operating systems to execute multiple tasks in a parallel or semi-parallel fashion. True parallel execution requires a multiple processor environment. Semi-parallel execution is achieved by distributing a processor's time between tasks (time slicing), creating the impression of concurrency.

Multi-threading   Multi-threading is similar to multi-tasking, except that it happens within a program. Several threads of a program, such as graphical user interface support, rendering of graphics, computations, database access, or network communication are executed in parallel or semi-parallel fashion. Multi-threading requires less overhead than multi-tasking because operating system services and switching between address spaces are not required.

Multi-tier   In a multi-tier application the components of the application are distributed among several tiers each located in a different computer in a network.

Namespace   A concept to place identifiers into a certain context. Namespaces are used to avoid name clashes.

Native code   Program code that can be executed directly by the hardware without intermediate software.

Object   See Instance.

ODMG   The Object Database Management Group is a consortium of object-oriented database management system (ODBMS) vendors and interested parties.

Object-oriented programming   In object-oriented programming (OOP) data structures are encapsulated with a set of access methods within a class definition. During execution several object instances (with different state) can be created from one class definition. Class definitions are ordered in class hierarchies by using inheritance. OOP started with Simula 67 in 1967. Popular examples are Smalltalk, C++ and Java.

Object–relational mapping   The mapping of the data structures of an object or a group of aggregated objects onto schemata of a relational database.

OLE (Object Linking and Embedding)   Microsoft's Object Linking and Embedding standard (OLE) is a set of services and mechanisms that define a component-oriented application architecture, implemented using [D]COM, Microsoft Foundation Classes, and OCXs or ActiveXs. See also [D]COM.

Object Management Group (OMG)   A consortium engaged in developing standards for distributed object computing. See `http://www.omg.org`.

OQL   The Object Query Language supports the querying of persistent objects stored in a relational database. OQL is closely related to the ODMG query language specification for object-oriented database systems and is almost fully compatible with retrieval constructs in SQL:1999(SQL-3).

ORB (Object Request Broker)   See CORBA.

OTS   Object Transaction Service. A definition of the interfaces that permit CORBA objects to participate in transactions.

Parameterized class/interface   A type parameter leaves the type of method parameters or of results undefined when the class/interface is defined. The type parameter is bound to a concrete type when the defined class/interface is applied. For example, it is possible to create a list class of generic elements, but when an actual list object is defined, it is defined as a concrete list of a specific type.

Persistence The property of objects to retain their states between independent requests or sessions.

Polymorphism A concept that allows the substitution of an object with an object of a subtype.

Pointer An address into a memory area, identifying a data structure or routine.

Relational algebra Used to model the data stored in relational databases and queries defined on the data. The main relational functions are the set functions such as union, intersection and Cartesian product, plus selection (keeping only some rows) and projection (keeping only some columns). Relational algebra was developed by E.F. Codd.

Relational database A database based on the relational data model. Queries in relational databases are formulated with SQL.

Repository A data store, typically based on a DBMS, where all development objects are stored. Repositories are typically used in integrated development environments (IDEs).

Resource manager Provides access to a set of shared resources. A resource manager participates in transactions that are externally controlled and coordinated by a transaction manager. Database management systems are examples of resource managers.

RMI Remote Method Invocation. A technology that allows an object running in one Java Virtual Machine to invoke methods on an object running in a different Java Virtual Machine.

RMI-IIOP A version of RMI implemented to use the CORBA IIOP protocol. RMI over IIOP provides interoperability with CORBA objects.

Rollback A rollback is the undoing of a partly completed transaction. See also ACID.

SAX The Simple API for XML provides methods for parsing XML documents and retrieving elements.

Serialization A method to export the inner state of an object as a stream of bytes.

Server

1. see Client–Server.
2. A computer which provides some service for other computers connected to it via a network.

Servlet Small application running on a web or application server. Servlets are used to generate content dynamically and interact with clients using a request–response paradigm.

Session A time interval during which several partners are connected with each other and interact. A session is typically implemented as a layer in a network protocol.

SGML The Standard Generalized Markup Language is a generic language for representing documents. SGML is defined in ISO 8879:1986.

Signature The signature of a method defines the parameters required when the operation is invoked. It consists of method name and parameter types.

Simulation Attempts to predict the behaviour aspects of a system by creating an approximate mathematical model of it.

SQL The Structured Query Language is used as an interface to relational database management systems (RDBMSs). A series of standards by ISO and ANSI culminated in SQL:1999 (SQL-3). While the original implementation of SQL in 1986 supported only flat tables, SQL:1999 strives to provide relational support for complex objects. The query constructs of SQL:1999 are almost fully compatible with OQL.

SSL Secure Socket Layer. A security protocol that provides privacy over the Internet.

State States are used to represent a situation or condition of an object during which certain physical laws, rules and policies apply. The state of an object is defined by the set of the values of attributes and relationships associated with that object. Associated with each state are one or more events which cause that state to change. Only states which are significant in determining the behaviour of the object are modelled.

State transition A state transition is a change in the state of an object caused by an event occurring to the object while it is in a given state.

Subclass An object class which inherits the attributes and operations of another object class (its superclass).

Superclass An object class from which other object classes (subclasses) inherit attributes and operations.

TCP/IP Transmission Control Protocol over Internet Protocol. TCP/IP encompasses both network layer and transport layer protocols. Telnet, FTP, UDP, RDP and HTTP are based on TCP/IP.

Thin client A simple client program or device which relies on most of the function of the system being located on the server.

Thread A single path of execution through a program, a dynamic model, or some other representation of control flow.

Transaction See ACID transaction, Long transaction.

Transaction manager Provides the services and management functions required to support transaction demarcation, transactional resource management, synchronization and transaction context propagation.

Two-phase commit See ACID.

Type A description of a set of instances that share the same operations, abstract attributes, relationships and semantics. A type may define an operation specification (such as a signature) but not an operation implementation (such as a method).

Type casting The conversion of a type into a different type.

UML (Unified Modeling Language) A set of semantics and notation for precisely describing system and business models.

Unicode A 16-bit character set standard. Unicode covers all major modern written languages.

URI A Universal Resource Identifier identifies a resource (typically a resource on the Internet) uniquely with a short string. URIs are defined in `http://www.w3.org/hypertext/WWW/Addressing/URL/URI_Overview.html`.
   The most common kind of URIs are URLs.

URL A Uniform Resource Locator specifies the address of an Internet resource, such as a web page, an image, a sound file, a script, etc. URLs consist of a transfer protocol specification, such as `http:` or `ftp:`, a domain name, such as `www.w3.org`, and a path specification, such as `http://www.w3.org/hypertext/WWW/Addressing/URL/`.

Value added network (VAN) A private network of leased lines, usually used for electronic data interchange (EDI). The provider adds value by providing extra services.

Videotex A system developed in the 1980s, combining telephone and TV set. Users could access remote information and send data using a keyboard or the TV's remote control.

Virtual machine A program that implements the design of an abstract machine. Code compiled for the virtual machine as the target machine is independent of the underlying hardware and can be executed everywhere a virtual machine of the given specification exists.

Visibility Visibility defines which objects may access and use the attributes and operations of any given object.

VisualBasic A popular event-driven visual programming system for Microsoft Windows. The underlying programming language is BASIC with object-oriented extensions.

VisualBasic Script VBScript is an extension of VisualBasic, used to automate tasks in Microsoft Office applications or web pages (Internet Explorer only). See also JavaScript.

W3C The World Wide Web Consortium is a non-profit organization responsible for the development of World Wide Web standards (recommendations).

WDM (Wavelength Division Multiplexing) Multiplies the potential capacity of fibre optics by filling a fibre with not just one but many wavelengths of light, each capable of carrying a separate signal. Experimental systems (Pirelli) allow 128 separate channels with 10 Gbit/s each to be squeezed into one fibre.

Wrapper A wrapper is a piece of object-oriented software that encapsulates something and manages the interaction with it.

XDBMS XML Database Management System. A database management system that uses XML as its native data representation.

XHTML eXtensible HyperText Markup Language. The successor of HTML 4.0. XHTML is based on XML and includes HTML functionality.

XLink The XML Link Language defines advanced link features for XML resources.

XML The eXtensible Markup Language is an initiative from the W3C for a simple dialect of SGML suitable for use on the World Wide Web.

XML Schema XML Schema is an alternative way to define the structure of an XML document. It allows data typing and provides mechanisms for inheritance between schema definitions.

XPath Describes the syntax for expressions that address XML elements.

XPointer The XML Pointer Language extends the URL concept, allowing single elements within a resource to be addressed.

XQL The XML Query Language extends XPath and defines query operations similar to SQL query operations on XML resources.

XSL The eXtensible Style Language defines the presentation of a single XML document or a set of XML documents.

Bibliography

Alexander C. et al (1977) *A Pattern Language*: *Towns, Buildings, Construction*. New York: Oxford University Press

Allaire J. (1999) *The Emerging Distributed Web, Part 4*. Allaire Corp.

Beca L. et al *TANGO Interactive – a Collaborative Environment for the World-Wide Web*. Northeast Parallel Architectures Center, Syracuse University

Berst J. (1999) Why Web Surfing is Down. ZDNet AnchorDesk

Bolding D. (1995) Network security, filters and firewalls. *Crossroads*, 2.1 September, ACM

Brandsma C. (1999) *ALS and the 'Digital Economy', Concepts for economic development in less populated areas*. Arizona Learning Systems

Breese, Heckermen and Kadie (1998) Empirical Analysis of Predictive Algorithms for Collaborative Filtering. *Microsoft Research Technical Report, MSR-TR-98-12*, October 1998 revision

Bons, R.W.H., Lee, R.M., Wagenaar, R.W. and Wrigley, C.D. (1995) Modelling interorganizational trade procedures using documentary Petri nets. In *Proc. 28 Annual HICSS Conf.*, IEEE, Computer Society Press

Box D. (1998) Essential COM. Reading, Mass: Addison-Wesley

Brockschmidt K. *Inside OLE*, 2nd edn. Redmond: Microsoft Press

Budd T. (1997) *An Introduction to Object-Oriented Programming*, 2nd edn. Reading, Mass: Addison-Wesley

Bush V. (1945) As we may think. *The Atlantic Monthly*, July

Casti, J.L. (1997) *Would-be Worlds*. Chichester: John Wiley & Sons

Chabert A., Grossman E., Jackson L. and Pietrovicz S. (1996) *NCSA Habanero – Synchronous collaborative framework and environment*. Software Development Division at the National Center for Supercomputing Applications

Chappell D. *Understanding ActiveX and OLE*. Redmond: Microsoft Press

Clark T. (1997) Xmas sales up for Net merchants. News.com

Codd E.F. (1970) A relational model of data for large shared data banks. *Communications of the ACM*, 13(6), June 377–87

Colan M. (1999) InfoBus 1.2 Specification. Sun Microsystems

Computer Technology Research Corp. (1999) *Internet2: The Future of the Internet and Next-generation Initiatives*

Cowan D. D. and Lucena C. J. P. (1995) Abstract data views, an interface specification concept to enhance design for reuse. *IEEE Transactions on Software Engineering*, 21(3), March

Dahl O.-J. and Nygaard K. (1966) Simula, an Algol-based simulation language. *Communications of the ACM*, 9(9), September, 671–8

Dijkstra E.W. (1968) Goto statement considered harmful. *Communications of the ACM*, March

Dourish P. (1996) Open implementation and flexibility in CSCW toolkits. *Dissertation*, Department of Computer Science, University College London

Eisenberg A. and Melton J. (1999) SQL: 1999, formerly known as SQL3. *ACM SIGMOD Record*, 1999(1), March

Euridis. (1999) Erasmus University Research Institute for Decision and Information Systems. Rotterdam

Fielding R., Gettys J., Mogul J., Frystyk H. and Berners-Lee T. (1997) *Hypertext Transfer Protocol – HTTP/1.1*

Foster I. and Kesselman C. eds (1998) *The Grid: Blueprint for a New Computing Infrastructure*. Morgan Kaufman Publishers

Galouye D.F. (1964) *Counterfeit World* (=SIMULACRON-3). Out of print

Gamma E., Helm R., Johnson R. and Vlissides J. (1995) *Design Patterns – Elements of Reusable Object-Oriented Software*. Reading, Mass: Addison-Wesley

Gates B. (1995) *Business @The Speed of Thought: Using a Digital Nervous System*. New York: Warner Books

Gelernter D. and Carriero N. (1989) Linda in context. *Communications of the ACM*, 32(4), April, 444–58

Gerstner L. (1999-1) IBM Annual Meeting of Stockholders. Miami, Florida

Gerstner L. (1999-2) Lou Gerstner addresses members of Congress, Washington, 1999

Gosling J., Joy B. and Steel G. (1996) *The Java Language Specification*. Reading, Mass: Addison-Wesley

Griswold D. (1998) The Java HotSpot Virtual Machine Architecture. White Paper, Sun Microsystems

Haake A. and Haake J. (1993) Take CoVer: exploiting version management in collaborative systems. In *Proc. InterCHI'93*, Amsterdam, Netherlands, pp. 406–13

Hammer M. (1995) Reengineering work: Don't automate, obliterate. *Harvard Business Review*, Jul/Aug, 104–12

Hammer M. and Champy J. (1993) *Reengineering the Corporation*. New York: HarperCollins

Harrison W. and Ossher H. (1993) Subject-oriented programming (a critique of pure objects). In *Proc. Conf. Object-Oriented Programming Systems, Languages, and Applications (OOPSLA'93)*, ACM, September

Hightower R. (1999) Developing with DCOM and Java. *Java.com Developer's Journal*, SYS-CON Publications

Hilderink G.H. (1997) Communicating Java threads Reference Manual. In *WoTUG-20*: *Parallel Programming and Java*, pp. 283–325. Amsterdam: IOS Press

Hills H. (1973) *An Introduction to Simulation using Simula*. Norwegian Computing Centre, Publication no. S55

Hoare C.A.R. (1974) Monitors: an operating system structuring concept. *Communications of the ACM*, 17(10), 549–57

Hoare C.A.R. (1981) The emperor's old clothes (1980 Turing Award Lecture). *Communications of the ACM*, 24(2), 75–83, February

Hoare C.A.R. (1985) *Communicating Sequential Processes*. Hemel Hempstead: Prentice-Hall International Ltd

Holmes D., Noble J. and Potter J. (1997) *Aspects of Synchronization*. Marquarie University, Sydney, Australia

Howe R.M. *Living in the Information Society, Banking In The Network Economy*. IBM

Howque R. (1999) Java, JavaScript and Plug-In Interaction using Client-side LiveConnect. NetScape Technote

Hoyle F. and Elliot J. (1962) *A for Andromeda*. London: Souvenir Press

Hürsch W.L. and Lopes C.V. (1994) *Separation of Concerns*: *Towards a New Paradigm of Software Engineering*. Boston, USA: Northeastern University

ISO (1986) *ISO 8879:1986 Information processing – Text and office systems – Standard Generalized Markup Language (SGML)*

ISO/IEC (1995) *ODP Trading Function*. Draft International Standard 13235, International Organization for Standardization, International Electrotechnical Commission, May

ISO/IEC (1997) *Information Technologies – Open-edi reference model*. ISO/IEC 14662

Jacobson J. (1992) *Object-Oriented Software Engineering*: *A Use-Case Driven Approach*. Reading, Mass: Addison-Wesley

Jacobson I., Christerson M., Jonson P. and Övergaard G. (1993) *The OOSE book*, *Object-Oriented Software Engineering*: *A Use Case Driven Approach*: Reading, Mass: Addison-Wesley

Jacobson I., Griss M. and Jonsson P. (1997), *Software Reuse, Architecture, Process and Organization for Business Success*. Reading, Mass: Addison Wesley Longman

Kay A. (1977) Microelectronics and the personal computer. *Scientific American*, 237(3), 230–44

Kay A. (1993) The early history of Smalltalk. The second ACM SIGPLAN history of programming languages conference (HOPL-II), *ACM SIGPLAN Notices*, 28(3), March, 69–75

Kiczales G. (1996) *Beyond the black box*: *open implementation. IEEE Software*

Kiczales G., Lamping J., Mendhekar A., Maeda C., Lopez C., Loringtier J.-M. and Irwin J. (1997-1) Aspect-oriented programming. In *ECOOP'97 – Object-Oriented Programming* (Mehmet Aksit and Satoshi Matsuoka, eds), 11th European Conference, vol. 1241 of *Lect. Notes in Comp. Sci.*, 220–42. Berlin: Springer

Kiczales, G., Irwin, J., Lamping, J., Loingtier, J.-M., Lopez, C., Maeda, C. and Mendhekar, A. (1997-2) Aspect-Oriented Programming. In *Proc. POPL Workshop on Domain Specific Languages*, Paris

Killen & Associates (1998) *The Responsive Information Technology Infrastructure*: *Impact on IT Business Planning and Markets in the New Millennium*

Kosiur D. (1997) *Electronic Commerce*. Redmond: Microsoft Press

Kurotsuchi, R.T. (1999) The wonders of Java object serialization. *Crossroads*, ACM

Lamb R.K. Evolving the web to mission critical. IBM UK Laboratories, Hursley Park, UK

Lea D. (2000) *Concurrent Programming in Java, Second Edition*: *Design Principles and Patterns*. Reading, Mass: Addison-Wesley

Lee R.M. (1999) InterProcs Designer, A CASE Tool for Designing Electronic Trade Procedures. Erasmus University Research Institute for Decision and Information Systems, Rotterdam

Lief V. (1999) *Anatomy of New Market Models*. Forrester Research

Lopez C.I.V. (1997) D: A language framework for distributed programming. *Dissertation*, Northeastern University

Matsuoka S., Wakita K. and Yonezawa A. (1990) Synchronisation Constraints with Inheritance: What is not possible? – so what is?, *Technical Report 10*, Dept. of Information Science, University of Tokyo

Mauth R. (1998) Mission-critical components. *Byte*, May

Meyer B. (1997) *Object-oriented Software Construction*. Upper Saddle River, N.J.: Prentice Hall

McNealy S. (1999) *How to .com – Executive Perspectives – Stop buying software*. Sun Microsystems

NASA (1999) Mars Climate Orbiter Mishap Investigation Board, Phase I Report. NASA, 10 November

Nielsen J. (1997) *Multimedia and Hypertext*: *The Internet and Beyond*. Boston: AP Professional

Nielsen J. (1999-1) *Designing Web Usability*: *The Practice of Simplicity*. Indianapolis: New Riders Publishing

Nielsen J. (1999-2) Do Interface Standards Stifle Design Creativity? Jakob Nielsen's Alertbox, 22 August

OBI Consortium (1999) Open Buying on the Internet (OBI). *Technical Specifications*, Release V2.0 (Draft). The OBI Consortium

OSF (1995) AES/Distributed Computing – Remote Procedure Call, Revision B. Open Software Foundation

Ossher H. and Tarr P. (1999) Multi-Dimensional Separation of Concerns in Hyperspace. *Research Report RC 21452 (96717)*, 16 April, IBM T.J. Watson Research Center

Papathomas M. (1995), Concurrency in object-oriented programming Languages. In *Object-Oriented Software Composition*, The Object-Oriented Series (Nierstrasz & Tsichritzis, eds), pp. 31–68. Upper Saddle River, N.J.: Prentice-Hall

Parnas D.C. (1972) On the criteria to be used in decomposing systems into modules. *Communications of the ACM*, 15(12), 1059–62

Pelegrí-Llopart E., Cable L. and Ahmed S. (1999) *JavaServer Pages, Specification, Version 1.0*. Sun Microsystems

Phipps S. (1999) Face to Face: Simon Phipps, Program Manager, IBM Center For JavaTM Technology. Sun Microsystems

Pressman R.S. (moderator) (1998) Can Internet-based applications be engineered? *IEEE Software*, September/October

Resnick, P. and Vaian H. (1997), Recommender systems. *Communications of the ACM*, March

Rolstadås et al. (1995) *Performance Management: A business process benchmarking approach*. London: Chapman & Hall

Rumbaugh J., Jacobson I. and Booch G. (1998) *Unified Modeling Language Reference Manual*: Reading, Mass: Addison-Wesley

Sakkinen S. (1998) On the darker side of C++. In *ECOOP '88 Proc. European Conf. Object-Oriented Programming*. (S. Gjessing and K. Nygaard, eds.) Berlin: Springer-Verlag

SAX 1.0: The Simple API for XML. Megginson Technologies, 1998

Schwabe D., Rossi G. and Barbosa S. (1996) Systematic hypermedia design with OOHDM. *Proc. ACM International Conf. Hypertext (Hypertext'96)*, Washington, March

Schwabe D. and Rossi G. (1998) *An Object Oriented Approach to Web-Based Application Design*. Departamento de Informática. PUC-RIO, Brazil and LIFIA, Fac Cs. Exactas, UNLP, Argentina

Shanesy C. and Compton L. (1999) *Web-Enabling CICS Applications, A Selection Guide*. IBM Dallas Systems Center

Simon K.A. (1998) Organizational Change and Information Technology. *Dissertation*, Göteborg University

Software AG (1999-1) *Bolero – The Application Factory for Electronic Business*. White Paper, Software AG

Software AG (1999-2) *EntireX. The Componentware for Enterprise Application Integration.* Fact Sheet, Software AG

Software AG (1999-3) *NaturalX.* Software AG

Software AG (1999-4) *Tamino – Information Server for Electronic Business.* White Paper

Stroustrup B. (1994) *The Design and Evolution of C++.* Reading, Mass: Addison-Wesley

Sun Microsystems (1996) Object Serialization Specification

Sun Microsystems (1997) JavaBeans

Sun Microsystems (1998-1) Java Message Service, Version 1.0.1

Sun Microsystems (1998-2) XML Library

Sun Microsystems (1999) *The Top 25 RFE's,* September

Taenzer D., Ganti M. and Podar S. (1989) Problems in object-oriented software reuse. In *ECOOP'89 – Proc. 1989 European Conf. Object-Oriented Programming,* July, pp.25–38. Cambridge, UK: Cambridge Univ. Press

Treese G.W. and Stewart L.C. (1998) *Designing Systems for Internet Commerce.* Reading, Mass: Addison-Wesley

Udell J. (1994) Component software. *BYTE,* 19(5), 46–55

US Department of Commerce (1998) *The Emerging Digital Economy*

US Department of Commerce (1999) *The Emerging Digital Economy II*

Venables M. and Bilge U. (1998) *Complex Adaptive Modelling at J Sainsbury: The SimStore Supermarket Supply Chain Experiment.* Warwick: ESRC Business Process Resource Centre, Warwick University

Vijghen P. (1997) Experience of EDI for documents: the role of SGML. In *Conference Proceedings of SGML '97,* December 1997, pp. 213–18

Virginia University (1996) *WWW beyond the basics.* Virginia Polytechnic Institute & State University

WAP Forum (1998) *Wireless Application Protocol Architecture Specification.* Wireless Application Protocol Forum Ltd

WAP Forum (1999) *Wireless Application Protocol, Wireless Markup Language Specification, Version 1.1.* Wireless Application Protocol Forum Ltd, June

Welch P. H. (1998) Java threads in the light of OCCAM/CSP. In *WoTUG-21: Architectures, Languages and Patterns for Parallel and Distributed Applications,* pp. 259–84. Amsterdam, IOS Press

White House (1997) Text of the President's message to Internet users. The White House, Office of the Press Secretary

W3C (1998-1) *Composite Capability/Preference Profiles: A user side framework for content negotiation.* World Wide Web Consortium Note, November

W3C (1998-2) *Document Object Model (DOM) Level 1 Specification.* World Wide

Web Consortium Recommendation, REC-DOM-Level-1-19981001

W3C (1998-3) *Extensible Markup Language (XML) 1.0.* World Wide Web Consortium Recommendation, REC-xml-19980210

W3C (1998-4) *XML Linking Language (XLink).* World Wide Web Consortium Working Draft, WD-xlink-19980303

W3C (1998-5) *XML Pointer Language (XPointer).* World Wide Web Consortium Working Draft, WD-xptr-19980303

W3C (1999-1) *Extensible Stylesheet Language (XSL) Specification.* World Wide Web Consortium Working Draft, April

W3C (1999-2) *HTML4.0 Guidelines for Mobile Access.* World Wide Web Consortium, March

W3C (1999-3) *Namespaces in XML.* World Wide Web Consortium, REC-xml-names-19990114

W3C (1999-4) *Platform for Privacy Preferences (P3P) Specification,* World Wide Web Consortium Working Draft, April

W3C (1999-5) *Voice Browser Activity Proposal.* World Wide Web Consortium, September

W3C (1999-6) *XHTML1.0: The Extensible HyperText Markup Language.* World Wide Web Consortium Working Draft, May

W3C (1999-7) *XML Path Language (XPath), Version 1.0.* World Wide Web Consortium Working Draft, August

W3C (1999-8) *XML Query Language (XQL).* Proposal to the World Wide Web Consortium, June 1999

W3C (1999-9) *XML Schema Part 1 & 2.* World Wide Web Consortium Working Draft

W3C (1999-10) *XSL Transformations (XSLT), Version 1.0.* World Wide Web Consortium Working Draft, August

XML/EDI Working Group (1998) *Guidelines for using XML for Electronic Data Interchange, Version 0.05.* XML/EDI Working Group

Yourdon E., Whitehead K., Thomann J., Oppel K. and Nevermann P. (1995) *Mainstream Objects, An Analysis and Design Approach for Business.* Upper Saddle River, N.J.: Prentice-Hall

Index

CD-ROM: Bolero Component Studio (Personal Edition)

Software AG's high-level business-oriented application development environment, Bolero, delivers distributed applications to the Java platform. Bolero means business for the development of server-side components used in complex, mission-critical mainstream systems.

Bolero supports all important industry standards like Servlets, Beans, CORBA, DCOM and others. Through its built-in database mapping it supports all leading databases (Adabas, Oracle, DB2 etc.)

Instead of focusing on technology Bolero users are able to focus squarely on solving their business problems, expressing their specific business logic in appropriately parcelled business objects.

Bolero Component Studio is currently available on Windows NT 4.0. Bolero applications can be deployed on a number of platforms (Windows NT 4.0, Solaris, HP/UX, Tru64 AIX, OS/390, Linux etc.).

Please note that this Bolero Personal Edition comes free of charge and might contain limitations in comparison to the full product.

What are Bolero's key technical features?

Bolero is an object-oriented platform for implementing and deploying mission-critical commercial applications in multi-client and multi-tier environments such as the Internet and the World Wide Web. Bolero is fully interoperable with Java, and Bolero object code is 100% pure Java byte code (Java Source Code Generation is also an option). A Bolero component can run on any platform for which a certified Java Virtual Machine is available and can cooperate with other distributed Bolero and non-Bolero components of various component models.

Component-based development and integration

Bolero is designed for the implementation of component-based commercial applications. The Component Studio provides seamless integration with the Java and DCOM worlds, so you can import Java classes and COM objects and at the flick of a switch generate JavaBeans and COM objects out of Bolero classes. CORBA is supported through the Java API.

Web integration

Bolero integrates with web operations through its ability to create applets and dynamic HTML pages to run in web browser clients. This also allows Bolero components to be called from browser scripting languages like JavaScript and VBScript. In addition, Bolero components can interface with popular web servers to allow backend processing.

Building robust commercial applications

Bolero emphasizes the development of mission-critical commercial applications, which is supported by Commercial Objects, Internationalization Functions, Programming by Contract, Long Business Transactions and Design Patterns.

Database access

Bolero allows the persistent storage of objects into relational databases through object-relational mapping. Bolero uses OQL (Object Query Language) both to retrieve persistent objects and to relieve the developer of the need to switch between the object paradigm and the table structure of relational databases. These OQL queries are checked at compile time (as opposed to pure JDBC commands), thus improving the quality of the code and reducing the development time required to build applications.

For Adabas customers an extra Adabas CLIP directly accesses Adabas by using the highly effective Adabas direct calls.

For more information please check the Bolero website at
http://www.softwareag.com/bolero